HOUSES AND GARDENS
BY E. L. LUTYENS

ISBN 0 902028 98 7

First published in 1913 by *Country Life,* London

Reprinted in 1981 for the Antique Collectors' Club
by the Antique Collectors' Club Ltd.
Reprinted 1985, 1987 and 1998

British Library Cataloguing-in-Publication Data
A catalogue record for this book is available from the British Library

Printed in England
by the Antique Collectors' Club Ltd., Woodbridge, Suffolk IP12 1DS
on Consort Royal Era Satin from Donside Mill, Aberdeen, Scotland

HEATHCOTE, ILKLEY: PART OF THE GARDEN FRONT.

HOUSES AND GARDENS BY E. L. LUTYENS

Described and criticised by

LAWRENCE WEAVER

ANTIQUE COLLECTORS' CLUB

PREFACE.

ARCHITECTURE is the most vital of the arts with which we, as a nation, have to do. The work of the men who practise it is the most important factor in the enlargement of the public mind on æsthetics generally. A foreign critic said not long ago that the domestic architecture of Great Britain to-day is not only a finer thing than that of any other country, but better than that of any period of history. It is a large claim, which it would be immodest for an English writer to repeat, were it not made by an outside observer. As it was, it may be examined in a detached spirit. The praise is strictly limited to domestic work. In the larger field of civic building and in the planning of towns, in the exercise of the Grand Manner, Great Britain lags deplorably. The very individualism that is expressed so intimately in domestic building may be a handicap to us as a people when we come to deal with schemes of a municipal or national sort. Our street architecture from that point of view is too often a confused expression of unrelated eclecticisms. The Palladian manner stands cheek by jowl with Tudor fancies, which are so much constrained by the urgent bands of Building Acts and commercial needs that they lack the life and sincerity of the originals. One massive club-house in the dress of the French Renaissance competes with another that recalls an Italian *palazzo*. Quiet elevations that have survived from the days of Robert Adam and of the English Regency are overshadowed by towering monuments of a nondescript classicism, tortured to fit the plans demanded by business enterprise. The quiet and regular brick facades of the eighteenth century disappear with alarming rapidity and are replaced by a restless assortment of warring elements. It is all very gloomy, and it is not clear whence help will come.

We turn, therefore, with refreshment, as did the foreign critic, to the field where individual taste may find its just expression in building without running the risk of destroying a neighbour by unhappy contrast—to the country house. In this direction the debt which the twentieth century owes to the nineteenth and to such great architects as Norman Shaw, Eden Nesfield, George Devey and Philip Webb cannot be exaggerated. They relit the torch which is being carried on by a new generation of men, among whom Mr. Lutyens fills a large place. Their work was essentially that of pioneers. They not only re-established principles of traditional domestic design which had been drowned in the fervours of the Gothic Revival, but they set out to rediscover the right uses of material. As men of their own time, they had to adjust the new outlook to an infinite variety of pressing problems in the planning and equipment of houses. An ever-increasing standard of comfort demanded of them a machinery of living which, could an Elizabethan or Georgian architect revisit us, would leave him dumb and nerveless. A mass of mechanisms has to be built into walls and floors without making its ugly presence known. The house must show fronts unsullied by a wealth of contrivance. How well such practical difficulties have been solved is clear when we remember how ingeniously the necessities of modern comfort are kept from obtruding their presence. It is an aspect of house-building which quite escapes the amateur and the doctrinaire.

When we turn to the greater question of design, it is wiser to look on each succeeding style as, in its way, the just expression of its generation. As the inheritors of a great tradition of long development, we are at liberty to ransack the centuries for the architectural expression which best represents our outlook on life and manners. It seems unreasonable to choose any one moment in the centuries and claim for it an essential rightness of inspiration to be denied to others. Rightness in modern design can best be shown by the wise handling of these varying motifs, by the absorption of their essentials, and by a fresh expression of the chosen outlook in the same language, but in new phrases. Architecture can no more invent a new style than literature can create a new language. Just as a modern writer will abjure the precise imitation of Elizabethan forms, though he may seek to express as richly and strongly the spirit of his day out of a vocabulary but little changed, so does the architect set his skill to solve new problems with old materials, and from the same elements to create new compositions. Guided by tradition, but stimulated by fresh needs to make a new architecture rather than mere copies of the old, the architects of to-day deserve well of their generation. Among them are many men of outstanding ability. Each has his own gift and personal note. To one some early phase of traditional building most appeals by its welding of simplicity with elasticity of plan. Another is at home with the more restricted opportunity given by the balance, symmetry and sobriety that came in with the full Renaissance. It is because Mr. Lutyens has achieved a large and equal success in many manners that his work is especially worthy of close study. His wide range and fertility of invention provide the critic with a long series of illustrative texts on which may be built a general discussion of the aims and tendencies of modern domestic architecture.

It is from no lack of appreciation of the widespread ability which informs the house-building of to-day that I have now attempted a separate monograph on the work of one man. I may, perhaps, claim to have done something to enlarge public appreciation of the admirable houses which are being built up and down the land, by illustrating and describing the work of nearly two hundred architects in the pages of *Country Life*.

It is because the influence of Mr. Lutyens is good, strong and increasing, and because his art gives me a large personal pleasure, that I have ventured on the difficult task of presenting his domestic work as a whole. The moment seems appropriate. He has lately been elected an Associate of the Royal Academy, at an age when that honour has come to few, but there is a more cogent reason for publishing the book at this comparatively early stage in his career. The year 1913 sees him in some sort at a parting of the ways. After nearly twenty-five years of work almost entirely devoted to houses and gardens of many types and sizes, he has been appointed joint architect with Mr. Herbert Baker of the new Imperial City of Delhi. As he has an amazing capacity for work, we may believe, as well as hope, that he will continue to build fascinating houses and that this side of his work will show a continuous development.

This is a convenient time, therefore, to attempt a survey of his past achievement in domestic architecture. Perhaps this word of personal explanation may be allowed to a writer who has attempted an unusual task, unusual because it is our habit to bury Cæsar before we praise him. I could not have attempted to publish this book if I had not a deep, but I trust not uncritical, admiration for what Mr. Lutyens has done and is doing. My only complaint is that he has hindered rather than helped me, by being very sparing of information and by refusing to read proofs. While this does honour to his modesty, it is somewhat disconcerting to a writer who attaches importance to accuracy of detail, which in this case he has not always been able to check. What I have written about the houses illustrated has followed visits made to them in all but a few cases, and those not very important.

The list of his works (page 318) is believed to be reasonably complete and accurate. It is so long that I have not attempted to illustrate more houses and gardens than seemed needful to explain the development of Mr. Lutyens' art. Chapters XXII. to XXVI. are given up in part to work in other fields than domestic architecture, in order that his outlook on different problems of design may be indicated, but the scope of the book forbade any attempt at full illustration or description.

Many of the subjects discussed are now illustrated for the first time. Others have appeared in various technical papers and in the pages of *Country Life*. I have to thank my friend Mr. H. Avray Tipping for allowing me to incorporate in my chapters, notably that on Hestercombe, some parts of articles written by him.

LAWRENCE WEAVER,

November, 1913.

CONTENTS.

CONTENTS—*continued.*

LIST OF ILLUSTRATIONS.

FIG. I.—EARLY PICTURESQUE MANNER. CROOKSBURY, 1890. ENTRANCE FRONT.

INTRODUCTION.

A General Survey of the Development and Character of Mr. Lutyens' Work.

THE writing of a book about the work of a living artist presents obvious difficulties, but one of them can be avoided by giving to it as little as possible the character of a biography. It will be enough, therefore, to set down here that Edwin Landseer Lutyens was born in London in March, 1869, the eleventh of a family of fourteen. His father, Mr. Charles Lutyens, after leaving the army, became a painter. His pleasure in experimenting with various techniques marks an interesting point in artistic heredity, for his architect son has always been swift to try fresh combinations of materials. Mr. Lutyens was educated at a private school, studied for two years at South Kensington, and was a year in the office of Messrs. Ernest George and Peto. As early as 1888 he did a little work on his own account in the alteration of a cottage at Thursley. Other small works followed until 1891, when he received his first serious commission from Mr. A. W. Chapman, for whom he built Crooksbury, his first house of any importance, illustrated in Fig. I. and in Chapter I.

The general state of architecture to-day does not vary greatly from the condition of things five and twenty years ago, except that the level of individual work is markedly higher and æsthetic achievement is far more widely spread. In 1890 Norman Shaw and Philip Webb were old men nearing the close of their artistic careers. They still shed, however, a large influence by personal contact with the present generation. It has been said that the fusion into one personality of these two artists would have achieved the perfect architect. Shaw was a master of design, and had the architectonic sense in a high degree ; Webb's vision was not large, but his reverence for tradition, his sense of material and his unflinching devotion to his æsthetic ideals have had an influence none the less great for being barely suspected. Of these two men Mr. Lutyens was a close student in his earlier years, and his first works clearly show how he was swayed by one or the other. He soon acquired the elasticity of design which was so marked in Norman Shaw and so notably absent in Philip Webb ; but his reverence for Webb was at the root of his rapidly increasing mastery of materials and their influence on design, an aspect of his art to which Norman Shaw never gave much attention.

The development of his outlook had its starting-point in what may roughly be called the picturesque manner. It derived in some sort from reminiscences of a childish love for the gabled houses in Randolph Caldecott's drawings, which were the means of making architecture significant to many of us, and from the half-timber work of such modern houses as Norman Shaw's *Wispers*. Among such early buildings, not illustrated, Munstead Corner deserves a reference. It was designed in March, 1891, and finished about a year later. The walls are of Bargate stone, with the upper storey of half-timber. A little bay projecting from the drawing-room has a very immature look. Another good example is Sullingstead (Fig. IV. and Chapter I.), built in 1896, but the use of half-timber did not last many years, and wisely, for it has little real significance in a country where most of the timber used is imported. This studied picturesqueness is observed throughout the work of 1888–1900, but as a factor of lessening importance. The early reminiscences of gothic detail in the garden porch at Crooksbury were soon abandoned, as were also the broad white barge boards (Fig. I. and Chapter I.) which now look rather aggressive. The stables at Little Tangley, a gardener's cottage at Crooksbury, the additions to The Corner, Thursley, and a cottage at Littleworth seem to have been the first works illustrated. Photographs of them were reproduced by the *Architectural Illustration Society* in *The Architect* of December, 1890. They show that in the Little Tangley stables classical instead of gothic detail was used in the half-timber gable.

Ruckman's Farm is of interest as showing a first essay in a field where extraordinary skill has since been shown—the repair and enlargement of old houses. The first additions to this typical little Surrey farmhouse were begun in 1894, and show the early stages of that tireless experiment with simple materials which was later to bear such notable fruit. It has been said that the red brick fireplace was invented at this date. That, of course, is nonsense. There are numbers of mediæval examples, and Philip Webb built them in the Red House for William Morris as long ago as 1859. Webb also re-introduced the use of roofing tiles for diversifying wall-building and for other half structural, half decorative purposes. Mr. Lutyens, beginning where Philip Webb left off, brought a gaiety and freshness to the unusual employment of hand-made materials, which has had an immense influence on modern building.

One of the important happenings in his artistic career was his early acquaintance with Miss

FIG. II.—FIRST IMPORTANT GARDEN SCHEME : WOODSIDE, CHENIES, 1893.

Jekyll. Her great gift for gardening served as a stimulus to his appreciation, and led him to give the large attention to garden design which has developed so notably, from Woodside, Chenies to Hestercombe.

It would be difficult to exaggerate the importance of her influence. Architects find in gardens a just sphere for design, but they cannot be expected to have a wide knowledge of horticulture. Miss Jekyll added to this knowledge an intimate sense of design, and Mr. Lutyens' association with her in the joint labour of design and planting led not only to splendid results in individual gardens, but also to the widening of his outlook on the whole question. It was an ideal partnership. It is in the main to Miss Jekyll that we owe the rational blending of the formal and the natural in garden design, which has harmonised the theories of two contending and often acrimonious schools. It is enough to say that the gardens illustrated in the succeeding chapters would never have been created without her help.

One of the results of this friendship was that he built for Miss Jekyll the house at Munstead

Wood which is illustrated in Chapter I. At Fulbrook, built in 1897, he made a further experiment in classical motifs by treating the interior to some extent in that fashion, while the exterior was still moulded on picturesque lines. The additions to Crooksbury House mark not only a first serious essay in a classical exterior, but a growing preoccupation in

FIG. III.—FIREPLACE IN FARMHOUSE MANNER AT MUNSTEAD WOOD, 1896.

the choice of fine materials. The design of the new wing shows a study of the domestic work of the middle of the seventeenth century, of that fascinating time when casements had not yet been disestablished in favour of sliding sashes. Just as the first part of Crooksbury House was Mr. Lutyens' first building of any importance, so the additions to it mark not only a break away from the mere pursuit of the picturesque, but a growing grasp of the principles of abstract design.

FIG. IV.—HALF TIMBER AND TILE-HANGING, SULLINGSTEAD, 1896.

In Chapter II. are illustrated four notable examples of Surrey building in the vernacular manner. Still picturesque, they show a growing breadth of treatment, a greater reticence in detail and a growing richness and variety in the management of the gardens.

Experiments in the very different traditional manner of East Anglia are discussed in Chapter III. At the same time was built the entertaining little chapel shown in Fig. VI. In the same year (1898) was built "Les Bois des Moutiers," Varengeville (Fig. VII.) which shows an interesting treatment of very tall and narrow oriel windows, an echo of Norman Shaw.

The work of the years 1900-1 (Chapters IV. to VI.) was varied, and shows an all-round development and a growing facility of design. The Deanery Garden was the last important essay in half-timber work, and may be regarded as one of the best, if not the best, of the modern houses built in this manner during last century. The garden also shows a growing skill in the treatment of water. Homewood, Knebworth, shows a rare surrender to a foreign influence. It owes a little to Cape Dutch architecture, but in spirit only, not in the letter, which is *sui generis.*

The exterior of Marshcourt (Chapter V.) shows a most characteristic Tudor mood. It is superb in its own manner, but the growing tendency to adopt a more restful basis for design is clear from the classical flavour of the interiors. Their treatment, however, is markedly immature when compared with later work, and shows a somewhat undisciplined richness and variety of material. Grey Walls (Chapter VI.), though less striking and showing a less exuberant invention, is more satisfying. It shows a growing restraint in the exteriors, but in order to achieve this effect, some sacrifices of convenience were made in the planning of the rooms. On the other hand, the ingenuity of plan shown in overcoming difficult aspects and approach is very notable and is discussed in its proper place.

To the years 1902-3 (Chapter VII.) belongs the exquisite house of Little Thakeham, with its exterior in the late Tudor manner, but yet instinct with personal feeling. The interior is frankly Palladian and shows a growing tendency towards austerity of treatment and a more visible scholarship. The Hoo, Willingdon, is a case of enlargement of an old house, and perhaps shows less than the usual skill.

FIG. V.—EARLY PICTURESQUE MANNER (1896) ON RIGHT. MORE CLASSICAL
TREATMENT (1903) ON LEFT. SULLINGSTEAD, SURREY.

The sun-trap type of house plan causes many problems, on which architects delight to test their ingenuity, and Papillon Hall (Chapter VII.) shows how skilfully the many difficulties which beset this type of plan have been avoided. On the general question of planning it is fair to say that in the earlier houses convenience of arrangement was sometimes sacrificed to a preconceived idea of exterior treatment. It is impossible to avoid the belief that design proceeded from elevation to plan, instead of in the logical way, from plan to elevation. This was probably due to the fact that Mr. Lutyens began to practise without that grounding in the hard facts of design which is part of a regular and organised architectural education. Impelled into architecture by a natural passion for the art, he gathered knowledge of some of its more practical aspects by experience rather than by training. His later work shows none of those rather irresponsible tricks of planning which are a defect of his earlier essays. This is the more notable because the later manner, with its reliance on symmetrical arrangements, presents far more difficult problems in the disposition of rooms than the less restrained type of picturesque and traditional buildings with which the earlier part of his career was occupied.

Daneshill (Chapter VII.) is one of the earlier houses in which careful attention is given to the actual bricks used, to their size, shape and texture, which has led to an amazing growth of interest and of achievement in brick building.

The normal size of bricks in England is 9in. by 4½in. by 2¾in., which gives, when allowance is made for the mortar joint, a depth of 1ft. to every four bricks. In some parts of the country the thickness is increased to 3in., which makes matters worse. These two stock sizes, the ugliest conceivable, are dictated by

FIG. VI.—NONCONFORMIST CHAPEL, OVERSTRAND, 1898.

utilitarian reasons. Anything bigger, such as a tile brick 12in. by 12in. by 1½in., would take two hands to lift, and the size of 9in. by 4½in. by 3in. has secured the mastery because it is the largest that a man can easily lay with one hand. A little brick, say, 7in. long by 1¾in. thick, is perhaps of the ideal proportions ; but a bricklayer can, in fact, handle and lay very few more of these in an hour than of the larger size, and consequently a wall so built costs more in labour. It is, at the same time, more expensive in material, because the little bricks cost practically no less than those of normal size, which is all very unfortunate for the interests of art in building.

In connection with their revived use, it may be well to point out that we owe it to a man whose influence and pioneer successes are hardly represented by the volume and quality of his ultimate achievement — Eden Nesfield. In 1862, i.e., only three years later than Philip Webb built of red brick The Red House for William Morris, Nesfield began Cloverley Hall, Shropshire. It is a house in the Elizabethan manner, but with a French accent in its dormers, and that touch of Japanese feeling in some of its decoration that marked also some of Norman Shaw's early work. The point of immediate interest is that the bricks were all made on the estate, and far thinner than usual.

FIG. VII.—LE BOIS DES MOUTIERS, VARENGEVILLE, 1898.

Nesfield's appreciation of the value of texture has further witness in his employment of thick mortar joints, which, as C. L. Eastlake wrote forty years ago, " resembled the style of work in old houses of the time of Henry VIII."

Monkton, Singleton, is important as marking an increasing bias towards the Georgian atmosphere, and of necessity a lessened use of gables and casements in favour of hipped roofs and sliding sashes (Fig. XV. and Chapter VII.). The influence of this house and others like it has been, and is, so increasingly effective that it is worth while to consider in some detail what is at the back of this return to the eighteenth century for inspiration.

Perhaps the case for the demure type of house, such as Temple Dinsley, Middlefield and Great Maytham, which take their spirit, though not necessarily their details, from the builders of the early eighteenth century, was never put better than in a letter of Robert Louis Stevenson. He has been at Chester visiting half-timbered houses redolent of gothic traditions. He liked the place, but says, " somehow I feel glad when I get

FIG. VIII.—EARLY USE OF BRICKWORK IN GARDEN ARCHITECTURE : PERGOLA
AT CROOKSBURY, 1898.

among the quiet eighteenth century buildings, in cosy places with some elbow room about them, after the older architecture. This other is bedevilled and furtive ; it seems to stoop ; I am afraid of trap-doors, and could not go pleasantly into such houses." He goes on to wonder how much of this feeling was legitimately the effect of the architecture. He supposes that the most part of his sensations are due possibly to associations reflected from bad historical novels and to the disquieting sculpture that garnished some Chester façades. As was inevitable for a man in whose life literature filled so great a part, he was inclined to belittle the direct appeal to his emotions of the architecture itself, and to cast about for more subtle explanations. It is an old saw that a reader takes out of a book no more than he brings to it, and the same is doubly true of the student of buildings. It is only after long observation and the getting of considerable knowledge that we can bring to architecture a judgment freed from the bias of sentiment. Our historical preferences give shape and direction to our taste.

FIG. IX.—PICTURESQUE MANNER DEVELOPED AND BROADENED, 1899 : ORCHARDS, GODALMING.

If we are most moved by the ascetic strength of monastic life in the early Middle Ages, we shall be greatly touched by the pure splendours of Cistercian buildings. If we are touched by the awakened humanism of the early Renaissance, we shall rejoice in the age of Inigo Jones. Perhaps the intellectual march and broadening civilisation of the eighteenth century chiefly attract us ; then the quiet shape of its domestic building will most satisfy. If we admit that architecture is the art which most surely expresses the life and tendencies of the people—and it is almost a truism—it is natural enough that one phase of it will make a more direct appeal than another. But to return to Stevenson and his comparison between eighteenth century houses and those of the Middle Ages. " I do not know," he writes, " if I have yet explained to you the sort of loyalty, of urbanity, that there is about the one (*i.e.*, XVIII. cent.) to my mind ; the spirit of a country orderly and prosperous, a flavour of the presence of magistrates and well-to-do merchants in big wigs . . . something certain and civic and domestic, is all about these quiet staid shapely houses, with no character but their exceeding shapeliness, and the comely external utterance that they make of their internal comfort. Now the others . . . are sly and grotesque, they combine their sort of feverish grandeur with their sort of secretive baseness,

FIG. X.—USE OF MASSIVE MATERIALS, 1900 : DEANERY GARDEN.

after the manner of a Charles the Ninth. They are peopled for me with persons of the same fashion. Dwarfs and sinister persons in cloaks are about them ; and I seem to divine crypts, and trap-doors." I have quoted at large from this letter because it reveals the effect of buildings on a mind singularly alert and sensitive. There is something boyish and a little over-strained in the vision of sinister persons summoned up by the buildings of Chester, surely not so theatrical as all that. Yet there is a substratum of truth in the outlined effect of gothic even in its quieter domestic shapes, when compared with the broad quietude of Wren and his followers. One question arises, perhaps rather literary than architectural, yet pertinent enough to be considered here. It may seem odd that a genius so ardently romantic as Stevenson's could turn with such obvious pleasure from the architecture of romance to the sedate houses of the eighteenth century. It is not really so. Stevenson, without any particular knowledge of the art of building, was swift to appreciate its power of expression. With all his delight in " fifteen men on the dead man's chest," his private outlook was influenced by the balanced spirit of intellectual enquiry which comes down from the eighteenth century. It was perhaps the unconscious sense that the desire for mental shapeliness was represented by " quiet staid shapely houses " that endeared them to Stevenson, as much as the more obvious expression which they gave to urbanity and orderly prosperity. For good or ill, the days of crypts and trap-doors are gone. For most people it is as difficult to hear the blind man's stick go tap-tap-tapping into the distance, as to listen for the knocking at the gate in *Macbeth*. Buildings that are " bedevilled and furtive " represent no very real or enduring emotions to-day. If we have arrived at another eighteenth century in our domestic architecture, it is because it is the

FIG. XI.—ELABORATION OF GARDEN DETAILS AND GROWING ATTENTION TO MATERIAL (1899) : GODDARDS, SURREY.

natural place for us. We have the right to ask, however, that the eclecticism from which architecture has suffered much shall be as good a servant now, as it was a bad master during last century's battle of the styles. Modern building dare not relapse into mere copyism of the eighteenth or any other century. It is to the honour of those who design such houses as Monkton that the urbanity and shapeliness of the late seventeenth and early eighteenth centuries find their echoes, while in plan all modern needs are met, and in decorative detail the modern provenance of the work is sufficiently expressed. If the subjective charms of a modern building are won at the price of apeing an old one, they are dearly bought. The architect of two hundred years ago was apt to show a magnificent disdain for comfort and convenience if they clashed with some preconceived idea of proportion. He showed therein a retrogression from the elastic planning of the Tudor men, so well fitted to the life of their day. Of modern architects we ask the best of both worlds, and, happily, do not ask in vain.

It may not be inappropriate, however, to sound a note of warning. The demure and balanced idea in house design slides with deplorable facility into timidity and dreariness. Unless it maintains a definite vitality by sheer effort of art and mind, repose will have been secured at too heavy a price. The town houses in Westminster illustrated in Chapter XXIII. go perilously

FIGS. XII AND XIII.—INCREASING USE OF SLIDING SASHES AND HIPPED ROOFS AT RUCKMANS, 1902. THE MUSIC ROOM FROM SOUTH-WEST——AND FROM SOUTH-EAST.

near dulness, and are saved only by a rightness of proportion which has no support from any other qualities save pleasant colour and texture. In hands rather less skilful, or in the same hands at a tired moment, the idea might easily miscarry altogether, and merely renew the spirit of Gower Street. The altar of restraint is ill-built if it is founded on the grave of romance and invention, and in such a case becomes only a monument to the spirit of middle age.

One of the earliest, as it is also one of the most important, works of repair and enlargement was Lindisfarne Castle, Holy Island. Begun in 1903, a further addition was made in 1912, but for convenience of illustration and description both parts of this work are described together in Chapter VIII. (Although the arrangement of the chapters is in the main chronological, it seemed impracticable to deal with separate works on the same building under different headings.)

Not the least successful part of Mr. Lutyens' achievement has been in the skilful repair and enlargement of old buildings. It is a field in which the modern architect is most open to hostile criticism, and deservedly so. The blight of " restoration " which robbed the majority of historical buildings of their character during the nineteenth century has now received its just condemnation. Ancient houses did not suffer such savage assaults as churches, because their

FIG. XIV.—VARIED USE OF MATERIAL—CHALK FLINT AND BRICK, 1901 : MARSHCOURT.

restoration was not approached in the half theological spirit which condemned all Renaissance work as savouring of corruption and calling for instant destruction.   Nevertheless, the failure to appreciate either the niceties of early design and craftsmanship or the æsthetic value of materials, when added to a lack of historical sense, wrought hideous havoc alike in mansion and cottage.   Reverence for ancient buildings as essential evidences of national development in art and manners was almost unknown until Ruskin, William Morris and others established it as a working theory.   Up to the nineteenth century succeeding generations had altered freely in accordance with their changing standards of taste, but always on the lines of a continuous and developing tradition.   We may regret that a house of Wren's time should have been remodelled in Adam's, but at least its new guise was authentic and good in its own right.   Our quarrel with the restorers is that in most cases they replaced authentic work by mean and lifeless copies, in what they conceived to be more reputable, because earlier, styles.   That these clumsy forgers made our national monuments ugly was an error in taste : that in the process they destroyed the evidences of national art was a crime.

FIG. XV.—MONKTON, SINGLETON, 1902.
(The symmetry of front is shewn by illustration on page 126.)

Thus it happens that the antiquary and the artist hear of the repair and enlargement of ancient houses with sinkings of heart. Happily, the steady efforts of the Society of Antiquaries and of the Society for the Protection of Ancient Buildings are establishing in the public mind, not completely as yet, but with increasing effect, the knowledge that it is an outrage to destroy old work.   Mr. Lutyens' record in this matter is clean.   His devotion to all authentic traditions of building is so sincere and knowledgeable that any works of simple repair are done with the smallest renewals consistent with stability and always with materials that accord with the old work.   His policy with regard to alterations and additions to old buildings seems to me wholly right, though it is by no means universally accepted.   When he has built a new wing to an old house, he has not sought to copy the original exactly.   While the addition has been in perfect harmony with the early work, it has revealed to the expert eye, though not necessarily to the casual observer, the fact that it is of the twentieth century.   Because he exerts a sedulous care in the choice of materials that conform in texture and colour with old standards, and because he has established in his building a quality of craftsmanship that recalls ancient methods, the juxtaposition of new and old achieves a real unity.   Slight differences in design, however, personal touches in mouldings and new uses of materials prevent that fraudulent suggestion of age which gives to so many clever additions a positively delusive quality.

The chapters which deal with his work at Lindisfarne Castle, at Great Dixter and elsewhere, describe his methods in detail, and it is enough here to sum up the qualities which distinguish

FIG. XVI.—MINGLING OF EARLY AND LATER RENAISSANCE MOTIFS : MARSHCOURT, 1901.

it as reverence, sincerity and a sure skill in making an old plan suit modern needs without veiling its original characteristics.   His practice of letting the old work stand out clearly to tell its own story is best seen perhaps at Lambay.

In connection with works of restoration something must also be said about his treatment of material, in so far as he gives it an appearance which we associate with age. Walter Pater wrote in *Notre Dame d'Amiens* : " In architecture, close as it is to men's lives and their history, the visible result of time is a large factor in the realised æsthetic value, and what a true architect will in due measure always trust to.   A false restoration only frustrates the proper ripening of his work."

The " faking " (an unpleasant but inevitable word) of buildings has become of late as fashionable and lucrative a business as the " faking " of furniture.   The craze for the " antique," to be distinguished clearly from a love of old work, has led to old buildings being treated on the

FIG. XVII.—A BRICK FIREPLACE :
DANESHILL, 1903.

analogy of the Chippendale chair which is acclaimed as old because it is built up from one original leg.   Both by the use of scraps of old materials, beams, bricks, tiles, ironwork and the like, laboriously collected from a score of demolished buildings, and by the sophistication of new stuff by onslaught with axes and hammers, the large fabric built round a little old cottage is made to masquerade as an original building which has undergone no more than necessary repairs.   When, furthermore, such a new-old building is built strictly on a historical plan, it is no more than a foolish forgery, which tickles only too readily the fancy of those whose love of the old is a romantic fad unsupported by knowledge.   This state of things tends to make even the love of antiquity vulgar, for it is " false restoration " in its most delusive and most insincere form.

Mr. Lutyens, recognising that " the visible result of time is a large factor in the realised æsthetic value," treats materials so that they surrender themselves in texture and colour more swiftly to Time's influence, but not by illegitimate means.   He has, for example, applied the sandblast to oak to remove the soft fibres from its surface, and has steeped it in lime to give it a soft grey tone, but the rough and cool-coloured surface thus secured is as justifiably sought as the unnatural smoothness and crude yellow tone which were in fashion thirty years ago.   He has never attempted to achieve a false air of age by contrived crudities of workmanship which are not only insincere but a studied essay in retrogression.

The largest scheme of garden design which has fallen to Mr. Lutyens' lot was at Hester-combe (Chapter IX.), and it is unfortunate that the gardens there have been laid out in relation to a Victorian house of no interest.   New Place, Shedfield (Chapter XII.), shows his skill in the handling of materials at his best.   It is in such a building that we see the inextinguishable pleasure that a born artist takes in the technique of his art.   While no one is more wedded than he to the great basic traditions of architecture, the originality which is brought to the treatment of

FIG. XVIII.—A TYPICAL WORK OF RESTORATION : LINDISFARNE CASTLE, HOLY
ISLAND, 1903 AND 1912.

ordinary materials fills the work with surprise and vitality. This attitude of mind it is that establishes a community of purpose between him in building and Robert Louis Stevenson in writing. Some advice that the latter gave to an art student seems so ripely to point the way to the success achieved and is of such wide application, that it is worth quoting. R. L. S. headed it, " Notes for the Student of Any Art," and after an appeal against a narrow devotion to one art to the exclusion of the others, and a warning against realism (which scarcely applies to building), he comes to technique. " Bow your head over technique. Think of technique when you rise and when you go to bed. Forget purpose in the meanwhile ; get to love technical processes ; to glory in technical successes ; get to see the world entirely through technical spectacles, to see it entirely in terms of what you can do. Then when you have anything to say, the language will be apt and copious." People do not realise how much success in any art is dependent on a grasp of sheer technique, and in the nature of things cannot realise it. Their general taste may enable them to applaud or reject broad effects without the joy in particular details that comes with *expertise.* An architect must, of course, have " something to say," a conception that is right alike in plan and proportion ; but unless he sees it through technical spectacles, and brings to his task an invention " apt and copious," the completed work is likely to miscarry.

FIG. XIX.—AN EXAMPLE OF THE EXCLUSIVE USE OF BRICK : NEW PLACE, SHEDFIELD, 1906.

Heathcote is dealt with fully in Chapter XIII., and it is needless to say more in this Introduction than to draw attention to the way this house at Ilkley shows an increasing reliance on sheer design as compared with the picturesque qualities and contrived haphazardness of the early building. The work from 1905 onwards is dealt with in considerable detail in its proper sequence, and it is needless, therefore, to discuss it comparatively here.

FIG. XX.—A LARGE GARDEN SCHEME : HESTERCOMBE, 1904. LOOKING TO SOUTH-EAST ACROSS THE GREAT PLAT.

It may, however, be noted that even the most recent work, austere as it is, shows no sign of any influence from that Greek revival which we associate with such names as Elmes and Cockerell.   In the architectural world to-day there is much talk of returning to Greek building for the inspiration of design.   Large homage is paid to these gifted men, who, in the first half of the nineteenth century, brought into their work something of Greek detail with results admittedly fine.   In the work under review, however, these influences, as far as *form and detail* are concerned, are not to be traced, and this seems to be right.   The Greek spirit is eternal and for all climes—it blossoms as much in a French cathedral as on the Acropolis—but English architecture throughout its long development kept its nationality, and it is to be hoped will continue to keep it.   The Greek spirit is an affair of ideals rather than of mouldings.   Walter Pater with his usual delicacy of insight put the case with a fine appreciation of underlying facts when he said : " Breadth centrality with blitheness and repose are the marks of Hellenic culture. Is that culture a lost art ? . . . Can we bring down that ideal into the gaudy, perplexed light of modern life ? "

It is function of the modern architect to secure for his buildings these four great qualities. Even in simple buildings we should not look in vain for breadth, centrality, blitheness and repose.   Perhaps especial stress may be laid on the quality of blitheness. Any excursion into the letter of the Greek law in architecture is likely to smother this sense, which belongs to the English tradition of building.   We see in the houses of Regent's Park what a direct Greek inspiration does for our domestic architecture. We may admit the breadth and repose, but it would take an enthusiastic eye to find any trace of blitheness.   This power is seen not only in buildings described in this book, but in the large influence exercised on the younger generation of architects.   To those who value a blithe humour in building as in life the strengthening of this influence will be welcome.

FIG. XXI.—A SMALL HOUSE RELYING WHOLLY ON MASS AND PROPORTION : MIDDLEFIELD, 1908.

The title of this book emphasises its concern with domestic and not with civic design, but it seemed well to give a little space to the latter, so that it may be seen from what point of departure is begun the immense labour of creating a capital city at Delhi.   The illustrations of Chapters XXIII. and XXIV., few as they must be lest the book should swell to unreasonable dimensions, show a grasp of the monumental aspect of design which encourages the admirers of Mr. Lutyens to believe that he will achieve as distinguished a success at Delhi as he has done in England.   He approaches the task with the finest of all equipments, an absolute devotion to his art, a wide experience of men and of affairs and that rarest of all qualities, a strong imaginative faculty.   There is no more impressive fact about his twenty-five years of work than its consistency and its unhurried development along inevitable lines.   The fertility of design and grasp of architectonic principles which mark his domestic work will be at the service of Delhi.   I have little doubt that the sterile talk of styles which has troubled the artistic world in this relation will cease when the joint designs of Mr. Lutyens and Mr. Herbert Baker are made public. The fact that they are only now in the making prevents—even if the scope of this book did not

FIG. XXII.—THE SALUTATION, SANDWICH, 1912 : GARDEN FRONT FROM THE SOUTH.

forbid—anything more than a general reference. On one aspect of so great an undertaking it seems proper, however, to say a word. It may have occurred to some who are not familiar either with the mental processes which affect architectural design or with the many-sided character of Mr. Lutyens' work, that there is a wide gap between the conception of a house and the creation of a capital city. That is true only in part, and undue emphasis on the difference would be misleading. It is one of the delusions of the half-educated that art should be subdivided and kept in compartments, that one man is a domestic architect and another an ecclesiastical.

Robert Louis Stevenson says in that acute essay, *A Note on Realism :* " The engendering idea of some works is stylistic ; a technical preoccupation stands them instead of some robuster principle of life." We may extend this criticism from the work to the worker, and recognise that with many able architects a devotion to some narrow, though it may be brilliant, outlook on their art unfits them for adventure beyond the field which their vision fittingly controls. With an artist of large achievement and wide sympathies such limitations are not, or at least need not be, operative. Once more the lucid mind of R.L.S. puts the point as I could not hope to do. He is writing of the perplexity and strain which beset the artist at the moment when he begins to execute a work of art. " Artists of indifferent energy and an imperfect devotion to their own ideal make this ungrateful effort once for all ; and having formed a style, adhere to it through life. But those of a higher order cannot rest content with a process which, as they continue to employ it, must infallibly degenerate towards the academic and the cut-and-dried. Every fresh work in which they embark is the signal for a fresh engagement of the whole forces of their mind ; and the changing views which accompany the growth of their experience are marked by still more sweeping alterations in the manner of their art." It is because this " fresh engagement " has marked Mr. Lutyens' essays in many manners that his admirers are not dismayed at the novelty and largeness of the problems which he has to face in the creation of an Oriental city. He has never suffered himself to be bound by stylistic considerations, and his art has grown steadily in a masculine austerity which will serve him well in the great task of creating an architectural symbol of the enduring greatness of Britain's work in India.

In all discussions about architecture the writer must sooner or later come to the question of " styles " and " style." On the question of how far any architect may properly work in various styles it may be useful to put in here a claim for wide choice. A writer, who was lately discussing the appropriateness of this or that style for the new Delhi, pointed out that a living architectural tradition is no more than a fashion which " may be ugly, but at its worst it has a certain dignity of the commonplace, due to the acceptance of a standard." He went on to " observe that when architects worked uniformly in the fashion of their day, they produced buildings which are, on the whole, pleasing. Bedford Square is dull, but it offends no taste ; on the other hand, the architecture of the last seventy years has produced a population of nightmares, varied by rare works of individual genius." He avowed himself an optimist, and saw no reason why a living architectural tradition should not be built up again. It would be pleasant to believe that his prophecy will come true, but the chances are against any such tradition winning anything like universal acceptance. More or less uniform traditions or fashions in the past have been the outcome of a fairly prevalent uniformity in the point of view of the average man about things in general. Opinion was more homogeneous. The spread of education has fostered the spirit of individualism in all literary and artistic matters. A coherent tradition implies the existence of authority, a quality conspicuously lacking in modern life. Tradition or fashion are due to the acceptance of a standard, but the increasing tendency is not to accept the standards set up by other people. This individualism may or may not be a good or a healthy thing, but it is here, and has to be reckoned with. An illustration may be taken from church architecture. The succeeding styles of Early English, Decorated, and Perpendicular not only marked inevitable æsthetic growth arising out of structural development, but perfectly expressed the change in the theological and social outlook of the time. Archbishop Laud's endeavour to keep the gothic spirit alive in church-building marked his brilliant perception of the relations between thought and art, but it failed entirely. Wren's cathedral and churches were the perfect expression of the flowing tide of humanism which comes out in the writings of the Caroline divines. Religious thought was becoming less homogeneous, but there was little or none at the end of the seventeenth century which did not find a fair counterpart in the spirit of Renaissance building. It is otherwise to-day. Butterfield's Church of St. Alban's, Holborn, and the Brompton Oratory each represent with singular faithfulness the outlook of the people who worship there ; both are flexible adaptations of authentic architectural traditions, and both are as wide apart in feeling as the Poles. If a building does not represent the views and emotions of the people for whose use it exists, it fails in part at least of its purpose. While opinion is free and diverse, and tending to show still sharper lines of cleavage, it seems unreasonable to expect that any one architectural tradition will be followed. We must be content if the threads of varying traditions are picked up faithfully and intelligently with due regard to changed methods of construction and new conditions of life and work. An architect, unless he is prepared to take the narrow view that the style he likes best should be imposed on all clients for all types of building, must show flexibility. Mr. Lutyens has never done " Gothic " building that follows text-book standards, because his mind does not work that way, but with that reservation

FIG. XXIII.—GRANITE ORIEL AT HOWTH CASTLE, 1910.

he has expressed himself in a variety of styles, and impressed on all of them an individual quality of design.

I feel strongly the difficulty of conveying by words the general impression in this relation which a broad yet detailed survey of his work has made on my mind. It is difficult to write

FIGS. XXIV. AND XXV.—LATER WORK IN VERNACULAR MANNERS. KENTISH BRICKWORK : LODGE AT KNOWLTON, 1912.

fruitfully, for the usual phrases of architectural criticism are not very helpful.   One general-
isation, however, may be made.   The buildings now illustrated clearly present one outstanding
quality—they are instinct with *style*, not in the usual meaning of the word that nails work to an
historical period, but as Pater used it—" for there is *style* there ; one temper has shaped the
whole ; and everything that has style, that has been done as no other man or age could have done
it . . . has its true value and interest."   For all his faithfulness to tradition, Mr. Lutyens
impresses on his work a personal quality that is unmistakable and that eludes the copyist.   " A
certain strangeness," says the same critic, " something of the blossoming of the aloe, is indeed
an element in all true works of art ; that they shall excite or surprise us is indispensable.   But
that they shall give pleasure and exert a charm over us is indispensable too ; and this strangeness
must be sweet also—a lovely strangeness."   It is precisely because Mr. Lutyens uses his power

FIG. XXVI.—FOLLY FARM, SULHAMPSTEAD, 1912 : ADDITION IN VERNACULAR
MANNER TO SYMMETRICAL HOUSE OF 1906.

of artistic surprise with reticence that it never becomes antic.   As soon as he has enlivened his
composition with a gracious touch of strangeness, he retires into a gravity which retains our
interest because it is unconscious, and never verges, as grave designing is apt to do, on dulness.
       The work of any artist, and perhaps of an architect especially, appeals to a variety of human
qualities.   Architecture throws a wider net than any other, for it is the expression of a more
complex group of needs, and we demand from it a more varied achievement.   Its art must
be grounded on a sure foundation of dexterous arrangement and practical skill in building ;
but, as Mr. Reginald Blomfield has wisely said, " architecture is something greater and more
profound than merely technical excellence, and though its appeal is more abstract and less readily

understood than that of the other arts, it is, like them, in the last resort addressed to the emotions." If this be admitted, and, indeed, the conclusion admits of no escape, we must agree with the same critic that, "Temperament, no less than imagination and intelligence, is an essential element in all good architecture." The word temperament, as well as its idea, has fallen on rather evil days. It is too apt to be associated with those wayward impulses which lead to disaster and form the raw material of so much modern art. A more sober meaning reveals it to us as "the force and passion within a man which drives him out to do certain things in a certain way and no other." This is only to say that temperament is at the root of originality, and it is to this quality that one must attribute the arresting power of any important work of art. No one can rightly understand modern architecture if the personal equation be neglected. In the Middle Ages the larger characteristics of buildings were mainly racial and national, and to a less extent local. Personal feeling appeared, but rather in small details of sculpture and painting than in the broad outlines and masses. The Renaissance changed all that. While, happily, national temperament has maintained some broad traditions in every country, and perhaps especially in England, the dominant influence on design and style has been since then the temperament of the individual. It has been the fancy of some architects that they could perpetuate the memory of their work by carving their names on its foundation-stones, and of others by the exaggeration of some ornament or group of details. To the architect who is an artist indeed there is no need of such adventitious aids. It is true that Mr. Lutyens has a special fondness for certain methods, but they have remained methods without degenerating

FIG. XXVII.—ADDITIONS TO ROEHAMPTON HOUSE, 1913.

into those dexterities and tricks which betray themselves as the spawn of an unreal originality. Vital art dare not keep to narrow paths or the traditions of the elders in any one selected style. Such houses as New Place, Shedfield, are conceived in the spirit of broad and dateless English traditions, yet with subtle differences in treatment which stamp it as the work of a modern. Others, like Great Maytham and The Salutation, Sandwich, are alive with the wide humanism of the age of Wren. In buildings of a more public sort Mr. Lutyens has clearly been mindful of the architecture of France and Italy, and there are echoes of the Grand Manner. Yet through it all there runs the vein of a marked personality, ever busy in invention and full of humour. It may be fairly said of his work, as did Walter Pater of one aspect of Italian art of the fifteenth century, that "it illustrates the faith of that age in all oracles, its desire to hear all voices, its generous belief that nothing which had ever interested the human mind could wholly lose its vitality." And it is in this word vitality that we may find the explanation of the appeal which this artist's buildings make. There will always be two broad tendencies in constructive art, the professional and the amateur. The former is best found in the work which in France and America is inspired by L'Ecole des Beaux Arts. Full of refinement and scholarship, as is much of it, it is yet apt to grow stiff in its reliance on formulas and its preoccupation with the realising of civic dignity. The architecture of England has always been, on the whole, the art of the amateur (the word being understood in its best sense). Into this category must be put the work of Wren, for the life of that great master was a long series of magnificent experiments, which never stiffened into a rule, or lacked the interest of a surging vitality.   In order to emphasise this by example, it may be noted that in the single department of church spires Wren created more types in the square mile of the City of London than the mediæval architects of the preceding five centuries in all England.   It is a kindred temperament, a like adventurous personality which Mr. Lutyens has stamped on scores of buildings up and down the country, while yet the weakness of lesser minds—self-repetition—has been avoided.   So much for invention, but it is more difficult to put into words the qualities which are the expression of humour. They are the outcome of a rich changefulness of idea.   Even so serious a person as Ruskin, with his insistent moralities, was not unregardful of this salt of humour in things æsthetic. In his usual pontifical fashion he has hailed the truth " that great art   . . .   does not say the same thing over and over again ; that the merit of architectural, as of every other art, consists in its saying new and different things . . .   and that we may, without offending any laws of good taste, require of an architect, as we do of a novelist, that he should be not only correct, but entertaining."   That the work here illustrated entertains us no one who studied the buildings, whether in being or in picture, can for a moment doubt.   We come continually on little conceits which relieve the prevailing and even sometimes austere simplicity.   It is not to be forgotten that the greatest artists of inventive temperament have relieved great conceptions by enchanting accessories, like Victor Hugo's butterfly which alights on the bloodstained barricade in " *Les Miserables.*"   Domestic architecture lives in an atmosphere of quieter and more gracious ideals, but none the less it needs its moments of relief, and these we find expressed, sometimes in a spirit of almost elfish charm, yet always without any strain on our sense of decorative proprieties.   It is a happy gift to keep these touches of humorous fancy in strict subordination to the main conception of a building, which is another way of saying that the work of the craftsmen is used to minister to a central idea, and is not regarded as an end in itself.   The function of architecture is not to apply ornament to building, but to create, in building, an artistic unity so pervading that it shall be impossible to detach any one quality or detail without an inevitable sense of loss.   In Mr. Lutyens' work, regarded as a whole, it is precisely the mastery with which he marshals the several elements of his art, without anything that can be called over-accentuation of parts, that touches us with the feeling of breadth and completeness, and explains the satisfying appeal which it makes not less to the emotions than to the critical judgment.

CHAPTER I.

TYPICAL EARLY WORKS—(1890–1898).

CROOKSBURY HOUSE ; RUCKMANS ; GARDEN AT WOODSIDE, CHENIES ; SULLINGSTEAD ;
MUNSTEAD WOOD ; FULBROOK HOUSE.

" THE spirit of place," to use a phrase of Mrs. Meynell, has a marked influence on the
work of any artist. It is idle to speculate on how Mr. Lutyens' work would have
developed if the early years of his practice had not been spent mainly in Surrey and
the nigh counties, but it is certain that it would have moved on rather different lines.
Crooksbury House was his first building of any size and importance. The plan is reproduced
in Fig. 4. To the right is shown the original house built in 1890. The eastern block to the
left and the connecting arm were added eight years later. I deal first with the house of 1890.
The influence of the picturesque way of building characteristic of Surrey is seen in the provision
of an ingle nook in the living-room and in the breaks in the lines of wall. There are some defects

FIG. I.—CROOKSBURY, 1890 : GARDEN PORCH ON SOUTH SIDE OF WEST WING.

in planning such as are expected of inexperience. The kitchen has its only window to the west, and the fireplaces are rather oddly disposed in some of the rooms. The treatment of the exterior is also rather uncertain. The little oriels in the half-timbered projection containing the porch look trivial enough in the light of later work. The roofing of the north wing (see

FIG. 2.—CROOKSBURY : PAVED GARDEN IN FIG COURT AND CORRIDOR BETWEEN THE WINGS : LOOKING NORTH.

first illustration in the Introduction), with the tiles sloping back under a broad white barge-board, may have some justification in old work, but it looks very awkward. These criticisms, however, are comparative only, and the house is sufficiently notable as the work of a youth

FIG. 3.—CROOKSBURY : THE FIG COURT. 1890 ON LEFT ; 1898 ON RIGHT.

of twenty-one. Indeed, it showed already a certain distinction which gave promise of better things. In 1898 Mr. Chapman wished to enlarge his home, and the new wing is illustrated, for the sake of convenience, here rather than at the end of the chapter. The first ten years of Mr. Lutyens' career were very appropriately closed by an addition to his first important building, for it marks his progress very decisively. It was characteristic of him then, as always, that he did not feel bound to do the new work at all in the manner of the old. A wing was wanted which should contain a library and several extra bedrooms. It was joined by a corridor to the original house so cunningly that the two manners cannot be seen side by side. The south end of the library wing was treated somewhat like the older work, and linked to it by a paved garden and a pergola. On the first floor there is an overhanging balcony with hood, which just appears at the right of Fig. 3. The new east front, however, shows a great development (Fig. 5). It recalls the houses of the middle of the seventeenth century, but the sense of balance was not yet so strong in Mr. Lutyens as to prevent

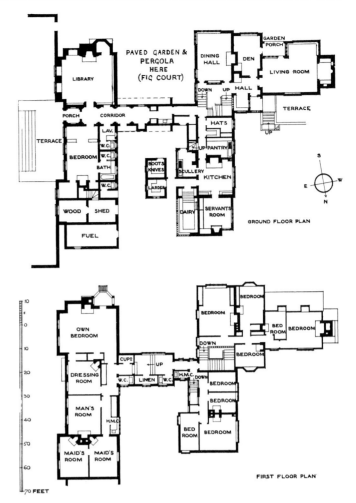

FIG. 4.—CROOKSBURY HOUSE : PLANS.

FIG. 5.—CROOKSBURY : EAST WING, ADDED IN 1898.

FIG. 6.—CROOKSBURY : 1898 WING FROM THE SOUTH-EAST.

him putting the garden entrance to one side. That position arose naturally out of the plan, but I have the feeling that if he were to face the same problem again, he would not have emphasised the garden porch so strongly. For all that, the front is a grave and delightful piece of building, and shows by its projecting quoins and by the quality of the brickwork generally a fine sense of the value of material. The setting of the house on the side of Crooksbury Hill made it ideal for garden making. It looks south to Hindhead, south-west to Trensham and west over the fat, green meadows, the stew-ponds and the big trees of Waverley Abbey. The house was built in a plantation of Scotch firs and birches, with undergrowths of heather and bracken. Terraces were built, which gave promise of the more brilliant work in this direction which was later to be done at Marshcourt and Hestercombe. There is a wealth of walls and gateways and pergola, and the handling of the fig court, with its pool and dwarf walls, is very successful (Figs. 2 and 3). I have, however, limited the illustration of the Crooksbury garden treatment to a few pictures, as the same characteristics appear in a more mature form in later houses.

FIG. 7.—RUCKMANS, 1894: GARDEN FRONT FROM THE SOUTH-WEST.

FIG. 8.—RUCKMANS: GROUND FLOOR PLAN.

Walls of original farmhouse are shown hatched and the new work in solid black.

RUCKMANS.

We must return, however, to work which was done earlier than the additions to Crooksbury. Ruckmans, Oakwood Park, Surrey, was built in 1894, and is interesting as being one of the first of the typical farmhouses which have taken new shape under Mr. Lutyens' hand. The plan (Fig. 8) shows that it was

FIG. 9.—RUCKMANS: OLDER PART (1894) LEFT; MUSIC-ROOM (1902) RIGHT.

FIG. 10.—RUCKMANS, 1894: THE STAIRCASE.

FIG. 11.—RUCKMANS : IN A BEDROOM.

FIG. 12.—IN THE DINING-ROOM.

originally a simple oblong with a small projection at the south-east corner. It possessed two chimney-stacks, one of considerable size in the middle, and was roofed with the heavy stone slabs which come from Horsham. The garden front, with its three gables and large expanse of tile-hanging, shows his early grasp of Surrey building traditions, but in some respects is rather immature. Very interesting, however, are the two brick fireplaces in the dining-room and one of the bedrooms (Figs. 11 and 12). They are early exercises in a manner which has become widely popular and has suffered no little caricature by unintelligent copying. The work begun in 1894 included the ample kitchen wing at the north-east corner, as well as the garden front (Fig. 7), on which a long verandah was provided. In 1902 some increase of the house was required in the nature of a room tall enough to make it satisfactory for music, which is not heard well in the low rooms proper to farmhouse design. As in the case of Crooksbury, Mr. Lutyens did not feel himself bound by his earlier adventures. The music-room was by its very character and dimensions a new and distinct feature at Ruckmans, and this distinction is marked by a change in the architectural treatment (see Fig. 9 and illustrations in Introduction). He has surrounded the

FIG. 13.—RUCKMANS : COTTAGE PLAN.

FIG. 14.—A COTTAGE AT RUCKMANS.

room with tall sliding sashes instead of with long rows of low casements. Instead of putting gables to the roof he has treated it with hips. This shows not only a faithfulness in the development of plan, but also a readiness to let a modern building confess its own history in a perfectly frank way. There is a tendency in some architects to copy themselves when making additions to their earlier works—a procedure which seems to lack justification. I also illustrate by plans and one photograph a simple little cottage built in the grounds of Ruckmans. (Figs. 13 and 14).

FIG. 15.—WOODSIDE: THE SUNDIAL.

WOODSIDE, CHENIES.

The first of the important gardens designed by Mr. Lutyens for an existing house was made in 1893 at Chenies, Buckinghamshire, for Adeline Duchess of Bedford. Woodside is plain and

FIG. 16.—WOODSIDE, CHENIES, 1893: FROM THE POND COURT, LOOKING EAST INTO RIVER GARDEN.

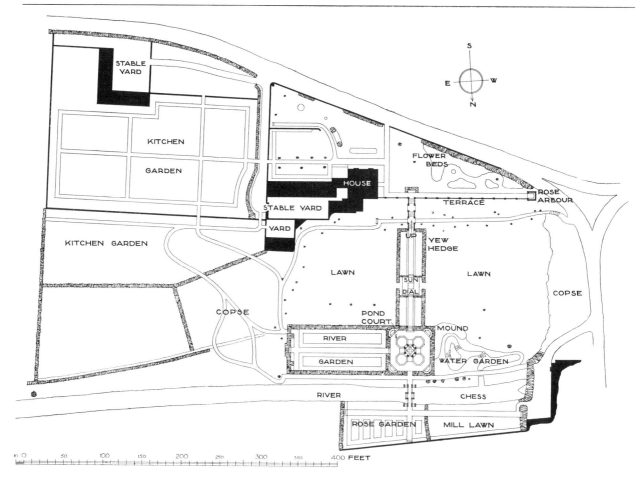

FIG. 17.—PLAN OF GARDEN AT WOODSIDE, CHENIES.

FIG. 18.—WOODSIDE: PERGOLA IN POND COURT, 1893.

FIG. 19.—THE POND COURT, LOOKING SOUTH-EAST, 1893.

FIG. 20.—SULLINGSTEAD : HALF TIMBER WORK, ON NORTH SIDE, 1896.

FIG. 21.—SULLINGSTEAD : ENTRANCE FRONT FROM WEST, 1896.

not impressive, but has a certain picturesqueness of outline which tells from every point of view in the new gardens. The slope of the ground suggested a terraced treatment, and it is to be observed that the design carried out embodies the character both of slope and terrace, of the natural and the formal. The green lawns leading down from south to north are the framework for the stepped descent. The scheme begins on the higher ground with a terrace running east and west and connecting the house with a rose arbour. From it a stairway leads down in three flights to a long sloping path flanked by flower borders which are backed by rich hedges. This slope is broken by a square terrace with three steps of approach and departure. Here stands a tall sundial (Fig. 15). At the north end of the sloping path we come to a square enclosure hedged with yews. In its midst is a round pond enclosed by four pairs of stone columns

FIG. 22.—SULLINGSTEAD : GABLED DRAWING-ROOM, ON RIGHT, 1896 ; HIPPED MUSIC ROOM, ON LEFT, 1903.

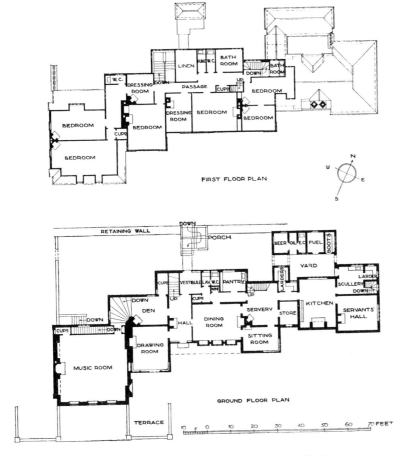

FIRST FLOOR PLAN

GROUND FLOOR PLAN

FIG. 23.—SULLINGSTEAD: PLANS—HOUSE, 1896; MUSIC ROOM, ADDED 1903.

FIG. 24.—SOUTH-WEST SIDE OF MUSIC ROOM, 1903.

on oblong panelled bases, which form with their heavy oak lintels an octagonal pergola (Fig. 18). The bases are set on the inner moulded kerbs of four octagonal flower-beds. The four corners of the pond court are occupied by brick-built seats with stone copings. An opening in the eastern hedge of the court leads by two steps to the river garden, which is also enclosed by yews (Fig. 16). On the west side of the pond court is a rock and water garden in the natural manner, which contrasts pleasantly with the formalism of the main scheme. Here irises and other water-loving plants find a congenial home. The north opening of the court leads across a bridge over the River Chess to a rose garden and mill lawn, which form the boundary of the garden.

In the light of later work, such as the gardens at Hestercombe, there is a slight hardness in the full detail of the stonework of the pergola, but as a whole the scheme shows a large grasp of the essential qualities of the formal garden at an early period of Mr. Lutyens' career.

SULLINGSTEAD.

Sullingstead, Hascombe, Surrey, was begun in 1896, and shows Mr. Lutyens following in Norman Shaw's footsteps, and making further experiments with half-timber work and tile-hanging. The house stands remote and sequestered, and we come upon it with a sense of surprise. The

FIG. 25.—SULLINGSTEAD FROM THE EAST.

entrance front is on the
north side, and the
ground slopes sharply
down southwards.
Standing well above the
house on the side of the
hill is a detached porch,
from which steps wind
down to the narrow
court before the front
door. The projecting
wing of the building
here is in oak and plaster,
set on a dwarf brick
wall, and seen in Figs. 20

FIG. 26.—MUNSTEAD WOOD FROM THE SOUTH-WEST.

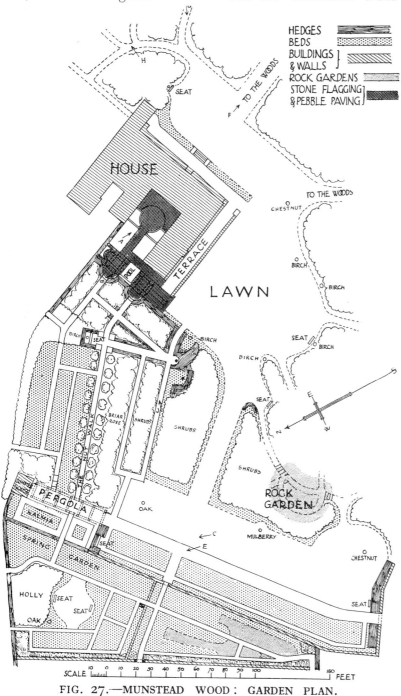

FIG. 27.—MUNSTEAD WOOD: GARDEN PLAN.

and 21. As in the cases of
Crooksbury and Ruckmans,
Mr. Lutyens was called in to
make additions at a time when
his design had developed, and
once again he did the new work
in his then existing manner.
In the design of the new
music-room at Sullingstead he
showed a notable judgment
(Fig. 22). Its big sash windows, prominent dormers and
hipped roof give it a character
wholly different from the
gabled tile-hung front which it
adjoins on the south front, but
the feeling of the older work
is carried on by the weather-
boarding which covers the
space above the cornice. When
we turn the corner and see the
boarded twin gables of the
west side (Fig. 24), the relation between new and old is
seen to be still more intimately
maintained, though the cornice
marking the later manner is
continued. In the result the
two distinct motifs of design
are mingled so subtly and yet
so rightly that the whole house
maintains its unity.

MUNSTEAD WOOD.

Mr. Lutyens began to de-
sign Munstead Wood for Miss
Jekyll in 1896. The site was
ideal for the purposes of a
simple country house which

FIG. 28.—MUNSTEAD WOOD, 1896.

FIG. 29.—THE SOUTH FRONT SEEN THROUGH THE WOOD.

should follow the building traditions of Surrey. It lies on a sideway which turns from the road leading from Godalming to Hascombe. Its chief feature is revealed by the name which the house now bears.

A clearing existed in a chestnut copse, and there the house and near garden were set. Paths were cut through the undergrowth and grassed, so that many aspects of the house are revealed at the ends of leafy vistas (Figs. 28 and 29). Much of the ground had to be laid out before it was known where the building was to stand, with the result that the garden plan shows some awkward angles. They have been ingeniously masked, however, and the immediate surroundings of the house were devised on formal lines. The space between the east and west wings is occupied by a paved court, with which are grouped two flights of stone steps enclosing a tank (Figs. 30 to 32). The court has a round pavement partly bounded by a raised step next the house, and the stairways on either side of the tank are punctuated by balls of clipped box (Fig. 30).

FIG. 30.—THE TANK.

"At the far end of the kitchen garden, where the north and west walls join at an uneven angle, stands a little building—a raised gazebo (Fig. 34). From inside the garden its floor-level is gained by a flight of steps that wind up with one or two turns. Its purpose is partly to give a fitting finish to a bare-looking piece of wall, and partly to provide a look-out place over the fields and the distant range of chalk hill to the north, for the region of the house and garden

FIG. 31.—PAVED COURT AND STEPS ON NORTH SIDE.

FIG. 32.--MUNSTEAD WOOD : TANK AND STEPS ON NORTH SIDE, LOOKING WESTWARDS.

FIG. 33.—MUNSTEAD WOOD : ON THE SOUTH SIDE, LOOKING WESTWARDS.

is so much encompassed by woodland that there is no view to the open country. The little place is most often used, when there is thunder about, for watching the progress of the storm, and an incised stone on the garden side bears its name of Thunder-house."

The last paragraph is quoted from the description of this garden in West Surrey which forms a chapter in *Gardens for Small Country Houses*. A full account of the planting of the garden is there given.

The house itself is built of the local stone, with a slight use of half-timber in the outer wall on the north side. Great play is made indoors with heavy oak beams, especially in the fine corridor on the first floor (Fig. 37), which is fitted with cupboards along its whole length. The house is entered on the east side by a long porch. From the inner vestibule a corridor leads to the hall (Fig. 35), from which the main staircase rises directly. There is a hint of the Gothic Revival in the canopied treatment of the fireplace. The disposition of the workroom, bookroom, dining-room, etc., are clearly shown on the house

FIG. 34.—THE THUNDER-HOUSE.

FIG. 35.—MUNSTEAD WOOD: THE HALL.

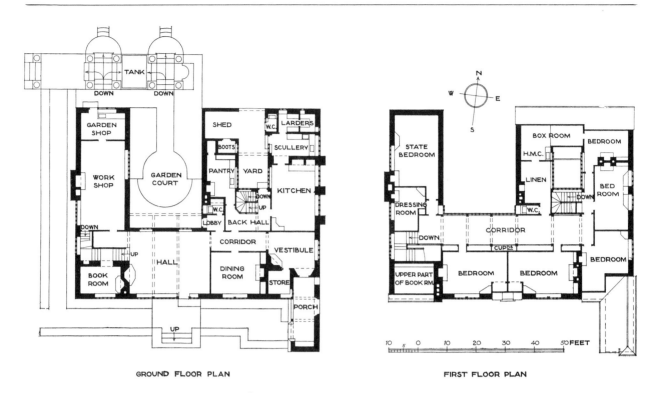

GROUND FLOOR PLAN   FIRST FLOOR PLAN

FIG. 36.—PLANS OF MUNSTEAD WOOD.

FIG. 37.—MUNSTEAD WOOD : UPSTAIRS CORRIDOR.

plans (Fig. 36), and needs not, therefore, to be described in detail. Some visitors to Munstead Wood have criticised the house on the ground that the windows are too small and the rooms consequently not light enough. That might be a reasonable criticism if the wishes of the owner had not been taken into account, but the house is the result of a

FIG. 38.—FULBROOK, 1897 : THE ENTRANCE FRONT.

perfect understanding between architect and client as to the sort of house to be built and its treatment. If the light is subdued in some rooms it is precisely because that was desired.

FIG. 39.—FULBROOK : WEST WING WITH OCTAGONAL TURRET.

FIG. 40.—EAST FRONT.

FIG. 41.—FULBROOK HOUSE, 1897: SOUTH FRONT.

FULBROOK HOUSE.

Fulbrook House, Surrey, stands a few miles south-east of Farnham, in a district which was once all forest land, and still keeps many characteristics of the wild. It shows Mr. Lutyens still in 1897 an urgent seeker of the picturesque and finding his way to his present consummate sense of the value of material. At Fulbrook, indeed, his pleasure in texture was so great as to lead to considerable restlessness. Too many techniques are employed at once. There are the stone of the walls, rubble and ashlar, the brick of the chimneys, tile-hanging and weather-boarding – truly, as Pepys would say, " a glut of pleasures." Also in the mass and outline of the house there is a somewhat too vigorous pursuit of the picturesque. It must be admitted that the south front—with its loggia and balconies set back under the main roof, the half octagons of the flanking rooms and the middle bay dividing the loggia—has a contrived charm which no one need seek to resist. It is delightful, but at what a cost of structural honesty. It is not

FIG. 42.—FULBROOK, 1897: HALL AND STAIRCASE.

necessary to adopt the bald Ruskin theories of sincerity in building ; but even if a large latitude be allowed for poetic licence, the loggia at Fulbrook House (Fig. 41) makes heavy drafts on the relation between facts and appearances. To what strange shifts Mr. Lutyens was put by way of ironwork concealed in the roof I do not know, but they must have been queer and considerable. It is not as though the amiable fraud were convincing. Anyone with an eye for structure can see that the four slim bracket-pieces cannot conceivably support the long horizontal beam. It is the less possible because the two from the bay do not even attempt to support it, but butt against its side. Few—perhaps, indeed, none—now demand that every constructional hook and eye shall be left naked, but struts that affect to carry a beam when the work of support is being done somewhere in the roof seem to make too vigorous a demand on our credulity. It is not the *suppressio veri* which catches the eye, but the *suggestio falsi*. The fault is more obvious when the game is played in a house of the vernacular sort. In a building which is based more or less on classical treatment we do not look for an excessive candour. We demand that it shall be structurally sound, and that its parts shall do the work demanded of them, without too critical an enquiry as to how they divide the labour, but the justification of evident brackets and beams is that they are working and not playing, that they are bones and not scenery. I have the less hesitation in setting down this criticism because such constructive jests as the Fulbrook loggia belong to Mr. Lutyens' *juvenilia*, and have long been abandoned for a more serious outlook. Happily, his work, even his most recent work, is full of amusing moments, but they are occasioned by frankly decorative features or by structural whimsies that do not attempt to deceive. The east wing of the entrance front is simple and satisfactory, but its effect is rather perturbed by the octagonal tile-hung turret at the corner of the west wing (Fig. 39). The next chapter illustrates other houses in the traditional manner in which Mr. Lutyens abandoned the pursuit of the picturesque, and consequently achieved it in a more convincing fashion.

The interiors of Fulbrook House show for the first time in a marked way an inclination to treat them in a classical fashion (Fig. 42) despite the purely traditional and picturesque handling of the exterior. The detail already shows skill but lacks the personal quality which developed later and is seen at its best in such houses as Heathcote, Ilkley.

CHAPTER II.

FOUR SURREY HOUSES OF 1899.

ORCHARDS, GODALMING; GODDARDS, ABINGER COMMON; TIGBOURNE COURT, WITLEY: AND LITTLECROFT, GUILDFORD.

ORCHARDS was begun in 1899, and took about three years to build. It is set on a wooded table-land, richly clothed with oak and fir and silver birch, to the east of Godalming town. Both the house and its garden show Mr. Lutyens still working in the spirit of the Surrey tradition of building, but with greater facility in the handling of materials, and with a readiness to let the mass and outlines of the building develop a natural rather than a contrived picturesqueness. The grouping of the house with its attendant and attached offices and walled gardens show the same spirit as that which animated the sixteenth century Englishman when he built, in native style, a house in which to dwell in native manner. Precisely the same careful attention to line and proportion, apt choice of

FIG. 43.—ENTRANCE TO ORCHARDS.
Way to stable yard on left and to courtyard on right.

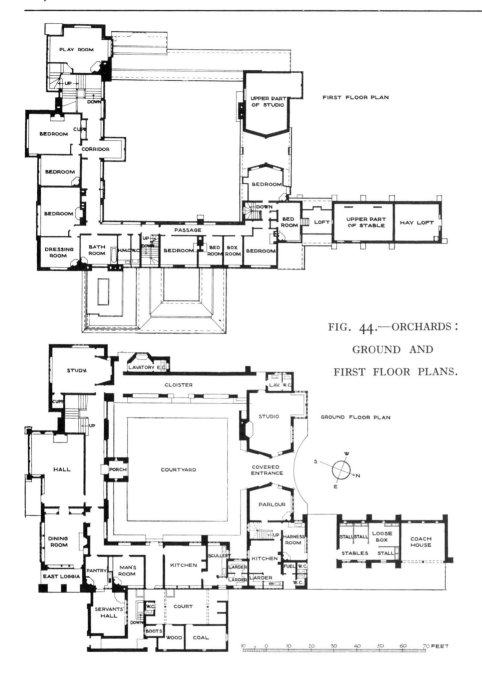

FIG. 44.—ORCHARDS:

GROUND AND

FIRST FLOOR PLANS.

FIG. 45.—ENTRANCE TO COURTYARD.

fitting material and right adaptation of features to their purposes are apparent round the whole compass of the buildings. As we enter the grounds we have on our left the stable building (Fig 43), stretching out towards us beyond the main square of the court, but connected and grouping with it. In front is the opening through the north side of the court (Fig. 45). It is a carriage-way, and rises up to the roof-plate, which is supported by oak brackets, and the whole reminds us of the entrance into the ample yard of an old coaching inn. In this case it admits to a quadrangle, around which there are in-habited buildings on three sides, but the fourth consists of a cloister (Fig. 47), which connects Lady Chance's studio, lying on the right of the archway into the court, with the main block of the house. This faces us on enter-ing the court, and a projecting two-storeyed porch (Fig. 46) occupies its middle. The material chiefly used for the walls is the small sized yellow rubble-stone of the district ; but above the windows and in many of the archways lines of red roofing tiles are built in. The garden piers and other architectural details are also done in the same tiles with which the buildings are roofed. Red bricks are used for the chimneys, and their fine shape and grouping produce the leading vertical lines of the composition. They contrast admirably with the simple and extended roof lines and with the long lines of oak casements. For the archway of the porch in the courtyard stone is introduced, but the upper part of this projection

FIG. 46.—PORCH AND CLOISTER IN COURTYARD.

shows an unbroken line of casements lighting the great bay in the upstairs gallery corridor. Downstairs a corresponding wide corridor, opening into a square whence the broad and

FIG. 47.—WITHIN THE CLOISTER.

FIG. 48.—ORCHARDS : LOOKING NORTH-WEST TO THE KITCHEN WING.

FIG. 49.—DIPPING WELL IN KITCHEN GARDEN.

FIG. 50.—THE SOUTH-EAST CORNER.

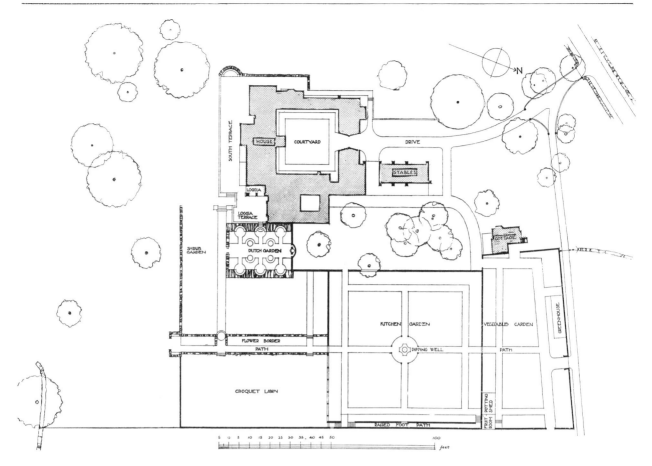

FIG. 51.—ORCHARDS: GARDEN PLAN.

FIG. 52.—A GARDEN ARCHWAY.

easy oak stair rises, forms the hall, and is set with oak dressers, chests, tables and chairs of seventeenth century character. From it are entered the three principal sitting-rooms, which all look out on to the south terrace. The centre of this southern front, with its gable projection, is the drawing-room, the mullioned windows of which end in a Tudor doorway forming part of

FIG. 53.—ARCH IN KITCHEN GARDEN WALL

the same oak framing. It gives access to the terrace, up to whose bank wild Nature stretches. There is no garden on this side, but an outlook upon and into the virgin wood, whose trees have been felled for a certain distance to give free play for light and air. Beyond the drawing-room, towards the east, is the oak-panelled dining-room (Fig. 59). Its casements are flush with the

FIG. 54.—ORCHARDS: HOUSE AND GARDEN FROM THE EAST.

outer face of its thick wall, the inner face of which is supported by dwarf oak columns rising from the broad window-ledge.   The same treatment is carried along the dividing wall between

it and the drawing-room. The recesses thus obtained form sideboard space for the display of a varied collection of pewter. The study fire-place is prettily treated with a great expanse of Dutch tiling, on which is pictured a pair of enriched pilasters with a frieze. These frame a plan of the house and garden (Fig. 58). The dining-room gives on to the loggia, which appears in many of the accompanying pictures, for it dominates the most choice part of the garden. This begins with a brick and stone paved plat, enclosed by a low wall where there are no buildings, and left free for sitting out in favourable weather. From here the glorious view may be enjoyed. Half the county of Surrey is seen beyond the garden, lying at the onlooker's feet. Steps from this plat descend

FIG. 55.—TILE-BUILT WALL FOUNTAIN AT ORCHARDS.

FIG. 56.—ORCHARDS FROM THE EAST.

to a small garden of the type often called Dutch, but unlike anything ever seen in Holland.   It is, indeed, essentially a creation of to-day, and the outcome of Mr. Lutyens' ingenuity.   Its guiding lines are fixed by three large semi-circular seats on each side of it, of which the central one on the house side forms part of the stepped descent from the sitting-out

FIG. 57.—STAIRWAY TO THE EAST LOGGIA.

plat (Fig. 57).   The circular idea adopted for the seats appears also in the intervening beds, and thus a segmental side is given to those that surround them.   The whole scheme of beds does not occupy too large a space, but is fitly restrained to allow of ample walking room, and a broad stone-paved alley runs down the middle of this little enclosure.   The dark yew contrasts well with stone and tile and bricks.   The latter are set in herring-bone patterns, and give relief and variety to the expanse of flagging. To the north this miniature pleasaunce is bounded by a tile-coped wall, which separates it from the kitchen garden. The middle of this wall is hollowed out into a curved recess, supported by tile-built piers and containing a tank, into which water pours from the mouth of a finely designed and wrought bronze lion head (Fig. 55). It is the work of Lady Chance, whose excellent craftsmanship in garden sculpture and ornament is well known. Form, rather than mass of colour, is the note struck by the "Dutch" garden. The right idea for such an enclosure is that it should form a projection of the dwelling-house into the realm of Nature; that it should partake mostly of the character of the former, but be tinctured with the spirit and the substance of the latter; that it should be a room with the sky as its roof and with living plants for its furniture and decoration. Shapeliness and restraint are, therefore, the right principles of its planting, and have guided this work at Orchards. Below the "Dutch" garden, and

FIG. 58.—A MAP IN TILES IN THE STUDY.

FIG. 59.—THE DINING-ROOM AT ORCHARDS.

backed and sheltered by yews, lies an ample
herbaceous border, exhibiting rich and varied
wares the long summer through. We have
scarce walked its length before the eye is
caught by an almost gayer picture lying before
it—a picture, indeed, duly and adequately
framed (Fig. 53). The kitchen garden wall
rises up to an added height to take a tall,
wide archway, whose great double oak-plank
doors stand open and reveal the bright borders
of the central alley. They are backed by
espalier fruit trees trained on an oak trellis.
On reaching the middle of this extensive plot
the alley takes a sweep round the coping of
an octagonal dipping-well (Fig. 49), and a
corona of posts and chain carries its bright
burden of rambler roses along its outer edge.
One other feature of the kitchen garden
needs mention. Its lower, or eastern, wall
blocks out the view at what is, perhaps, its
best point. Yet such a wall—and of great
height—is essential for the protection of the
garden from the ungenial wind. With
Mr. Lutyens a difficulty generally resolves
itself, not into a detriment, but into an added

FIG. 60.—STAIRCASE TO STUDIO.

FIG. 61.—ORCHARDS: MAIN STAIRCASE AND FIRST FLOOR CORRIDOR.

amenity, and so this wall is not left as an obscuring block, but is contrived into an elevated outlook. As in the "mount" of the early gardens, a walk runs along within a yard or so of the top, and it commands the whole prospect. At its further end—the north--east angle—a high peaked roof covers a building which in the sixteenth century would no doubt have been a garden-house; but Orchards is so amply supplied, at other

FIG. 62.—GODDARDS : ENTRANCE FRONT.

points, with buildings for pleasure that this one is reserved for utility, and is fitted as a fruit-room.

GODDARDS.

Goddards was built for Sir Frederick Mirrielees as a Home of Rest to which ladies of small means might repair for holiday. It was also used for invalid soldiers after the South African war, and has since been altered somewhat as a private house for Mr. Donald Mirrielees. Figs. 62 to 68 show the house as first built : Figs. 69 and 70 illustrate the

FIG. 63 —GODDARDS : BRICK MULLIONS AND HORSHAM HEELING, 1899.

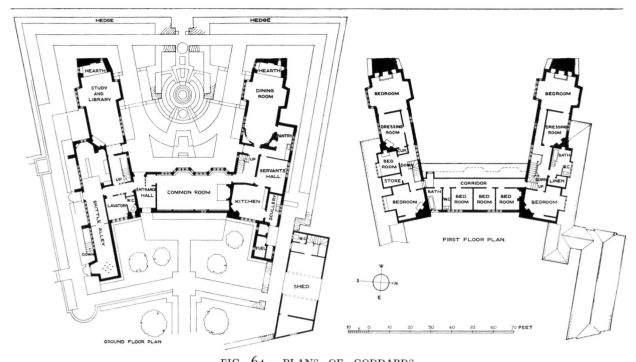

FIG. 64.—PLANS OF GODDARDS.

Showing house as built in 1899 and additions to north and south wings made in 1910.

additions made in 1910 and the greater growth of the yew hedged garden.   It stands on Abinger Common, which runs for a couple of miles south of Leith Hill, in Surrey.   The air sweeps up from the weald to this typical Surrey site over the nine hundred feet of elevation of the hill, and the house itself is nearly seven hundred feet above the sea.   The land was part of the

FIG. 65.—GODDARDS: GARDEN COURT FROM THE NORTH-WEST, AS BUILT IN 1899.

FIG. 66.—PAVING OF WEST COURT, 1899.

FIG. 67.—THE SOUTH WING: AS BUILT IN 1899.

FIG. 68.—GODDARDS : DIPPING WELL IN WEST COURT.

copyhold of the ancient manor of the Evelyns of Wotton, from whose descendants it was purchased by its present owner. The ancient name of the property was " Goddards," and that name it still retains. It shows a delightful variety both in plan and in the use and treatment of materials. What, for example, could be more charming than the western court, with its fine roof, chimneys, brick-mullioned windows and doors, or the garden there, with its pool, its curiously laid pavements and flowering plants like sea-anemones lying on a rock ? The house occupies three sides of a quadrangle, which is splayed open towards the west. The connecting arm between the north and south wings is occupied on the ground floor by what was originally the common room or dining hall. A new dining-room has lately been added to the north wing, and a library to the south. (Figs. 69 and 70.) An unusual and interesting feature is the skittle alley, which appears in Fig. 72. The fine carvings used as ornaments on the walls of the alley are dated 1707.

FIG. 69.—NEW WEST END OF NORTH WING, ADDED 1910.

FIG. 70.—FROM SOUTH WEST, SHOWING ADDITIONS TO WINGS IN 1910.

FIG. 71.—GODDARDS: THE COMMON ROOM.

FIG. 72.—GODDARDS : THE SKITTLE ALLEY, 1899.

FIG. 73.—GODDARDS : DOOR TO COMMON ROOM.

They came from the pediments of the gables of the old Wandsworth Manor House, now pulled down. The common room is a good example of heavy timber construction (Fig. 71).

TIGBOURNE COURT.

This house was built in 1899. Surrey has no fairer region than that which lies between Guildford and Hindhead, for it is a land watered by many streams in the green-gathering grounds both of the Wey and the Arun, a country varied in surface, rich in pasture, and embowered in much of the woodland of the ancient Weald of Surrey. Witley stands high on the road from Godalming to Petworth, and commands extensive views. To the south-west rise Hindhead and Gibbet Hill ; to the south-east lie wooded heights, parts of the ancient Weald ; to the north is the green valley of a tributary of the Wey with the long line of the Hog's Back beyond ; and on every side is a rich prospect of hill and dale. The Weald of Surrey is notable for its fine old farmhouses, relics of prosperous

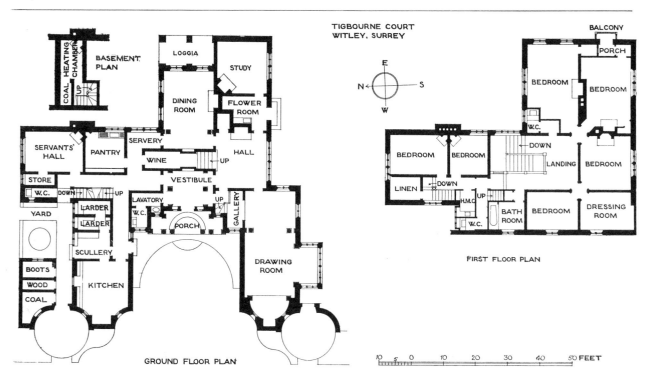

FIG. 74.—PLANS OF TIGBOURNE COURT.

FIG. 75.—TIGBOURNE FROM THE SOUTH-EAST.

days, for its hammer-ponds, the vestiges of
its disused iron furnaces, its many " folds,"
which were ancient enclosures for cattle in the
wood, and for its copses of oak and other
trees. Cobbett says of the district that it is
" a country where, strictly speaking, only three
things will grow well—grass, wheat, and oak
trees."

The site where Mr. Edgar Horne decided
to build the house was occupied by Tigbourne Cottage, which had a picturesque
garden. Its well-matured alleys of thuja or
Arbor vitæ and trained yew hedges were too
good for the cottage to which it belonged,
but the cottage was not sacrified to the new
house. It remains, and is suitable for the
coachman's residence as it adjoins the newly
erected stabling. The new house stands by
the road, and Mr. Lutyens has given to the
entrance front a more welcoming character
than in most of his later houses. It faces
west, and the pillared porch is set back
between projecting wings, which contain the
kitchen quarters on the north and the
drawing-room on the south. The plan is
very gay in conception. Not only are the
inner corners of the wings set out with
concave curves, but the gateway to the

FIG. 76.—THE DINING LOGGIA.

FIG. 77.—TIGBOURNE : PERGOLA AND WELL.

FIG. 78.—TIGBOURNE COURT : ENTRANCE FRONT FROM THE ROAD.

kitchen yard on the north and to the garden on the south are also made the occasion of great recessed curves. The walls are of Bargate stone, with garretted joints diversified by courses of roofing tiles disposed in half diamonds, and ingeniously used as keys to

FIG. 79.—THE BALCONY ON THE WEST SIDE.

the round arches. Some of the quoins are of brick, which also serves as filling to the little pediments, straight and curved, over the first-floor windows. The gaiety of this vernacular treatment of material and of the plan is sobered by the classical treatment of the porch with

FIG. 80.—TIGBOURNE COURT : THE TERRACE.

columns and entablature.   The planning of the vestibule and hall is a little confused, and the
relation of kitchen and dining-room leaves something to be desired.   The drawing-room, with
its little gallery reached from the vestibule by a private stair, is a large and important apartment,
in the main only one storey high.   A notable feature of the design is the dignity and sense of
largeness secured for a house which is not, in fact, large.   The first floor provides only seven

FIG. 81.—LITTLECROFT, GUILDFORD : ENTRANCE FRONT.   FIG. 82.—FROM FRONT DOOR.

FIG. 83.—LITTLECROFT : GARDEN FRONT FROM
SOUTH-WEST.

FIG. 84.—STAIRS FROM LOWER
HALL.

bedrooms, but there are others in the attic. The south front is attractive with its broad terrace, clipped yews, brick-mullioned windows and the glimpse of the convex face of the wing wall on the road side. On the west front, and opening from the dining-room, is an arcaded loggia (Fig. 76), and on the first floor a balcony carried on a brick bracket, and with a hipped canopy roof supported by iron balusters of delicate design (Fig. 79). The garden is made the more attractive by its pergola and well (Fig. 77).

LITTLECROFT, GUILDFORD.

Littlecroft is a small house on Guildown. It stands alongside the road winding round the hill, and the ground slopes to the south so very rapidly that what seems a low cottage on the entrance front (Fig. 81) becomes a tall house on the garden side (Fig. 83). The little polygonal oriel windows at the angles of walls show how strong Norman Shaw's influence was in 1899. The house is on a small scale, and simply equipped, but the nature of the plan, with its front entrance near the level of the bedroom floor, indicated that the staircase should be somewhat emphasised. The reception-rooms open from the lower hall (Fig. 84), and the staircase is used, therefore, by every visitor.

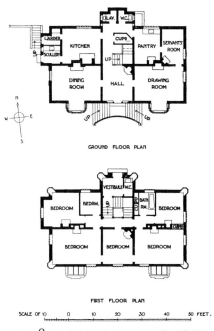

FIG. 85.—PLANS OF LITTLECROFT.

CHAPTER III.

TWO NORFOLK HOUSES, 1899.

OVERSTRAND HALL AND THE PLEASAUNCE, OVERSTRAND.

OVERSTRAND HALL, near Cromer, is of interest as the earliest example of any importance of Mr. Lutyens' vernacular work outside the Home Counties. The building traditions in East Anglia are as different as can well be imagined from those in Surrey. The county of Norfolk in particular is poor in building stone, but rich in flints and clay. It has, therefore, developed a very characteristic idiom of flint and tile building, and the treatment of the Fountain Court at Overstrand Hall shows an experiment in this manner. The walls are built of rough, unsquared flints, diversified by two strongly marked horizontal bands of roofing tiles laid in definite and varying patterns, one below the sills of the upper windows and one above the arcade of the fountain loggia. The window mullions are throughout of red brick. Fig. 89, which shows the garden front as seen from the north-east,

FIG. 86.—OVERSTRAND HALL : IN THE FOUNTAIN COURT.

indicates the variety of materials which have been used. The upper storey on the south side is built of timber framing, whereas the two bays at the corner have their white walls diversified by red brick quoins of broken outline.

The plan of the house is interesting and unusual. In general outline it is a quadrangle with an open fountain court in the middle and with a kitchen block added at its north-west corner. The house is approached from the west, and is entered by an interesting vestibule framed of timber with brick filling, which appears in Fig. 88. It is worth noting that the skeleton archway from this entry to the fountain court is designed in a fashion which was afterwards developed more skilfully at Marshcourt. From the entry the house may be reached either across the fountain court, on the east side of which a double flight of steps, circular on plan, gives access to an inner vestibule, or through a door to the right of the entry by a few stairs into the main hall.

The main staircase is in oak and designed in a Jacobean manner (Fig. 92). The hall fireplace is attractively modelled, and has a very low opening (Fig. 91). East and west of the hall

FIG. 87.—ENTRANCE FRONT FROM SOUTH-WEST.

FIG. 88.—FROM ENTRY TO FOUNTAIN COURT.

FIG. 89.—FROM THE NORTH-EAST.

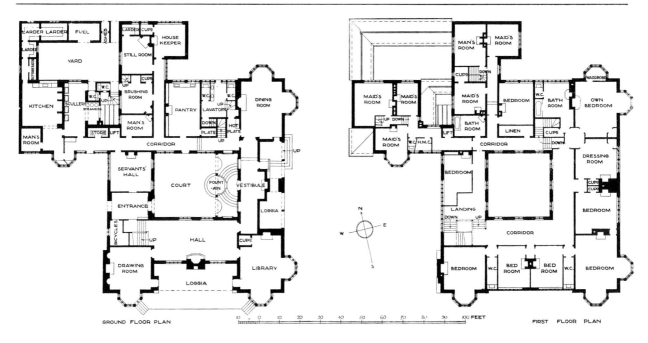

FIG. 90.—PLANS OF OVERSTRAND HALL.

are the library and the drawing-room : the latter has a beamed ceiling, and appears in Fig. 93. An interesting feature of the house is the ample provision of

FIG. 92.—OVERSTRAND HALL : THE STAIRCASE.

FIG. 91.—OVERSTRAND HALL : THE HALL FIREPLACE.

outdoor sitting-rooms. On the south side there is a wide loggia, with doors both from drawing-room and library. On the east side a pair of loggias was provided, the northern one of which is illustrated in Fig. 94. The other has since been glazed, and the wall shown on the plan between it and the vestibule has been removed, in order to provide a little tea-room. Overstrand Hall, though interesting in plan and attractive in its grouping, lacks evidence of that assimilation of local traditions which is so obvious in Mr. Lutyens' Surrey work done at the same time. The growing facility which came with large practice and wide experience of different local manners enabled him in his later work to absorb more rapidly the characteristics of other districts in which he has worked. It can hardly be said that at Overstrand he had grasped so fully the essential characteristics of East Anglian building.

THE PLEASAUNCE, OVERSTRAND.

The design of this house cannot be regarded as in any way typical of Mr. Lutyens' work, because there were many hampering conditions. There existed on the site two villas wholly lacking in architectural merit, and they had to be incorporated in the main body of the new house. The problem, therefore, was to make the best of the unsuitable plan to which he was tied, and to mask as far as possible the houses that already existed. It is easy to make the criticism that the

FIG. 93.—OVERSTRAND HALL : DRAWING-ROOM.

FIG. 94.—OVERSTRAND HALL : NORTH LOGGIA ON EAST FRONT.

FIG. 95.—THE PLEASAUNCE, OVERSTRAND.

FIG. 96.—THE PLEASAUNCE : THE PAVED GARDEN.

garden front, as it appears in Fig. 95, is markedly lacking in definite form, but that is due to the circumstances and not to any failure of the designer. The plan of the house is not illustrated because the conditions which hampered its development deprive it of interest. The garden is attractive, and Fig. 96 shows a skilful disposition of paving, shaped flower-beds and steps. In the treatment of the entrance porch a pleasant decorative use has been made of a shield of arms with gaily designed lambrequins.

FIG. 97.—THE PORCH.

CHAPTER IV.

WORK DONE IN 1900–1.

DEANERY GARDEN, SONNING ; FISHER'S HILL, WOKING ; HOMEWOOD, KNEBWORTH ;

ABBOTSWOOD, GLOUCESTERSHIRE.

THE Deanery Garden gave great opportunities, because it was enclosed by an ancient red-brick wall, and part of the site was covered by an old orchard. The name marks an early ecclesiastical ownership, but there was no fragment of building to suggest any definite characteristic for the house to be built there. The design made for Mr. Edward Hudson showed early a peculiar gift for welding together house and garden into a harmonious whole. The building has since been enlarged for a later owner, but as first built it marked the rapid development that was taking place in Mr. Lutyens' art in the opening year of the century. The Deanery Garden is therefore more instructive if considered in the form which it first took. Reference to the garden plan (Fig. 106) shows that the house was built on

FIG. 98.—IN THE TANK COURT, LOOKING SOUTH-EAST. ENTRANCE VESTIBULE ON THE LEFT.

the north-east side of the garden and adjoining the road. The door from the road opens to an entry vaulted in brick and chalk blocks, a treatment continued across the passage which connects the garden with the open court (Fig. 98). The latter has a round tank, and rising from it a statue which is set on a pedestal of refined detail. On crossing the vaulted passage the visitor reaches an inner vestibule, which gives access to the hall (Figs. 110 and 111). This is furnished

FIG. 99.—ON THE UPPER TERRACE.

with a solid screen built of heavy timbers with chalk block filling, seen in Fig 111. To the east of the screened space, which in a mediæval house would be called the " screens," is a sitting-room. At the other, or western, end of the hall is the dining-room. The hall itself is a fine two-storey apartment with a great open fireplace, crossed by a heavy beam framed with the main posts of the hall. The back of it is lined with roof tiles built in herring-bone fashion. To the south-west is a tall bay window of no less than forty-eight lights, and the topmost tier is carried along the main wall for another four lights on each side. Leading from the " screens " to the garden

FIG. 100.—THE DEANERY GARDEN, SOUTH-WEST SIDE : LOOKING UP TO THE TERRACE.

FIG. 101.—GARDEN FRONT FROM THE WEST.

is the round arched doorway, with six recessed brick members, which leads to the bridge and stone stair seen in Fig. 104. The delightful effect of the pierced parapet is very simply got by curved bricks arranged between low rusticated piers. At the south end of the bridge is a broad flight of steps, round on plan, which appears in Fig. 100. To the south-east of the bridge is a terrace supported by a brick retaining wall (Fig. 105). From

FIG. 102.— DEANERY GARDEN : THE CANAL AND TERMINAL POOL.

the pool crossed by the bridge, there runs a canal or rill parallel with the south-west front. It is interrupted mid-length by a square pool, and from it rises a pedestal occupied by a bronze boy bearing on his shoulder a dolphin, from whose mouth issues a jet of water. This appropriate ornament marks another axial line running from north-east to south-west, and finishes in a round tank backed by a double winding stair at the north-west boundary of the garden (Fig. 103.) Another scheme of formal gardening is worked out on the south-east side of the house. A broad paved way leads from the Tank Court under the vaulted undercroft (Figs. 98

FIG. 103.—TANK AT NORTH-WEST END OF GARDEN.

FIG. 104.—DEANERY GARDEN: HALL WINDOW AND TERRACE BRIDGE FROM S.W.

and 107) to a pergola which runs from north-east to south-west (Fig. 108).

Much could be written of the fine opportunities given to the enthusiast in every kind of gardening, and especially of wall treatment, but the successes achieved here, and the skilful planting which made them possible, have been fully described by word and plan in *Gardens for Small Country Houses*, and need not be repeated

FIG. 105.—RETAINING WALL AND STEPS: FROM VIEW POINT D. ON PLAN BELOW.

here. It suffices for me to say that Miss Jekyll worked with the architect in producing effects of singular richness. It may well be that it was the fine old enclosing wall of the Deanery

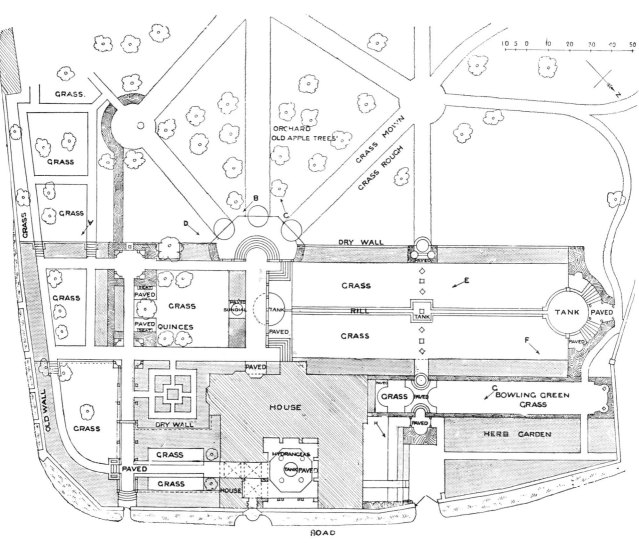

FIG. 106.—DEANERY GARDEN: SITE PLAN.

FIG. 107.—LOOKING NORTH-WEST : ARCHWAY LEADING TO TANK COURT.

FIG. 108.—SOUTH END OF PERGOLA.

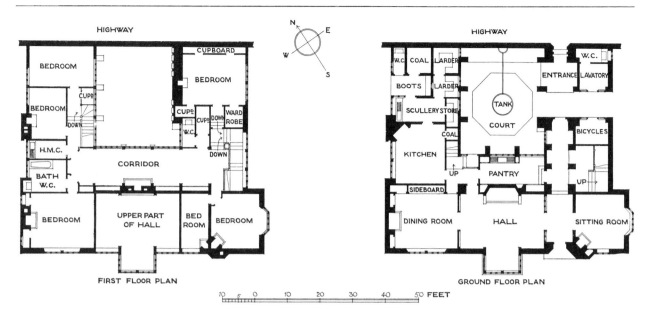

FIG. 109.—DEANERY GARDEN : HOUSE PLANS.

Garden, with its massive buttresses and well-wrought coping, which has since encouraged Mr. Lutyens to be generous with materials in the building of garden walls.

FISHER'S HILL, WOKING.

Fisher's Hill, Hook Heath, Woking, is a simple house of red brick, which calls for no special description. It has a broad terrace on the south side, on which abuts a projection containing

FIG. 110.—THE HALL FIREPLACE.

FIG. III.—DEANERY GARDEN: THE HALL FROM THE ENTRANCE.

FIG. 112.—FISHER'S HILL : THE PORCH.

FIG. 113.—ON THE TERRACE.

FIG. 114.—FISHER'S HILL : THE SOUTH FRONT.

FIG. 115.—FISHER'S HILL FROM SOUTH-EAST.

FIG. 116.—FISHER'S HILL, WOKING : PLANS.

a big dining-room flanked by loggias on either side. The running of twin chimneys up the face of the gable-end here is not a very happy piece of design. As Fig. 114 shows, the garden is richly furnished.

HOMEWOOD, KNEBWORTH.

At Homewood, built in 1901, the garden frames the house to admiration. The building owes its beauty largely to the skill with which it has been gabled. Nothing could exceed the welcoming charm of the entrance front. A short drive brings us from the road to a square gravelled space before the entrance, which is marked by a delightful round hood. The vestibule, with a lavatory opening from it, is unprotected by an outer door, and indeed there is no need for one. At its end, a door facing us leads to the kitchen quarters, so that the servants need not enter the hall when answering the door bell, and a door to the right gives the visitor entrance. The rooms are rather low, yet perfectly light, but the same cannot be said for the kitchen passages, which are not well planned. Very delightful are the quiet dignity of the staircase ascent and the treatment of the first-floor landing, as

FIG. 117.—HOMEWOOD, KNEBWORTH : TWIN GABLES ON SOUTH-WEST FRONT.

FIG. 118.—HOMEWOOD, KNEBWORTH : STEPS ON SOUTH-EAST FRONT.

Figs. 122 and 124 abundantly show. It is, however, the handling of the exterior which shows an especial daring. The south-east front with its loggias is a conception of extraordinary grace. There is a hint of the South African stoep in the broad space in front of the dining-room windows. No roof hangs over the latter to keep out the sunshine, as the pair of loggias stand clear at the sides, and nothing checks the view from the windows over the quiet rolling landscape.

The brilliance of the design of this front is in the neighbourhood of Ionic pilasters to the simple elements of roof and gable, which are the essence of a treatment characteristic of farmhouse traditions. Like so much that

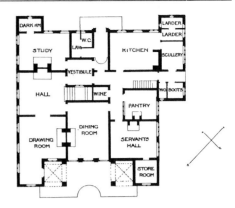

FIG. 119.—HOMEWOOD: GROUND PLAN.

FIG. 120.—HOMEWOOD: ENTRANCE FRONT.

FIG. 121.—SOUTH-EAST SIDE.

Mr. Lutyens does, it was an experiment that few would have dared to make, and fewer brought to satisfactory achievement. People sometimes talk as though architecture had come to an end, as though there is nothing to be done except to copy the work of our fore-fathers. This garden front of Homewood is a small, albeit delightful thing in itself, but it is symptomatic of much. It proves, what people are slow to believe, that in the new arrangement of traditional forms, perhaps themselves of widely differing provenance, there is room for infinite originality. We do not want new forms, but new light on the old, a new perception of their possibilities, and it is precisely this illumination which the work of Mr. Lutyens affords. Happily, the days are gone when they talked of " pure styles " and the work of some periods (notably English of the fifteenth century) was dismissed as " debased." In Mr.

FIG. 122.—FIRST FLOOR CORRIDOR.

FIG. 123.—ENTRANCE DOOR FROM SOUTH-WEST.

Mallock's *New Republic* the makers of modern taste were happily touched off for us under pseudonyms which concealed little. Walter Pater was made to masquerade as Mr. Rose, and

if the portraiture is a little malicious in its delicate parody of the Pateresque position, Mr. Rose's dicta are luminous even when they are exaggerated. A sly hit is made at æsthetic posing, by now almost entirely buried under a mound of ridicule. Mr. Rose was expatiating on the joys of upholsterers' shop windows : " I seem there to have got a glimpse of the real heart of things ; . . . indeed, when

FIG. 124.—HOMEWOOD, KNEBWORTH : HALL AND STAIRS.

I go to ugly houses, I often take a scrap of some artistic cretonne with me in my pocket as a kind of æsthetic smelling salts. . . . " This is simply admirable fooling, but in his pontifications about the architecture that should glorify the New Republic, a note of truth sounds clearly.

"If you will just think of our architecture, and consider how that naturally will be——"

"Yes, said Mr. Luke, "I should be glad to hear about our architecture." (Luke was Matthew Arnold.)

"How that naturally will be," Mr. Rose went on, " of no style in particular."

"The deuce it won't!" exclaimed Mr. Luke.

"No," continued Mr. Rose, unmoved. " No style in particular, but a renaissance of all styles."

This should not be read as a plea for eclectic imitations, but rather for an organic fusion of differing motives. It was precisely this readiness to use all elements that made Sedding so successful with Holy Trinity Church, Sloane Street, and it appears to be in the same spirit that Mr. Lutyens applies a Greek order to the front of a vernacular English cottage, and achieves a certain success. In his later work he has played on the same string in a more assured fashion, but never

FIG. 125.—ABBOTSWOOD : THE MAIN ENTRANCE DOOR.

in a more winning way than at Homewood. A further word by way of description must be added. The boarding of the great gables has weathered to an exquisite silver grey, through which the grain of the elm is wonderfully pictured, and on the sunless north front the dripping rain has marked the boards with bands of greenish stain. On the south-west elevation fig trees and peaches flourish, protected from the winds by the raised lawn. Over one loggia pavilion a broad-leaved American vine climbs freely, and even in late September the garden is brilliant with colour and rich with quick scents. As one walks round the house every step shows a fresh picture, and the low spreading roofs fall into a new grouping. For all its diversity of mass and the shadows which its broken outlines throw, there is an underlying gravity which comes of the considered symmetry of every front. Add to that the subtle massing of colour, the simply whitewashed brick at the base, the broad spread of silvery boarding and the medley of red roofs, and Homewood stands revealed as a notable work.

ABBOTSWOOD, GLOUCESTERSHIRE.

Abbotswood is a nineteenth century gabled house of no interest, to which Mr. Lutyens made some additions, begun in 1901 and finished the next year. He also laid out the gardens which appear in the accompanying pictures. On the entrance front he built the projection with a gable running almost to the ground, a somewhat immature treatment, which he has not repeated elsewhere. The entrance doorway is a pretty piece of scholarly design,

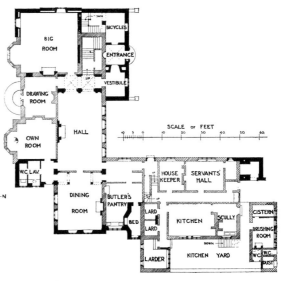

FIG. 126.—GROUND FLOOR PLAN OF ABBOTS-WOOD.

Old walls shown hatched, additions in solid black.

but it can hardly be thought appropriate in relation to the great gable above it. More successful, though not without uncertainties of touch, is the elevation facing the lily pool. The gables look rather small, rising from the panelled ashlar blocks above the cornices, but the pedimented window above the

FIG. 127.—ABBOTSWOOD: ENTRANCE FRONT FROM NORTH-EAST.

FIG. 128.—THE WEST FRONT.

FIG. 129.—IN THE PAVED GARDEN, LOOKING NORTH.

fountain is very successful, as are the unwindowed walls on either side of it.   The lily
pool is set in a broad paved terrace with dry stone retaining walls, and the dome-
shaped recess of the fountain is an idea which was developed further at Hestercombe
in 1904.   On the stone rim of the pool, tubs of pink hydrangeas in parallel lines
are mirrored in the running water, and bring to mind a feature somewhat similar in the
gardens of the Generalife at Granada.   The remodelling of the principal rooms shows
Mr. Lutyens gradually feeling his way to a more classical treatment.   The work done
was not extensive, but the new hall and dining-room (Figs. 134 and 135) are of interest.   The
fluted Ionic pilasters of the hall arcade and the entablature are dignified, but there is more
invention in the repeated projections of the overmantel (Fig. 134).   The white painted
panelling of the dining-room is broadly done, but the rather small Ionic columns on pedestals

FIG. 130.—ABBOTSWOOD : THE PERGOLA.

(Fig. 135) are not a success.   It is worth while comparing such details with those of Heathcote,
Ilkley, illustrated in a later chapter.   Only so can the rapid development between 1900 and
1906 be appreciated.   The work at Abbotswood is good but tentative and uncertain : six years
later those qualities had given place to a sure and personal grasp of classical detail which gives
the student continual pleasure.   For the garden there can be nothing but praise, and here
Mr. Lutyens was peculiarly fortunate in his client.   Mr. Mark Fenwick is a master of all
cultural mysteries.   Not only are the architectural bones of the garden most richly clad, but
its outlying parts show natural treatment at its best, and in pleasant contrast with the formal
lines of paved rose garden and the like which frame the house itself.   A broad terrace walk,
studded with slender Irish junipers, flanks the entire house front, and a flight of descending
steps leads to the square flower garden on a lower level.   At the inner corners of the grassed
court four conical yews give a note of contrast and restraint to the surrounding beds of

shimmering roses.   Beyond this tangle of colour appears a rich herbaceous summer border, showing above the retaining wall that encloses the tennis court, on a yet lower level.   All levels and flights of levels, planned with skill and purpose, descend in quiet progression from the upper terrace walk to the flower garden, to the herbaceous border, to the sunken tennis court, and beyond into the surrounding park land of oaks and elms, leading the eye, still

FIG. 131.—THE LILY POOL AND FOUNTAIN.

descending, through Bourton Vale, then up to the sky-line where the ridge of Eyford Hill frames the picture.   To the east and west are levels also; the bordered pergola with its clematis, vines, roses and honeysuckle, its oil-jars filled with dwarf roses; and the paved rose garden.

FIG. 132.—ABBOTSWOOD : GARDEN HOUSE OVERLOOKING TENNIS LAWN.

FIG. 133.—GARDEN HOUSE FROM LOWER LAWN.

FIG. 134.—THE HALL.

FIG. 135.—ABBOTSWOOD : THE DINING-ROOM.

Again we descend to the familiar flower court, then mount to a higher level to balance the parallel paved court, a little old-fashioned garden with box-edged beds filled with summer flowers, and four middle beds of roses surrounding an old stone urn. From this upper terrace, espaliered by a rose-screen of inverted segments, the entire series of gardens is revealed.

FIG. 136.—ABBOTSWOOD : THE HALL ARCADE.

CHAPTER V.

MARSHCOURT, HAMPSHIRE, 1901.

M ARSHCOURT is a house of peculiar interest, not only because of its intrinsic beauty, but also because it is the last and most important of the houses which Mr. Lutyens deliberately built in the Tudor manner. Since then he has done much work which is akin to it, but only when he has added to an old house which

set the note or when, as at Drewsteignton, begun in 1913, his client has specifically desired a building in an early manner. The record of his work, in the chapters following this, marks an increasing reliance on the motifs which informed the design of the eighteenth century. Marshcourt shows the art of Mr. Lutyens in its gayest mood. It is, indeed, the richest expression of his earlier manner, when the romantic quality of Tudor building influenced him most strongly. It was built at a time when he had already developed that

FIG. 137.—FROM PORCH TO FORECOURT.

FIG. 138.—THE NORTH SIDE.

FIG. 139.—FROM THE WEST.

full mastery over material which has done so much to give freshness and distinction to his work. It is one of the conditions of health in the career of any artist, whether painter, architect or sculptor, that it should develop along orderly lines, and the change is generally in the direction of an increasing devotion to the classical idea. The late Norman Shaw went that way—there are centuries between such houses as Cragside and Chesters. Even Mr. Philip Webb, rooted as he was in the principles

FIG. 140.—THE EAST WING.

of the Gothic Revival, and the exponent in architecture of William Morris' mediæval outlook, betook himself in later life to classical forms at Rounton Grange. Architects, or at least the

FIG. 141.—THE LOGGIA.

greater among them, show in the development of their life-work the tendency which prevails during each long period of architectural activity. It took five centuries of English history—from the thirteenth to the eighteenth—to run through all the moods of architecture, from Gothic, in its most soaring manifestation, to a re-creation of classical ideals, modified only by changed needs. It was a secular procession from the sway of imagination and adventure to the rule of law. When the classical spirit became so attenuated in the beginning of the nineteenth century that it ceased to produce an art that convinced and inspired enthusiasm, the reaction of the Gothic

FIG. 142.—THE HALL BAY FROM SOUTH-EAST.

FIG. 143.—PART OF SOUTH FRONT SEEN ACROSS POOL GARDEN.

Revival became inevitable. There are many students who regard it as a mere exercise in archæology, and as a wholly unreal and unfortunate movement, which represented no sound or abiding quality in our national life. This seems to be a short and unhistorical view. The antiquarian spirit is a pious one, but without æsthetic enthusiasms, even though they may be misguided, it will have no driving power. The Gothic Revival had its failures and its absurdities, but it seems wiser to regard it as a real and inevitable movement, which scored its

FIG. 144.—ENTRANCE FRONT FROM NORTH-WEST.

FIG. 145.—THE SUNK POOL GARDEN.

FIG. 146.—FROM THE SOUTH-WEST.

own triumphs and left some noble monuments of the skill of its protagonists. The power of its influence is unchallengeable. It is impossible to imagine a building like Marshcourt, save as the logical outcome, after many days, of the Revival. It was a necessary upheaval, if only to prepare the way for the new Renaissance of the classical spirit, which is making such notable headway now. Artistic development to-day

FIG. 147.—POOL GARDEN : LOOKING SOUTH.

moves with uncertain and even with incoherent steps, but it moves with extraordinary rapidity. In fifty years of the last century the Revivalists covered the same field of design

which had taken five centuries of normal development. Admittedly, it was a period of copyism, of random raking amid the valley of dry bones, if haply some new formula might be constructed which might faithfully be hailed as a new creation. At the end of it all we are back at a restatement of the old principles and mainly in the old language, but there is this difference. The career of a single man may well show a development of

FIG. 148.—THE TILE-BUILT PERGOLA.

design which represents centuries of change in æsthetic outlook. It took sixty years of Norman Shaw's full and splendid career to travel from his early work in the Gothic manner to the fine classical flavour of his last house, Chesters. With the younger men the speed of development is greater. In twenty-five years Mr. Lutyens has passed from his early exercises in traditional cottage-building to the broad austerity of Heathcote and Great Maytham, and is now setting about the designing of Delhi on lines which it is safe to believe will produce a monumental conception. Marshcourt may be regarded as the best example of his skill in the vernacular manner ; it is as obviously the result of an imaginative outlook, as his later work is an expression of law and intellect in architectural design.

The house seeks its effect by ingenious combinations of local materials, by sharp contrasts of colour—white chalk, black flint and red

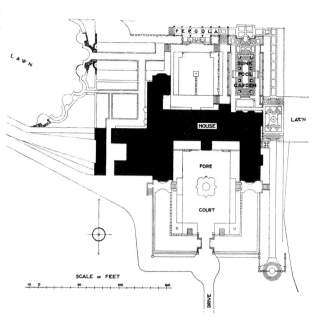

FIG. 149.—GARDEN PLAN.

FIG. 150.—LITTLE POOLS UNDER PERGOLA.

brick—by daring groupings and by the juxtaposition of features of varying scales. Experience shows that such a conception, unless handled in a bold and masterly way, is bound to fail from lack of that essential unity which is needful in any perfected work of art ; but Mr. Lutyens has essayed a *tour de force*, and has achieved it. It is by the elimination of the non-essential that a fine architectural style achieves unity, and experience tends to drive the artist who is forming his manner along lines which harmonise with the classical ideal. He is forced to concentrate, to develop the sense of order in preference to the picturesque,

FIG. 151.—PLANS OF HOUSE.

to see more in mass than in detail, and thus unconsciously to derive his inspiration more and more from the great traditions of Greece and Rome.

Marshcourt stands on the spur of a hill which overhangs the river Test, where it wanders past Stockbridge. It looks across the reedy water-meadows that fringe the river, dotted with large silvery willows. The site needed very careful handling lest the extent and presence of the house should overwhelm the situation. It demanded in a pre-eminent degree an architectural treatment of the garden which should soften the break between the house and the hillside. There are places so enriched by Nature with bastions of rock and fringes of natural growth that an elaborate scheme of terraces and balustrades, of retaining walls and paved walks,

FIG. 152.—THE VESTIBULE.

FIG. 153.—FIRST FLOOR CORRIDOR.

seems not only un-
necessary, but imperti-
nent. At Marshcourt,
however, the garden
setting which Mr.
Lutyens devised was
essential to success, and
the accompanying pic-
tures show how com-
plete such a success can
be. The building is
supported by a series of
terraces with flights of
steps connecting and
long balustrades bound-
ing the various levels.
The house is laid out
on an H plan, but with
the omission of one arm
at the south-west corner.
The walls are of chalk,
glittering white in the
sunshine, and relieved
here and there by

FIG. 154.—STAIRCASE FROM BILLIARD-ROOM.

chequer-work in red brick and surmounted by a fine red roof and by gaily modelled red brick
chimneys. The entrance front looks due north. Its two deep projecting wings enclose a
broad paved forecourt, which is approached by a bridge crossing a fall in the ground.

Fig. 138 shows the long, low front, with windows symmetrically placed and a projecting
porch. The skeleton arch of the latter, tied to the chequered vault by three long keystones,

FIG. 155.—AN UPPER STAIR.

FIG. 156.—STAIR DOWN TO BASEMENT.

FIG. 157.——THE MAIN STAIRCASE.

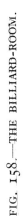

FIG. 158.—THE BILLIARD-ROOM.

is a fascinating detail. Perhaps an even better picture could have been secured from within the entrance door ; but when both the photographer and I visited Marshcourt the swallows were nesting over the lintel, and the door was locked until their domestic duties were finished for the year. The ground slopes downwards from the west wing, but there is a rise to the north-west, an accident of levels which drove Mr. Lutyens to devise the charming scheme of steps and balustrading which appears in Fig. 144. It is, however, on the south side that the architectural treatment of the garden finds its most notable development. The lily pool, sunk in a setting of steps, and surrounded by a balustraded wall, makes a retreat rich in architectural fancy. From whatever point of view the building is seen, the tall chimneys of moulded brick group in romantic fashion with bold bays, broad overhanging eaves and great stretches of mullioned windows.

The planning of the house owes nothing to Tudor models, but is frankly modern. Entering through the porch (Fig. 137) the visitor finds a long vestibule, at the right-hand end of which is the main staircase (Figs. 155 to 157). To the left are openings to the big hall (Figs. 161 and 162), and, through a short passage, to the dining-room (Fig. 160). The whole of the east wing is occupied by the kitchen

FIG. 159.—DINING-ROOM DOOR.

FIG. 160.—MARSHCOURT : THE DINING-ROOM.

FIG. 161.—THE HALL SCREEN.

FIG. 162.—THE HALL, LOOKING EAST.

offices, save for smoking and gun rooms at the south end. The west wing is given up to the drawing-room and billiard-room (Fig. 158). The staircase is an echo of Elizabethan influences, built massively in oak with simple detail in baluster and panel. In the hall there is a burst of richness such as we associate with late Jacobean work. Marshcourt dates from a time when Mr. Lutyens was giving a more close attention to details of craftsmanship than is demanded by his later work in a more austere manner. The rich, perhaps it is fair to say heavy, plaster-work of the hall ceiling, and the exquisite carving of the long chalk frieze panels at the two ends of the hall (Figs. 161 and 162), with their swags and clusters of the wild flowers that grow about Marshcourt, show a vigorous sense not only of decorative values, but of the contrasting play of various textures. Of the ceilings in the downstairs rooms the most successful is that in the billiard-room, and the table itself with its great moulded base is a *tour de force* in the use of chalk in a new way. The dining-room is lined with great panels of quartered walnut, and the detail here is admirably restrained, prophetic, indeed, of later work in the Wren manner (Fig. 159). It escapes the charge of slight restlessness which may not unfairly be brought against the treatment of the hall.

Of its kind, however, the interior of the house is admirable, because it indicates a strong grasp of the right uses of a varied craftsmanship. The rooms upstairs show the same vigorous character. Some of the furniture was designed by the architect, but that can be more conveniently discussed in a later chapter.

I left Marshcourt with the feeling that for all its wealth of Tudor fancies it stands confessed as a work of modern days, which is wholly as it should be. Whether the freedom of such a phase of architectural feeling or the straiter bonds of classical ideals be chosen, the critic has the right to demand that the artist's own personality shall inform the work and mark it for his own. If a modern house cannot be distinguished from one of the sixteenth or eighteenth century by anything but the obvious newness of its materials, architecture as a living art has merely borrowed the clothes of antiquity and has failed to express a truth ; but in this regard Mr. Lutyens does not fail us.

FIG. 163.—STONE SUNDIAL WITH LEAD INLAY.

CHAPTER VI.

GREY WALLS, GULLANE—(1901).

GREY WALLS is a small, albeit dignified, holiday home standing on the famous Muirfield Links, the home of the Honourable Company of Edinburgh Golfers, which was instituted even earlier than the Royal and Ancient Club of St. Andrews. It was built for the late Mr. Alfred Lyttelton, but went afterwards into the possession of the late Mr. William James. The position of the site with reference both to the links and the road, as well as the difficulty of catching both the sun and the view to the north, drove Mr. Lutyens to some engaging shifts in planning, the outcome of which is at once original and attractive. The feeling of poise which comes from symmetry he secured in the entrance court; but even by setting out the front of the house on a curve it could not have a direct relationship with the approach road without disarranging its elevation to the links. The waywardness of the natural lines was therefore masked by an attractive group of lodges and garage at the south corner of the site arranged to form an outer forecourt (see Fig. 179). Between two of these the drive leads through a walled garden of interesting shape to the curved entrance front, flanked

FIG. 164.—THE HOUSE FROM THE OUTER COURT.

FIG. 165.—FROM THE NORTH.

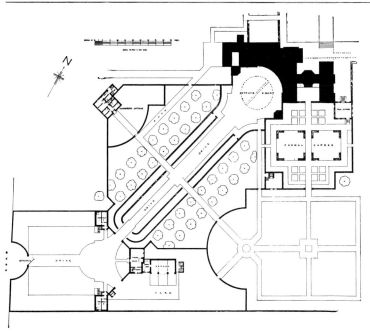

FIG. 166.—GARDEN PLAN.

by low pavilions. This front faces south, and as it is obviously inconvenient to have the chief rooms looking on to a forecourt, Mr. Lutyens threw them out eastwards and broke up their plan into H form, so that the round projection of the corridor, which serves as a sitting-room, might have a south-east aspect. The eastern stroke of the H is the drawing-room, a long, narrow apartment with windows that face to every quarter and enjoy views both of the links and of the formal garden. At its east corner and built against the garden wall is an open-air tea-room, with glazed windows to the north and east and openings filled only with rolling shutters to the south and west. Fig. 171 shows how attractively the western opening frames a picture of the recessed south side that looks across the formal garden. The rubble walls are built of stone of a rich cream colour, while the roofs are covered with grey Dutch pantiles that give an effect altogether delightful. Everywhere there is evidence of ingenious new uses of materials. Set in the window lintels are sections of grey pantile, which by their repeating curves give touches of interest, and between them is a garretting with dots of red tile. The round pillars of the tea-room are built up of thin shards, set in thick mortar, of the same green slates that are hung on some of the walls. On the north-west side, between the east wing and the links, is a sunk garden rich with the scent of sweet briar.

Not least of the merits of Grey Walls is the way the subsidiary buildings take their places faithfully and naturally in the general scheme. Beyond the west wall of the great middle court

FIG. 167.—ENTRANCE FRONT FROM SOUTH-WEST.

FIG. 168.—THE ENTRANCE FRONT.

FIG. 169.—THE SOUTH-EAST SIDE.

FIG. 170.—THE TEA-ROOM FROM THE FORMAL GARDEN.

FIG. 171.—THROUGH THE WEST WINDOW OF THE TEA-ROOM.

is a gardener's cottage, which appears in Figs. 177 and 178, but special attention must be drawn to the ingenious way in which the glass awning of the garage has been managed (Fig. 175). This can be seen from the road. In order to avoid the ugliness of the usual sloping glass roof, the gutter

FIG. 172.—PART OF THE NORTH-WEST FRONT.

has been set in the middle of it, instead of at the outside. In the result nothing but a thin edge appears, and, indeed, that is hardly true, for the whole awning is almost invisible except from close at hand. It is by devices like these, which are as practical as they are helpful from the æsthetic side, that Grey Walls appears as a house of singular charm. Whether in the broken mass of the north-west front or in the symmetries of the south-west side that looks across the formal garden, and especially in the sweeping lines of the entrance front, the design is satisfying.

If one seeks to define the quality that most penetrates Grey Walls it would seem to be rhythm. It emerges the more obviously when the building under review is, like the entrance front of Grey Walls, symmetrically conceived. Goethe says, in a phrase which has a large basis of truth, " Art is but form-giving." With John Addington Symonds we may enquire, " To what does it give form,

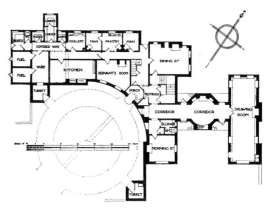

FIG. 173.—GROUND PLAN OF HOUSE.

what does it express or present ? " and accept his answer, " Art gives form to human consciousness ; expresses or presents the feeling or the thought of man. Whatever else art may do by the way, in the communicating of innocent pleasures, in the adornment of life and the softening of manners, in the creation of beautiful shapes and sounds, this, at all events, is its prime function." It may, however, be admitted at once that architecture, by reason of the fact that it ministers primarily to human uses, is the art least obviously fitted for the subtler expression of thoughts and feelings. Its appeal is large rather than subtle. Symonds touches this when he says that " into the language of arch and aisle and colonnade, of cupola and facade and pediment, of spire and vault, the architect translates emotion, vague perhaps but deep, mute but unmistakable. When we say that a building is sublime or graceful, frivolous or stern, we mean that sublimity or grace, frivolity or sternness, is inherent in it. The emotions connected with these qualities are inspired in us when we contemplate it, and are

FIG. 174.—THE CORRIDOR SITTING-ROOM.

FIG. 175.—THE GARAGE.

FIG. 176.—TWO OF THE LODGES (A AND B SHOWN IN FIG. 179).

FIG. 177.—GREY WALLS: THE COTTAGE: NORTH-EAST CORNER.

presented to us by its form." While this seems true enough, the question as to how far those who developed the styles consciously desired to materialise the emotions that inspired them, is not susceptible of a very ready answer. It seems more likely that the characteristics of different periods and of emergent personalities unconsciously found their expression, and that only so far does architecture present to us through form the human spirit. Walter Pater takes up the same parable after his own delightful fashion: "Architecture, which begins in a practical need, can only express by vague hint or symbol the spirit or mind of the artist. He closes his sadness over him, or wanders in the perplexed intricacies of things, or projects his purpose from him clean-cut and sincere, or bares himself to the sunlight. But these spiritualities, felt rather than seen, can but lurk about architectural form as volatile effects, to be gathered from it by reflexion ; their expression is not really sensuous at all." This is only an enchanting way of saying that the art of building does not permit the expression, at once categorical and complex, of an idea such as is possible to the sculptor, the painter and, still more exactly, to the poet. The form that an architectural idea

FIG. 178.—GARDENER'S COTTAGE FROM THE SOUTH-WEST.

must take is so restricted by the practical purposes of the building that the material clothing tends to overcome the thought, which thus flickers indistinctly. This is naturally more markedly true of domestic architecture, with its insistence on the practical setting of life, than of Greek temple and Christian church, where the dominant idea may repose or soar less hampered by material needs. At the other end of the scale lies the unhampered art of music, where practical things have no need to be expressed, and the way is free for the translation, " with the utmost attenuation of detail," of every delicacy of thought and feeling. There is, of

course, the power in architecture to make plain, by the aid of symbolism, spiritual ideas of some simplicity, but that is mainly with the aid of the sister arts of sculpture and painting. Walter Pater attached large importance to a dictum of his that, literary precisian though he was, he emphasised with italics, " *All art constantly aspires towards the condition of music.*" This condition, he asserts, is the mingling of the matter with the form so intimately that the understanding is able to blot out the distinction between them. Putting it another way, we look in fine art for the quality that makes us forget how our imagination is struck, and we remember only the pleasure that it brings. If, then, the possession of a quality of music is in any sort a standard for other arts, for which of them can we fairly look in architecture ? Perhaps more than one, but certainly, and perhaps pre-eminently, rhythm. A simple definition

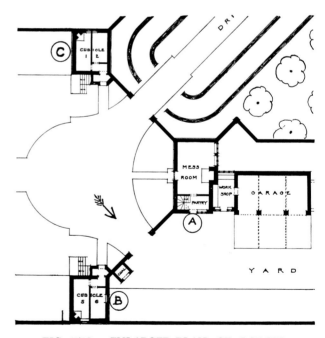

FIG. 179.—ENLARGED PLAN OF LODGES.

can be made that fits it alike to architecture and music—a combination of forms producing harmony at recurring intervals. And this brings us back (after struggling uncomfortably with abstract phrases, the unhandy machinery of criticism) to a plain question. Have we any right to look for such qualities in the simple face of a stone building, or is the whole idea a mirage invented for the confusion of the plain man, who hates subtleties of words ? I believe not, and claim that the pleasure to be got from a building like Grey Walls, which is intrinsically good, is greatly increased if a little trouble be taken to analyse the charm which it exhales.

CHAPTER VII.

WORK DONE IN 1902–3.

LITTLE THAKEHAM, SUSSEX ; PAPILLON HALL, LEICESTERSHIRE ; THE HOO, WILLINGDON ; DANESHILL, HANTS ; MONKTON, SUSSEX.

LITTLE THAKEHAM shows a marked development in Mr. Lutyens' handling of Tudor elements of design. It is smaller than Marshcourt, but there is an increase in restraint of treatment which is not accounted for merely by difference of size and the more modest decorative scheme appropriate in a smaller house. The exterior claims our attention first. There is altogether less exuberance of fancy in the quiet masonry of the walls and the simple brickwork of the chimneys. Marshcourt gives the suspicion of a feeling that Mr. Lutyens was determined on the *tour de force* which he certainly achieved there. It seems to have been designed " at the top of the voice." In that respect, indeed, it resembles more closely some of its late Tudor prototypes, which, despite the glamour which age has thrown over them, still seem

FIG. 180.—LITTLE THAKEHAM : WITHIN THE FORECOURT.

FIG. 181.—THE STAIRCASE LANDING.

FIG. 182.—LITTLE THAKEHAM : THE HALL BAY.

to protest their charms too freely. Little Thakeham, by contrast, bears no mark of effort. Its elevations seem to have happened so. The rooms show no less that Mr. Lutyens was progressing in 1902 towards a more mature manner of interior treatment. The late Jacobean richness which inspired the hall at Marshcourt has given place to the more quiet methods of the age of Wren. In less able hands this mingling of styles, of Tudor and Palladian, would have led to disaster, but Mr. Lutyens has always shown a particular skill in combining different manners and yet in achieving unity of effect.

The house is entered on the north, and a flagged path across the forecourt connects the drive with the porch. The general plan of the building (Fig. 183) is based on an H with a broad connecting stroke, the kitchen offices being grouped round a distinct court to the east of the

FIG. 183.—HOUSE PLANS OF LITTLE THAKEHAM.

FIG. 184.—LITTLE THAKEHAM : THE HALL AND SCREEN.
(The balcony above the fireplace opens from the first floor corridor).

main house.   The front door opens on to a broad corridor, which runs across the house from east to west.   Of the considerable area of the " stroke " nearly three-quarters is occupied by this corridor, by the porch and stairs and by the space behind the screen.   About one-quarter only is left for the hall itself, and it is overlooked by the open screen, the staircase balcony and the upper corridor balcony.   It can only be used as a public room.   If such planning is to be judged on economic grounds it obviously fails, for a large proportion of the cubic space is, as

FIG. 185.—LITTLE THAKEHAM : LIBRARY FIREPLACE.

FIG. 186.—IN THE PARLOUR.

an economical planner would say, wasted. Waste, however, is a relative word, and takes no account of æsthetic purpose. If the disposition of the hall, etc., at Little Thakeham had been devised for a hotel where every cubic foot of space had to earn a dividend, it would manifestly have been bad planning. As it was for a private house, the owner of which wanted to secure a distinct and distinguished architectural effect, it was not only good but brilliant planning. Planning must always be judged with special reference to a client's aims and views, and cannot be considered *in vacuo*. The arrangement at Little Thakeham would not suit all family habits and needs, and was not intended to. The whole composition is not only peculiarly attractive and successful, but relies for its effect on the spaces provided for passageways, etc., with so liberal a hand. The merit of the detail in the hall is considerable, and seems to be the best Mr. Lutyens had done up to that time.

The stone used comes from the neighbourhood, and has the composition of a marble

FIG. 187.—THE SOUTH FRONT AND PERGOLA.

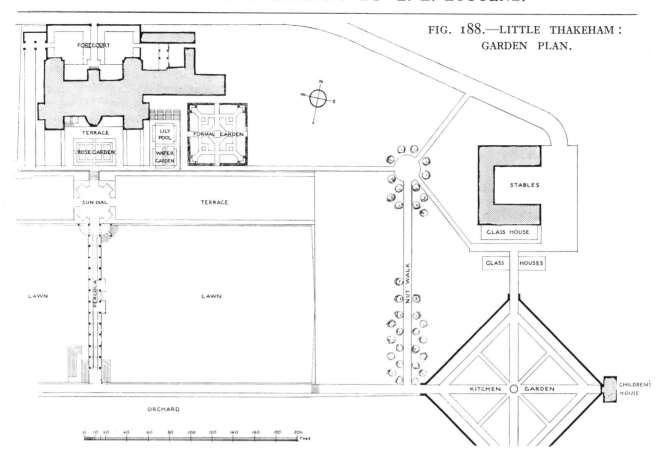

FIG. 188.—LITTLE THAKEHAM :
GARDEN PLAN.

FIG. 189.—GARDEN FRONT FROM THE SOUTH-WEST.

FIG. 190.—LITTLE THAKEHAM : THE SOUTH-WEST DESCENT FROM THE PERGOLA.

FIG. 191.—LILY POOL AND IRIS MORASS.

It is rather brittle, and is made up of harder and softer particles not very firmly welded together. It therefore permits itself to be wrought, but will with difficulty take a highly dressed surface or sharp angles. Mr. Lutyens has given it the value of its qualities, and though the forms are Palladian, they are treated simply, while the finish and texture remind one of the work of seventeenth century handicraftsmen of country training. The dignified doorways have their architrave mouldings broken by rustication, and are surmounted by keystone and pediment. But there is no attempt at carving or small detail, and therefore they compose perfectly with the plain mullions of the great oriel and are not too stately and palatial to consort with the modest and untransomed windows and with the general absence of decoration that prevails throughout the building. The wrought iron of the hall balconies forms one of the rare and reserved points of ornament. The screen and staircase space is divided into compartments, all of which, as well as the parlour beyond, have a stone door-case of the same character as those of the screen. The vista from the hall—the oak boards of whose floor are carried right through to the parlour—is very telling. The parlour occupies the southern half of the west wing and the library the north half. The fireplace in the library is of the same type as the structural features of the hall. A mantel-piece of Sussex marble is moulded in the manner of Wren and polished. Raised panels of oak surround it, the two upright ones turning on pivots and forming the doors of cupboards. About the parlour there is nothing Palladian, the wide fire-arch, which is its principal feature, being evidently inspired by a late mediæval kitchen. The stone arch, of which the keystone reaches the ceiling, seems too big for the height of the room, while the beam below has insufficient work to justify its size. The tiling of the interspace is well devised, but the close juxtaposition of three materials and four pronounced lines of different curvature is a little worrying. The materials are all delightful, and each one is deftly used ; but the combination just misses that reserve and mastery of right line which Mr. Lutyens generally achieves. The hearth itself, with tile panel and a tile platform for its iron plate, is wholly pleasing, and on the iron plate stand excellent examples of old Sussex ironwork. The hall is not of the full height of the two storeys in the east and west wings, and allows of a suite of lofty roof rooms above it. The upper and lower corridors divide the height of the hall, and are therefore low, depending on a horizontal character for their effect. Great stone door-cases give feature to the entrance from the porch and to the hall screen. The suites of rooms at each end of the upper corridor are approached up flights of stairs so as to reach the level above the sitting-rooms.

The garden at Little Thakeham is very successful. It lacks the elaborate architectural elements which are so notable a feature at Marshcourt, and this reticence is the more suitable because the owner, Mr. Ernest Blackburn, is a gardener of exceptional skill. The extraordinary profusion of growth which that skill has encouraged would have veiled unduly any elaborate architectural features in the garden. Mr. Lutyens' task was to provide a broad framework to be clothed, and this he has done well. The house stands on an easy slope facing south. The garden enclosure has been divided into three sections at different levels, and dry walling, formed of local stone, composes the divisional bulwarks, and offers a wide field for the exhibition of sun-loving shrubs and alpines. The two lower levels are little else than stretches of unbroken turf, but that which lies directly in front of the south side of the house is treated in more detail. A portion, the length of the central block of the house, is laid out in flagged paths framing square and oblong beds planted with dwarf roses and edged with stonecrops and other sessile growths. On either side of this are grass plats sheltered by hedges of rambler roses on posts and chains, which emphasise the lines of the projecting wings. Beyond the west wing is a square devoted to the cultivation of the taller perennials—larkspurs, hollyhocks and many another. Beyond the east wing the building continues, somewhat recessed, as the office annexe. In front of this a broad stairway, divided into three by platforms on which stand tubs of flowers, descends to a set of oblong water-pools, set round with flagging, in which nymphæas, arums, Iris Kæmpferi and other water-loving subjects disport themselves. One pool has deep water, and the other two are kept rather in the state of morass in order to meet the varying requirements of their denizens. The detail of both the laying out and the garden treatment of this feature is clearly shown in Fig. 191, on the left-hand side of which the luxurious growth and profuse blooming of the Romneya Coulteri are to be noticed.

It was felt that two flat stretches of lawn, merely broken by plant-clothed dry walls, would be an arrangement too entirely lacking incident to afford adequate support to the house. A strong feature was needed to carry something of an architectural feeling forward to the garden boundary, and a pergola was chosen for this purpose. Now a pergola may be a few posts stuck in the ground topped by rustic boughs or unwrought poles. So modest a construction would here have been quite out of place. Something of great presence and solidity was called for. At the same time it must harmonise with the rustic simplicity of the general garden work. The desired effect has been perfectly attained by setting massive oak beams, squared and slightly

FIG. 192.—LITTLE THAKEHAM : NORTH FRONT FROM THE ROAD.

cambered, on to stone pillars of large diameter built up out of local stone roughly hewn and faced. Even this would have been quite inadequate without its being set up on a platform and dignified by great stairways. The lie of the ground not only permitted but suggested this. Facing the great oriel, which forms the centre of the south front of the house, a few steps lead from the first parterre to the first grass plat, of narrow width but great length. Across this a flagged way is taken, and then spreads out into a

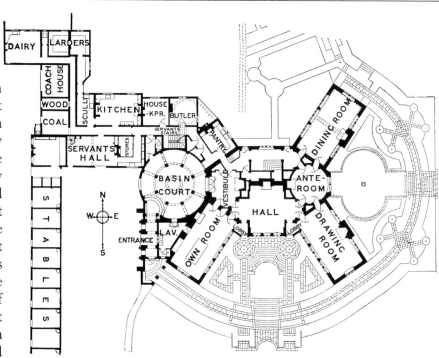

FIG. 193.—PAPILLON HALL: GROUND FLOOR PLAN.

FIG. 194.—PAPILLON HALL : THE BASIN COURT.

FIG. 195.—PAPILLON HALL: FROM PORCH TO BASIN COURT.

FIG. 196.—PAPILLON HALL: EAST FRONT.

semi-circle on which the T-shaped head of the pergola is built. Segmental stairways, divided by the pergola pillars, start right and left from the platform and descend to the lawns on each side of the pergola, of which the long body starts from the centre of the semi-circle. Its ample breadth is flagged throughout, and it is raised on a dry stone

FIG. 197.—PAPILLON HALL: GARDEN HOUSE AND GATE PIERS.

FIG. 198.—PAPILLON HALL : LILY POOL ON SOUTH SIDE.

retaining wall which becomes higher as the pergola extends its level length down the south slope.   Thus, when it reaches the boundary between the garden and the orchard, it is no longer raised seven but fourteen steps above the lawns, and these are reached by most generously proportioned flights of steps, that give the idea, with their mass of masonry, of being the outer bulwark of the house.   It is this large and serious manner of establishing a single central incident that entirely saves the situation.   Here the principle that a country house is much more than the square block forming the house has been fully appreciated, and has been carried out with rich result but thrifty means.   It is, indeed, a question whether the scheme of planting sympathetic to the owner, and therefore reflecting his tastes and stamping the place

FIG. 199.—PAPILLON HALL : THE DRAWING-ROOM.

as his home, would have consorted so well with the garden design if the latter had been of a highly finished architectural character.

PAPILLON HALL.

I turn now to another house in which exteriors treated in a simple gabled fashion have been combined with interior elements of a richer and more dignified sort—Papillon Hall, near Market Harborough.   Lay students of architecture are apt, and naturally enough, to judge buildings only by the impression made by their elevations and decorative treatment.   In so far as the plan attracts their attention it is usually only by reason of its practical convenience.   There is, however, an actual beauty of plan which is well worth study, and Papillon Hall shows that beauty in large measure.   The diagonal wings suggest a butterfly, and the name of the house, which comes, however, from an earlier owner of the estate, is therefore appropriate.   The type is not original, for Norman Shaw employed it when he remodelled Chesters.   Mr. Lutyens, however, has used the air with variations of his own, the most notable of which is the round

FIG. 200.—THE DINING-ROOM AT PAPILLON HALL—   FIG. 201.—AND STAIRS.

Basin Court on the west side. This court has two practical merits, as well as its architectural charm. It serves to connect the main part of the house with the kitchen offices, which form a projecting block at the north-west corner, and it provides a dignified interlude between the entrance lobby and the vestibule, through which access is given to the sitting hall. It is of one storey only, and the middle of the court is open to the air. There is a roof to the covered part with access from the first-floor rooms. This flat is in connection with the nursery suite, and forms an outdoor playroom. The problems presented by a butterfly plan are many, because the diagonal placing of the important rooms creates a number of angular spaces between them and the central block. The absorbing of these, without making the rooms themselves of an odd shape, requires considerable ingenuity—a quality which is not sought in vain at Papillon Hall. Two of the angles have been taken up on the south front by the provision of lobbies between the hall and the paved garden, and these are as convenient with their five sides as they would have been if rectangular. Other corners were masked by making the ante-room on the east side circular, while the remaining odd spaces are used either as cupboards or for lavatory and similar accommodation. A very

FIG. 202.—THE HALL.

delightful feature of butterfly or suntrap plans is the partly enclosed garden spaces which are formed by the wings. On the south front this area has been filled with paved work and a shaped pool, which appear in Fig. 198, and show Mr. Lutyens in a characteristic mood as garden designer. A dolphin serves as fountain and is poised on a pipe which leads the water to its mouth. The pool is pleasant with broad-leaved water plants. In another part of the garden paved walks are divided from broad herbaceous borders by turf, and one of them leads past a summer-house with conical roof

FIG. 203.—THE HOO: GARDEN HOUSE AND BALCONY.

to a pair of brick piers (Fig. 197). Surmounting them are leaden figures that might have stepped from a Watteau canvas. They are not unlike the famous shepherd and shepherdess in lead which are to be seen at South Kensington Museum and elsewhere. In the eighteenth century, as we learn from J. T. Smith's *Nollekens and His Times*, they were wont to paint their lead figures in natural colours, but that needs a more robust sufferance of bright decoration than finds favour to-day. Lead, if left to the kindly touch of wind and rain, will weather in silvery patches that accord better than anything else with green surroundings. It is pre-eminently the English material for garden ornaments. The hall is a delightful apartment. There is a window over the fireplace, which yields a view to the staircase beyond,

FIG. 204.—THE HOO, WILLINGDON: GABLES AND STEPS.

and the flues are carried right and left of this opening. The drawing-room is particularly attractive with its barrel vault, decorated with ribs of modelled vine pattern. The whole treatment of this room suggests the influence of Mr. Philip Webb, and its charm is accentuated by the beautiful furniture collected by its owner, Mr. Frank Belville.

THE HOO, WILLINGDON, SUSSEX.

The Hoo is an interesting example of work done in 1902, but it shows some uncertainty of touch. The weather-boarded " saw-cut " gables on the middle of the garden front rhyme a little awkwardly with the hipped roofs and bold dormers of the flanking wings, but perhaps this was intentional. Mr. Lutyens' task was not to create a new house, but to build round an old one of no particular interest. The gables were imposed on the existing front, and a break in treatment between that and the wings has the merit of emphasising the history of the place. The house stood close to the high road and has secured a certain privacy and charm by the little walled courtyard formed on two sides by the addition of spurs containing servants' quarters, etc., and on the third by the roadside wall. The garden is long and its steady southward slope made occasion for some attractive terracing. The groups of round stairways which lead down from the house terrace are ingeniously planned. The middle level is bounded on the south by a wall pierced at its middle by a long balcony of wrought iron, and flanked by a pair of pavilions which head the stairways to the next level below. At the end of this terrace is a charming brick-built seat with stone dressings, built round a round pavement whereon stands a sundial. From this level another double stair leads down to the lower part of the garden (Fig. 207).

DANESHILL, OLD BASING.

This is a good example of Mr. Lutyens' skill in the employment of brick as the sole material of a house. Mr. Walter Hoare was the fortunate possessor of a fine brick earth, and started an industry at Old Basing with intent to emulate the beautiful small hand-made bricks which at that time could be got only from Holland. His success in recapturing the quality of the bricks of Tudor times was complete, and he was greatly helped by Mr. Lutyens, who designed a number of special shapes for jambs, mullions, sills, parapets and the like. By careful study of technical methods Mr. Hoare secured a notable texture and a fine colour, in which reds blended in subtle fashion with purples. The

FIG. 205.—THE HOO, WILLINGDON : ENTRANCE COURT.

FIG. 206.—THE TWO PAVILIONS FROM MIDDLE LEVEL.

FIG. 207.—STEPS AND PAVILION FROM LOWER LEVEL.

FIG. 208.—THE HOO : SEAT AND SUNDIAL.

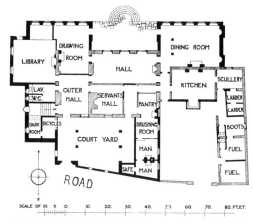

Old house shown hatched ; new work in solid black.

FIG. 209.—THE HOO : GROUND FLOOR PLAN.

slight hint of cushion shape given to the bricks produced a play of light and shade on the wall surfaces which gave brickwork a new charm and character. The varied designs of the fireplaces at Daneshill show considerable invention, and Fig. 213, as well as an illustration in the Introduction, indicates their character. Mr. Lutyens cannot be held responsible for the ineptitudes of his imitators, but these fireplaces have not been an unmixed blessing. They are justified by the beauty of their material and the reasonableness of their design and scale. I have, however, seen copies of them in bad machine-made brick, with rough and ragged mortar joints, and of a Gargantuan size which made ridiculous the little rooms where they were fixed. Even when he uses a rough material Mr. Lutyens' sense of scale and skilful design bring refinement to the finished thing. Some of his imitators succeed only in producing an effect of crudeness and barbarity, as, for example when they use a raw brick fireplace and window

FIG 210.—THE HOO, WILLINGDON : THE GARDEN FRONT.

FIG. 211.—DANESHILL : WEST SIDE.

openings, with the mortar guttering at the joints, in a drawing-room, the walls of which are covered with white-painted panelling, based on Wren's work at Hampton Court. No doubt in good time

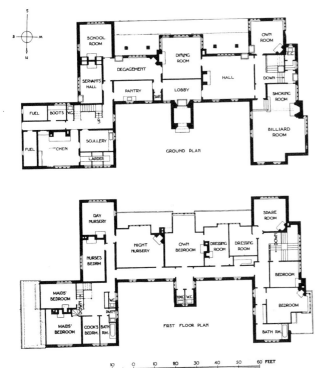

FIG. 212.—PLANS OF DANESHILL.

FIG. 213.—AT DANESHILL.

FIG. 214.—ENTRANCE FRONT OF DANESHILL, OLD BASING.

the wheel will revolve : a decent coat of plaster will cover the window mullions and a wood mantel-piece the fire opening, but meanwhile it all looks rather absurd and marks the danger of fashions little understood.   The design of Daneshill itself is interesting.   The north or entrance side is successful, but less can be said of the south front.   The windows seem excessive in size, especially the twelve-light gabled dormers, which, moreover, do not rhyme

FIG. 215.—DANESHILL : GARDEN FRONT FROM SOUTH-EAST.

well with the eighteen-light window on the first floor between them (Fig. 215). The latter would probably have been more happy in effect if it had been built with brick mullions, leaving wood mullions to be used for the dormers; but that would have involved the omission of the two inner wing lights. The south front of Daneshill is, indeed, one of Mr. Lutyens' less successful works, but the west front with its absence of gables is more restful.

MONKTON, SINGLETON, SUSSEX.

It is doubtful where Sussex can show a more enchanting wood than is threaded by the road leading to Monkton House. The ground slopes rapidly to the left. Through the near trunks, straight and thickly set, the eye rests on the vivid green of distant tree tops that in high summer shimmer brilliantly under the sun. The house is only a few miles from West Dean Park, the chief home of the late Mr. William James, and was built to serve as a shooting-box and a place for quiet days. Set high in typical Sussex country, Monkton owns a superb view that sweeps round southwards from Portsmouth to Chichester. Though the house is not large, the modesty of its entrance front

FIG. 216.—MONKTON, SINGLETON: FROM SOUTH-EAST.

FIG. 217.—LOGGIA AND BALCONY.

FIG. 218.—THE BALCONIES.

FIG. 219.—UNDER THE LOGGIA.

FIG. 220.—THE EAST GARDEN ROOM.

makes it look even smaller. An L-shaped loggia on the south and the minor offices connected with the kitchen form a little courtyard, which is sunk slightly below the level of the entrance drive. Through the vestibule we reach the hall, with which runs parallel the servants' passage, and from the hall there open the dining and drawing rooms. All these are simply and agreeably decorated, but our chief admiration goes to the loggia on the south front. It is formed into three compartments by two square piers built of brick and thin tile, with carved stone capitals. The end bays are divided from the middle space by open archways, and the south openings are filled by big windows. At the first-floor level there are balconies with doors from the four chief bedrooms, and a balustrading of refined design. Special reference must be made to the treatment of the bedroom which is shown in Fig. 223. The fireplace stands in the middle of the room. It thus forms in effect a bed recess, which can be screened from the front of the room by drawing a curtain, while yet remaining perfectly lighted by the window to the right. Altogether Monkton shows a delightful and characteristic scheme of bedroom planning.

The house sits on the side of the hill, and a considerable bastion had to be built to make place for a small garden. This best appears in Fig. 224A, taken from the opposite hill.

Very sheltered and inviting is the stretch of turf and paving, shut in by the low-roofed outdoor rooms that flank the body of the building. It would be difficult indeed to devise a house so admirably fitted for the open-air life, or more attractive with its red walls and roofs in a green setting of trees. The needful contrast is given by the white windows and balconies, and by the white flints of the terrace walls.

It is appropriate to close this chapter with Monkton because it helps to mark the

FIG. 222.—ENTRANCE FRONT OF MONKTON.

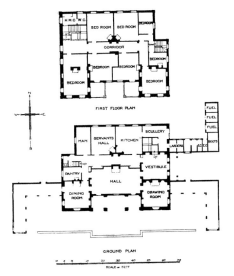

FIG. 221.—PLANS OF MONKTON.

FIG. 223.—A BEDROOM.

growing severity and symmetry which in 1902 were taking hold of Mr. Lutyens' outlook on design. Little Thakeham and Papillon Hall combined gabled exteriors with interiors which show a rising tide of later motives. Monkton is one of the earliest houses in which Mr. Lutyens abandoned the gable altogether in favour of hipped roofs. At the Deanery Garden the big bay of the hall is hipped, but the main roofs are gabled. At The Hoo, Willingdon, hips and gables are mingled. At Littlecroft, Guildford (page 46), the hipped roof alone

FIG. 224.—THE HEAD OF THE STAIR.

FIG. 224A.—MONKTON FROM THE SOUTH.

is employed, but the nature of the site led to the house being treated in a less balanced fashion than we find at Monkton, where the long, broad, hipped roofs give a convincing sense of repose.

CHAPTER VIII.

LINDISFARNE CASTLE, HOLY ISLAND.

Restoration Begun 1903 and Finished 1912.

BEFORE I describe the work done by Mr. Lutyens at the enchanting castle of Lindisfarne it is important that some history of Holy Island shall be set down. It will help the reader to capture the spirit of the place, and to realise the atmosphere of romance in which Mr. Lutyens worked. By the permission of my friend, Mr. P. Anderson Graham, a Northumbrian whose sympathy with his county's history is as deep as his knowledge is wide, I borrow an outline of what he has written about the island :

" In the history of Lindisfarne there are three well-defined stages. Chapter I opens in the year of grace 635, when Aidan was asked to choose the seat of his Bishoprick. Already he had made acquaintance with Bernicia, the northern part of Northumbria, having, with Oswald as his interpreter, taught the Gospel there. Aidan was a man of the ancient apostolic type, simple in thought and habit, full of the love taught no less by Colum, the founder of the Monastery of the West, than by his Master—one who took no thought of earthly rank or riches, but who believed with deep enthusiasm in that eternal Treasure which is found where neither the moth

FIG. 225.—LINDISFARNE CASTLE : FROM THE SOUTH-EAST.

nor the rust doth corrupt. We must try to look through his eyes to understand why his choice lighted upon the island. Probably the greatest consideration was that it reminded him of Iona.

"In Lindisfarne the evangelist monk beheld a new Iona like the old one, but with one or two different and remarkable features. It lay closer to the mainland, from which it is divided by a tract of flat sand that the flowing tide conceals and the ebb lays bare twice every day. Aidan must also have seen a great bare hump of basaltic rock that formed a centre round which the rest of the island landscape is naturally grouped.

"There was more to see. We can imagine the young Bishop climbing this bare crag—it is that on which the castle now stands—and gazing at the objects which interested him as he listened to the water sobbing among the rocks or watched it flowing over the sands. On the friendly shore within an hour's sail rose the Royal vill of Bamburgh, not as we know it, but as it was built by Ida and dwelt in by Oswald. Further off were the Farnes, dark and, according to the belief of the time, devil-haunted rocks rising ominously from a dangerous sea. He rejoiced in them, but not as a modern poet, a Swinburne or a Victor Hugo might have done. The monk of that period was convinced that the way to Heaven lay through self-imposed penances. Fasting and solitary prayer were the means by which he hoped to subdue the lusts of the flesh and get into communion with the Unseen. For austerities such as these Nature might have purposely brought forth these bleak and melancholy isles.

FIG. 226.—THE CASTLE IN 1728.

"In this spirit the See of Lindisfarne was founded, and with little essential change it existed for two centuries and a half. There were in all sixteen Bishops, and of these the most famous was Cuthbert. He was a shepherd boy on the Lammermoors when Aidan died, and the Venerable Bede says that on that night he saw stars falling. Comely in appearance, thoughtful in habit and of an inborn piety, he soon attracted the notice of great ecclesiastics as one of the chosen of the Lord. Eata, Abbot of Lindisfarne, made him Prior, a great step upward for the erstwhile shepherd lad; but humility was of the very essence of the man.

"As Aidan had done, Cuthbert turned his eye on Farne, the name island of the Farne group, which is now identified with House Island. On a rocky slope Cuthbert built his cell. Here for nine years he lived the anchorite's life, and when the King came in person, accompanied by Archbishop Truman, and begged him to accept the See of Lindisfarne, he yielded with the greatest reluctance, and with the due ritual and solemn pageantry of the Church was consecrated at York.

"The end of this portion of island history came in tragedy. Unmolested during the troubled centuries of their existence by the fighting people among whom they were placed, the monks at last fell victims to the Danish marauders. When the harried monks fled from the island, they took with them their dearest possessions, viz., the bones of Saint Cuthbert and the Gospel that had been hidden in his grave.

"Interesting as is the second stage of the history of Lindisfarne, we may not linger over it. 'The Holy Isle which was the mother of all the religeuse places in that part of the realm' now became 'a hand-mayde to Durham.' In 1082, Bishop William Carileph by charter bestowed on his newly established cell of Benedictine monks *inter alia* 'The Church of Lindisfarne which had been originally the Episcopal See.' Until now the island had been known as Lindisfarne, but under Benedictine rule it was called Holy Island 'in consequence of the sacred blood shed upon it by the Danes.' The new owners, as soon as they were established, cleared away the decaying remains of the old cathedral and built upon it the priory

FIG. 227.—FROM THE NORTH-EAST, SHOWING THE LOWER BATTERY.

whose ruins still remain. The foundation was probably laid in 1093 or 1094.

"The second period in the history of the island lasted from 1082 till about 1538. Holy Island for four centuries was ruled from Durham. There was no Aidan or Cuthbert in the second period. High ideals and romantic enthusiasms were now replaced by humdrum routine; fasting and penance gave place to good living. The Saint had been content with pulse and sometimes gave that to the eiders, which came to be known as St. Cuthbert's ducks. Fat beeves and sheep and porkers, capons, ducks and geese, malt for strong ale and store of wine ' for the solace of the brethren and strangers' were not too good for his successors. They no doubt said their orisons and chanted their daily Psalms with great regularity, but without the madness of devotion which had distinguished those of the older monastery.

"No band of freebooters ever rode a foray into Holy Island. They harried and wasted the land whence the revenue came, but they never touched the island, even though they knew, as they must have done, that the monks could have

FIG. 228.—THE WAY UP TO THE LOWER BATTERY.

FIG. 229.—LOOK-OUT FROM ENTRANCE TO LOWER BATTERY STAIR.

FIG. 230.—LINDISFARNE CASTLE FROM THE NORTH-WEST : THE UPPER BATTERY ON THE RIGHT.

made no effective resistance. Indirectly, however, the marauders robbed the church. The Priory drew tithes and land-rents from the mainland. Never were these dues collected without some of the farmers being unable to pay, owing to their being wasted by the Scots. In one year, 1584, the whole country-side was laid waste, and from the site of the present castle, then a bare rock, the monks must have watched the Scots burning and harrying.

" It was not till after the Dissolution of the religious houses that the need of a fortress in the island was urgently felt. Raine is most likely right in concluding that the castle owed its existence to the Order in Council (1539) that ' all havens should be fensed with bulwarks and blockehouses.' But the work was not immediately begun. What forced the island upon military attention was the preparation for Hertford's tremendous raid in 1543.

" The main embarkation took place at Berwick, but on the way to it two thousand two hundred troops were landed on Holy Island, and in October, 1543, ten English line of battle-ships were in the haven. In the previous year was made the first attempt at a serious fortification of the island, under the direction of ' Robart Rooke of Barwik.' The plan was to make two bulwarks, the one to be set in such place as would command the roadstead, the other in the most favourable situation for defending the island. In the report of the master mason and Robart Rooke, it was said that ' there is stone plentie and sufficient remayning of the olde abbey lately dissolved there to make the bulwark that shal defend the eland all of stone if it maie so stand with the good pleasure of the kinges said majestie.' We find the Castle mentioned for the first time in the Border Survey made by Sir Robert Bowes in 1550. He writes exactly in the manner of one looking at a newly-built fortress : ' The Fort of Beblowe, within the Holy Island, lyeth very well for the defence of the haven theire ; and if there were about the lowe part thereof

FIG. 231.—THE ENTRY HALL, LOOKING SOUTH-WEST.

FIG. 232.—THE ENTRY HALL, LOOKING NORTH.

made a ring, with bulwarks to flancke the same, the ditch thereabout might be easily watered towarde the land. And then I thinke the said forte were very stronge, and stood to great purpose, both for the defense of the forte and annoyance of the enemies, if they did arrive in any other parts of the Island.' Later, in 1675, a second fort was built upon the east end of the Heugh, but it was soon allowed to fall into ruins. In the third year of her reign Queen Elizabeth had a survey made, which paints a scene of desolation. Only a few emblems and remnants remain to tell of the importance of Lindisfarne during days when it was a famous seat of learning and the home of a powerful monastery; the castle armoured with culverins and demi-culverins, sakirs and falcons, but never assailed—its history since Aidan's day is being obliterated. In the reign of Elizabeth's successor, when Scotland and England became united under James, the island lost importance even from the military point of view. The castle, it is true, remained a Government fortress, and the parish register shows, by the frequent entry ' a soger died,' that a military garrison was maintained, the soldiers being probably strangers to the fisher community. During the tragical reign of Charles I. we obtain an unexpected peep at it. This is to be found in the diary of John Aston, who was attached to the suite of Charles I on his expedition through the counties of York, Durham and Northumberland, in the first Bishops' War of 1639. On May 25th, 1639, the King's Army was encamped at Goswick.

" Charles did not join the camp, but Aston went there, and from it made an expedition, the account of which shows exactly what the island and the fortress were like in 1639 : ' Hence wee went to view the Holy Island, and about 10 a clock, when the tyde was out, wee rode over to it and divers walked on foote into it. It is about 5 mile in compasse, a levell ground

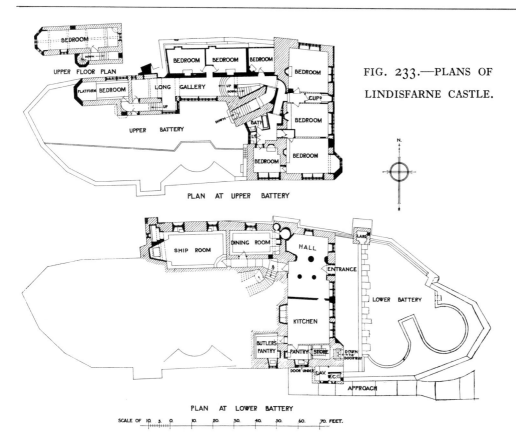

FIG. 233.—PLANS OF LINDISFARNE CASTLE.

PLAN AT UPPER BATTERY

PLAN AT LOWER BATTERY

SCALE OF 10. 5. 0.   10.   20.   30.   40.   50.   60.   70. FEET.

with a short greene swade upon it, noe part of it tilled nor affoording any thing but conies. . . . There is a pretty fort in it, which upon this occasion was repaired and put into forme. There are 2 batteries on it, on the lower stood mounted 3 iron peeces and 2 of brasse, with carriadges and platformes in good order. On the higher was one brasse gunne and 2 iron ones with all ammunition to

FIG. 234.—THE DINING-ROOM.

FIG. 235.—THE SHIP ROOM.

them. There are 24 men and a captain kept in pay to man it, the common souldiours have 6*d.* per diem, and the captain [*a space is left here*]. The captain at our beeing there was Captain Rugg, knowne commonly by his great nose.'

FIG. 236.—THE STAIRWAY UP TO GALLERY LOOKING WEST.

" We can now clearly apprehend the three chapters of the island, of which Chapter I beholds the opening in an unworldly splendour where monks, humble in heart, zealous in belief, unflinching in penance, sent the message of the Galilean to the most barbarous corners of the North. Follows Chapter II., with priests trading on the sanctity of their predecessors ; epicene and luxurious, they enjoy the fruits of the earth and sea like stalled oxen consuming their provender witless of the fatal poleaxe. Chapter III is but the history of decay."

So much for the island's story in bygone days. When its present owner, Mr. Edward Hudson, saw it first the state of dilapidation was extreme, but the main fabric was sound. The accompanying plans (Fig. 233) show the original walls by hatched lines and the new work in solid black. They are a little difficult to understand owing to the variety of levels and the somewhat wayward run of the stairways, but the following description will, I trust, make fruitful a study of the plans and photographs. The castle is approached by a sloping way which

FIG. 237.—A CORNER IN THE GALLERY.

runs up from east to west on the south side of the rock (Fig. 228). It brings the visitor to a stone platform and a portcullised door (Fig. 229). Going through this he ascends to the lower battery by a flight of stone steps which run up under the pantry and store. This battery remains, with its gun emplacements, as it was left when the castle ceased to be a defensive place, but the guns themselves have disappeared. The east wall of the castle lacked windows. It was, moreover, in a very unsatisfactory state, and as it appeared to date chiefly from some later reconstruction of the building, most of it was taken down. Built into its core were found some fragments of Tudor worked stone, too decayed, however, for re-use. The combined outcome of the alterations made in 1903 and 1912 has been to give, at the lower battery level, a fine entrance hall (Figs. 231 and 232) and a roomy kitchen. Attention may be drawn to the delightful treatment of the bases of the new hall columns, which die away into the floor. They emphasise Mr. Lutyens' skill in giving a new significance to old forms. Walter Pater wrote in *Notre Dame d'Amiens :* "The massive square pillars of a Romanesque church, harshly angular, obstruct, sometimes cruelly, the

FIG. 238.—THE GALLERY, LOOKING EAST.

standing, the movements of a multitude of persons. To carry such a multitude conveniently round them is the matter-of-fact motive of the gradual chiselling away, the softening of the angles, the graceful compassing, of the Gothic base, till in our own Perpendicular period it all but disappears." Fig. 232 shows that at Lindisfarne this lessening of the base is carried still further, and only enough remains to avoid the harshness of a baseless column, and to establish the organic relation between floor and pillar. From the hall a door leads to the foot of the old stone stair which ascends to the upper battery. First, however, the visitor goes along a passage to the two original vaulted rooms, now the dining-room and the ship room. Neither has been materially altered, but in both the original little openings have been enlarged and fitted with traceried windows : the ship room also was lengthened a little at its west end, and new fireplaces were built in both (Figs. 234 and 235).

FIG. 239.—ONE OF THE BEDROOMS.

The stairway to the upper battery from this level has a branch to the right some six steps up, which leads to the first floor rooms on the upper battery level. At the head of this branch is a passage which leads eastwards to the old rooms. Westwards is a flight of four steps, curved on plan (Fig. 236), which gives access to the gallery. This is wholly new and connects the

FIG. 240.—ON THE UPPER BATTERY, LOOKING WEST.

east and west blocks of the castle, which were originally separate. The western building was a separate guard-house, approached from the upper battery. On the north of what is now the long gallery was another battery known as Elizabeth's. This has been occupied by three new bedrooms, built in 1912. The gallery is a delightful apartment, and has a new archway and fireplace (Fig. 238). The three steps which are seen in Fig. 237 are at the foot of the staircase to the upper floor, which is occupied by a long bedroom. A new octagonal stair turret leads to the roof of this room. From the upper battery (Fig. 240) there is an enchanting view across to Bamburgh Castle, over the village which groups round the ruins of the priory church of Lindisfarne, and cunningly disposed steps enable us to climb on to the leaded roofs of the castle and thence to sweep the sea view to the Farne Islands and beyond to the horizon.

Needless to say, Nature and the Tudor builders of Lindisfarne had given to the castle a romantic quality which no modern building could hope to achieve, but it was Mr. Lutyens' happy gift so to alter and enlarge what he found that a rude blockhouse has become a home of reasonable comfort. This he has done without qualifying its original character, though he has increased the domestic, as opposed to the defensive, note by giving the new north bedrooms a pitched and dormered roof of red pantiles.

Fortunately, his client, Mr. Edward Hudson, entered with a lively enthusiasm into the spirit of the work, and did not demand that wealth of modern devices which some people insist on installing in the most ancient fabrics. But he did more. His discriminating taste has furnished the castle with authentic oak furniture of the sixteenth and seventeenth centuries, and the walls are gay with domestic objects of brass and pewter. Nowhere could these things look more apt and pleasant than at Lindisfarne Castle. Both architect and owner, indeed, may be congratulated on having treated a unique building on a unique site with the utmost judgment and taste. I have set out, in Mr. Graham's words, the three chapters of the history of Holy Island, from the days when it shone like a star of hope on the Northumbrian shore to the time of its decay. Mr. Hudson and Mr. Lutyens have furnished its story with an epilogue which tells of the return of the castle to a state of architectural honour.

CHAPTER IX.

THE GARDENS AT HESTERCOMBE. 1904.

NORTH of the plain on which Taunton is set, the spurs and outlying hillocks of the Quantocks thrust themselves out upon the level. Among them, admirably placed to get the southern sun and avoid the northern blast, and with broad outlook upon the immediate lowlands and the distant hills, Hestercombe is set. Coplestone Warre Bampfylde was in possession of Hestercombe when Collinson wrote his *History of Somerset* at the close of the eighteenth century, and the picture of the house and its environment in that publication was drawn by its owner. It appears as a great square structure pierced by rows of sash windows, but having architraves, pediments and other good architectural features of the classic type. An indication of a balustrade standing in front of the house suggests that there may have been a narrow terrace to the south. Otherwise the house rises sheer out of its undulating park set with a few clumps of trees and with a rolling woodland rising behind it to the

FIG. 241.—LOOKING SOUTH FROM WITHIN THE ROTUNDA: THE CANAL OF THE EAST WATER
GARDEN IS JUST VISIBLE IN THE DISTANCE.
(From view-point A on plan. See Fig. 243.)

FIG. 242.—MAIN TERRACE AND RETAINING WALLS BELOW THE HOUSE, LOOKING EASTWARDS.

At the foot is the beginning of the great plat, north end. (From view-point B on plan.)

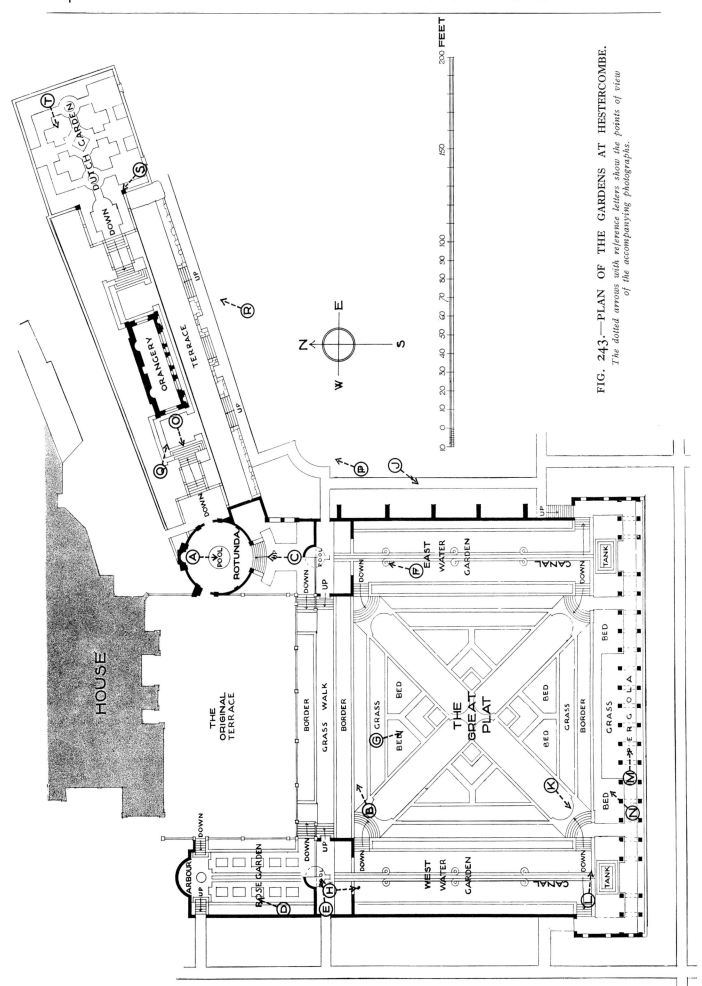

FIG. 243.—PLAN OF THE GARDENS AT HESTERCOMBE.

The dotted arrows with reference letters show the points of view
of the accompanying photographs.

north. These were days of the severest classicalism in architecture and of " Capability " Brown's " natural " style in gardening, and the arrangement at Hestercombe so fully came up to these ideals that Collinson describes it as " most admirably improved by art, and exquisitely embellished by taste." The place is now transformed. The eighteenth century house, which was fairly

FIG. 244.—LOOKING NORTH INTO THE ROTUNDA.
(From view-point C on plan.)

good of its age, was added to and overlaid in the nineteenth century, and this was not done at a fortunate moment or by a happy hand.' It is a most ample, comfortable and well placed home, but architecturally and decoratively it is one of those many products of the Victorian age which is an example to avoid rather than to copy. The chief feeling it excites is one of regret that it did not escape such drastic ill-treatment, in order that it might have come under the same guidance and within the same scheme as the new gardens. Their fine architecture emphasises the contrast rather strongly. The difference between house and garden is more than one of shape and structure. It lies deeper. It is in the spirit and the essence. The architect who altered the Bampfylde classic house did

FIG. 245.—RILL AND ARBOUR IN ROSE GARDEN, LOOKING NORTH.
(From view-point D on plan.)

not understand what style was, and he lacked feeling both for form and surface. The original windows must have made, with their moulded architraves and thick sash bars, part of a considered composition in conjunction with rusticated quoins, bold cornice and pedimented parapets. Their effect was destroyed by the insertion of plate glass, and the

FIG. 246.—WALLED POOL ENCLOSURE AT NORTH END OF WEST WATER GARDEN.
(From view-point E on plan.)

FIG. 247.—LOOKING NORTHWARDS INTO THE WALLED POOL ENCLOSURE AT THE NORTH END OF THE EAST WATER GARDEN, AND SHOWING BEGINNING OF CANAL AND FIRST LOOP POOLS

The piers and pedimented niche of the rotunda are seen on the upper level. (*From view-point F on plan.*)

new windows show no relation to the older ones.   The tower may have some affinity with French Renaissance, but none with English Palladian work.   We turn from them to the more structural parts of the new gardens, to the orangery, the rotunda and the retaining walls at the head of the two water-terraces.   The first thing that strikes us about these is that they undoubtedly possess style.   Moreover, it is apparent that the style is informed by two all-important characteristics.   It shows a full knowledge of, and a loyal adherence to, the principles and the practice of past ages of architecture, yet there is no mere copying. The whole realm of formal gardening, Italian, French and English, has been industriously and intelligently surveyed.   But Mr. Lutyens has then thought for himself.   He has weighed the full possibilities of the site, the peculiar character of local materials and the manifold methods of modern gardening, and he has brought to the design invention and ingenuity, imagination and learning.   That is why it has style.   It is the work of a particular man in a particular place.

FIG. 248.—THE GREAT PLAT, LOOKING SOUTHWARDS FROM BELOW THE MAIN TERRACE.
(From view-point G on plan.)

In view of the unsatisfactory character of the house it must have been difficult to determine the basis of the garden design.   The pictures show that Mr. Lutyens has had in mind the period of William III and of Anne.   It was the time when expansion first became the aim of English gardeners.   Elizabethan and Jacobean gardens were elaborate, but small.   A man of large mind and princely ideas like Lord Bacon could plan one that covered thirty acres, but neither he nor any of his contemporaries could carry it out ; Wilton, with its ten acres, was considered prodigious at the time.   The French, however, did things on a more ambitious scale.   Even under Louis XIII great men, such as Richelieu at Rueil, and Gaston d'Orleans at the Luxembourg, made vast gardens.   Under Louis XIV Le Nôtre gave further extension to this system, and French ideas became dominant in England after the Restoration.   In the middle of the seventeenth century John Rea considered that an acre and a half was ground enough even for a nobleman's flower and vegetable gardens.   Before the end of the century many of the

FIG. 249.—THE WEST WATER GARDEN, LOOKING SOUTHWARDS FROM THE POOL ENCLOSURE SEEN
IN FIG. 246, AND SHOWING FULL LENGTH OF CANAL.

(From view-point H on plan.)

FIG. 250.—BUTTRESSED RETAINING WALL ON EAST SIDE OF EAST WATER GARDEN, AND STAIRWAY UP TO EAST END OF PERGOLA.

(From view-point J on plan.)

extensive schemes of grounds depicted by Kip were completed or in hand. An Elizabethan atmosphere should, therefore, be reserved for designs that include only a small space. Where, as at Hestercombe, a complete formal scheme of considerable extent is to be carried out, a later style is certainly preferable, and Mr. Lutyens did right to choose it. But though the orangery, the pedimented alcoves, the inserted niches, the great gateposts, are strongly reminiscent of the age of Anne, we

FIG. 251.—STEPS AT SOUTH-WEST CORNER OF GREAT PLAT UP TO PERGOLA AND WEST WATER GARDEN.

(From view-point K on plan.)

cannot fail to note the originality of the architectural treatment. The old formalists aimed at banishing Nature, just as the landscape school banished formalism. Mr. Lutyens combines the two. In the choice and treatment of his material, he has succeeded in bringing about the desired partnership of Nature and of Art. He has taken what was near at hand. For all dressed work he has used Somerset's splendid ashlar from the Ham Hill district. For the general walling a rough self-splitting and unworked stone from the neighbourhood is employed. But the totally different proportions and different manner in which these two contrasting substances are used in the case of a roofed edifice and in the case of a mere retaining wall give the keynote of the leading idea. The orangery is a house, a complete building, a work of man in his most artificial mood, *i.e.*, in a classical mood. Here is no place for natural ruggedness, but for fine material delicately wrought. Ham Hill stone therefore largely predominates, and is treated with a good deal of elaboration. There are pilasters, niches,

FIG. 252.—TANK AT SOUTH-WEST CORNER OF GREAT PLAT: LOOKING EASTWARDS.
(*From view-point L on plan.*)

architraves, pediments, all well moulded, and the ends have the further ornament of crisply carved festoons of fruit and flowers and coats of arms in boldly designed cartouches. But though the orangery is essentially a thing of conscious design, its position in the general scheme of being the first step from artifice to Nature is not forgotten. It stands on a base of rough, thinly laminated rubble stone, the mortar joints of which are kept so well back from the surface that it almost looks like dry walling. Panels of the same work are also introduced above, and the rustication of the pilasters is done in stone of similar quality, but slightly wrought and surface pointed. As the orangery is the most polished piece of building in the gardens, so is the outside walling of the main terraced garden the most rugged and simple. It is all of rubble stone, taken as it comes. The buttresses are of primitive type (Fig. 250), the wall is uncoped, and the doorways and roundels are all roughly treated in the same material. It is the last

outwork of man on the edge of Nature.   Half-way between these two extremes is the treatment
of the rotunda and of the head walls of the water-terraces.   Here the walls are coped with
moulded Ham Hill stone.   Of the same material are the balustradings, the niches, the arches
and the great keystones with masks spouting water.   But the whole of the walls are of rubble
roughly used, while they are slightly wrought for pilasters, architraves and end pillars.   The
feeling that garden architecture should exhibit some kinship with Nature was represented in the
old work by artificial rustications and grottoes.   It is reached at Hestercombe by using the most
natural-looking materials that were to be found, and by leaving them as far as possible in the
most natural state.   The stairways liberally used and many shaped, which crop up at every rise
in the ground, and the great extent of flagged spaces and pathways, are all of rough-edged and

FIG. 253.—LOOKING EASTWARDS UNDER THE PERGOLA.
(From view-point M on plan.)

rough-surfaced paving such as readily becomes weathered and mossed.   Thus, though the lines
are straight and shapes formal, Nature is not extinguished or enchained, but allowed free
activity within recognised limits.

So much by way of indicating the spirit in which Mr. Lutyens approached the design and
the way that he handled the materials available for building.   We come next to a detailed
description of the garden in the light of the plan and photographs.   The points from which
the latter were taken have been indicated on the plan (page 142) by lettered arrows, to which a
reference is given under each illustration.   The pictures cannot be understood fully unless the
lie of the ground and the relative position of the various parts of the garden be first realised.
The house occupies a middle elevation on the hill-land which forms the southern declivity of

the Quantocks as they drop to the Taunton plain. The view looking south out of the rotunda (Fig. 241) gives an idea of the broad outlook over the rich vale beyond the park. High ground, fully and beautifully timbered, rises behind the house ; a rapid fall of open land lies in front.

FIG. 254.—LOOKING NORTH-EAST ACROSS THE GREAT PLAT TO THE ORANGERY FROM UNDER THE PERGOLA.

(From view-point N on plan.)

But there is not merely a general slope from north to south ; there is also a succession of much-varied hollows and swells from west to east. The house stands on a swell. The orangery occupies the middle of the adjacent hollow. The Dutch garden is on the flattened

summit of the next swell (Fig. 260).   It looks down westward on to the orangery (Fig. 258) and
eastward into a timbered glen where Nature is left untouched.   Full advantage of this triple
lie of the land has been taken in order to give character and variety to the three chief sections
of the lay-out.   A single terraced parallelogram was long ago constructed in front of the south
elevation of the house (lettered on the plan " the original terrace "), and from here we may start
our tour of inspection.   It is below this terrace that the new main garden lies.   It consists of
a great plat, two side terraces and a southern pergola.   To the sides of the old terrace have been
added, on the west a little plat set with roses and headed by an arboured alcove (Fig. 245), and
on the east the rotunda (Fig. 244).   There is a drop of about four feet from the old terrace to

FIG. 255.—LOOKING WESTWARDS FROM WEST END OF ORANGERY
UP TO ROTUNDA.
(From view-point O on plan.)

the rose garden, itself
standing eight feet above
the long water-terrace
directly below, which is
reached by a double flight
of steps at the side.   The
rotunda is on the same
level as the original
terrace, but its south
stairway leads to a terrace
on the same level as the
rose garden, and from
that a similar double
flight of steps leads to
the water-terrace level.
These two east and west
water gardens are identi-
cal in plan, and each
begins with a little walled
enclosure on the south
side of which the walls
ramp down and leave the
centre open (Fig. 247).
The north end of each
has a water-jet playing
from the keystone of an
arch into a round pool
below, half of the cir-
cumference of which lies
in the scooped-out wall
and half in the open, an
ingenious arrangement
yielding much play of
light and shadow on the
water (Fig. 246).   The
overflows of the pools

are carried down the centres of the water gardens for one hundred and forty feet in canals
(Figs. 247 and 249) filled with water plants, edged with paving-stones and ending in oblong
tanks (Fig. 252) abutting on to the pergola which runs from end to end of the southern boundary
of this garden.   The water-gardens are the protecting bulwarks of the great plat—a square of
one hundred and twenty-five feet—which is reached from each end of either terrace by a stairway.
Half-way down these descents are platforms at the level of the pergola, which lies three feet lower
than the terraces.   The further drop is made practical by sets of steps segmentally arranged
at each corner of the great plat (Fig 251).   This cornerwise entry dictates the oblique disposition
of the flag-bordered stretches of grass (Fig. 248) and the triangular arrangement of flower-beds

FIG. 256.—THE ORANGERY FROM THE SOUTH-WEST.
(From view-point P on plan.)

FIG. 257.—WEST END OF ORANGERY.
(From view-point Q on plan.)

in the great plat. Mr. Lutyens first sketched a scheme of many parallel and cross grass paths framing a whole series of oblong beds. It was after the manner in which such gardens are habitually laid out and gave no value to the corner segmental stairways. It is merely mentioned here in order to contrast it with the final design, which makes the corner entries not merely possible, but imperative. If it lessens the space dedicated to plants, it makes the planting far more effective by grouping it into four sections well separated by restful stretches of grass. Moreover, the introduction of narrow paved ways edging the beds and shaping the grass plots emphasises the geometrical character of the most geometrical part of the gardens. This æsthetic quality is joined to an eminently practical advantage. The paved ways serve the double purpose of permitting the visitor to saunter everywhere dry-footed in damp weather, and of dividing the grass from the plants. The latter can therefore keep their natural growth and broken outline, and need not be subjected to the harsh straight line given by the shears, or to the bruises and tearings inflicted by the

FIG. 258.—EAST END OF ORANGERY AND STAIRWAY GOING NORTH-EAST UP TO DUTCH GARDEN.
(From view-point R on plan.)

passing mowing machine. The main plat is an undoubted triumph; it has richness and repose, breadth and variety. There is a good deal of design and pattern, and yet no undue sacrifice of simplicity. Without the use of any architectural features—of which there is an abundance elsewhere—a quite uncommon manner of treating a plain and perfectly flat square has been devised, which gives it adequate form and dignity, and avoids conceits and fussiness. Indeed, one of the merits of this section of the gardens is that, while full of incident and interest, it is not restless. There is no multiplication of objects, no frittering of effects, no cluttering of garden ornaments. Those elements were chosen which the site and the environment recommended. The rest were resolutely put aside. Mr. Lutyens was therefore able, having an acre and a half to deal with, to use the parts in a large manner, and blend them into a dignified whole. The natural levels were taken as a basis; they were accentuated and formalised. The ascents and descents are therefore expected rather than surprising. The treatment of the water is decidedly happy. At so considerable an elevation, and on so rapid a slope, sheets of water or lengths of broad canal would have been uncomfortable, though they might have been

FIG. 259.—AT THE WEST END OF THE DUTCH GARDEN.
(From view-point S on plan.)

adequately fed. It is a position where water should have a certain degree of the precious, and that is given to it by the narrowness of the ways along which it is brought and by the use of thin rills—and of the little loop pools breaking the harshness of the line—for the necessary irrigation of the water-weeds. The size, too, of the pools, which begin and end the canals at the top and bottom of the water-terraces, is satisfying, while the architecture of the little enclosures at the head of these terraces centres in the tiny rill dropping from the masks into the round pools with a sound that modestly calls attention to it.

The whole architectural composition is charming.   The balustrade telling of an upper walk, the side niches—intended, of course, for the future reception of busts—the semi-circular arch framing the segmental scoop into the wall, the circular pool of limpid water, are all as good as can be.   But the water does not drop in quite a happy place : it would have been better if the jet had been contrived to fall into the middle of the pool rather than close to the margin, but that is a small point.

Before we leave the great plat and its enclosing features we shall glance down the fine vista afforded by the pergola (Fig. 253) and see how pleasantly the diagonal grass paths with the sundial at their intersection are framed by its posts (Fig. 254).   Our tour of the main garden began at the rotunda, and we return to it as the feature which connects the original terrace alike with the main plat and water-gardens and with the orangery and Dutch garden.   These look to the south-east and in front of them is a natural tree-set lawn, levelled in two places for the purposes of croquet and tennis.   As it is a slight hollow, there is a rise at its west and east boundaries as well as to the north or main hillside.   The buttressed retaining wall of the main formal garden, which we have just left, forms the western boundary, but it is not at right angles to the northern boundary.   These boundaries are not artificial lines set out on the drawing-board, but are dictated by the lie of the land.   The upper or northern end, which thus fails to form a right angle with the western side, is used for the remaining portions of the formal gardens.   Immediate access to it by straight flights of steps out of any of the levels of the higher terraces to the west could only be obtained at the cost of an awkward effect.   Hence the rotunda.   Its walls screen the obtuse angle, and its exits are arranged to open centrally and at right angles to the stairways to south and east.   Its eastern stairway, with its several flights and ample and increasing breadth, descends on to the orangery terrace (Fig. 255).   At the eastern end of the orangery a similar stairway rises to the little elevated Dutch garden (Fig. 258).   This pretty little enclosure is an example of Mr. Lutyens' power of seizing on an unpromising feature and turning it into a valuable one.   The mound it occupies was an old rubbish heap which was to have been removed as an eyesore.   Mr. Lutyens saw its possibilities and incorporated it into the general scheme.   The strip of ground occupied by this composite and many-levelled arrangement, starting with the rotunda at one end and finishing with the Dutch garden at the other, is sixty feet wide and three hundred feet long.   It gives a sense of being very fully occupied, but not overcrowded.   Behind it, and here and there within it, rise tall trees of great size and importance.   They cast a desirable air of humility over the works of man, which they over-shadow.   Yet they do not lessen the importance and the dignity of the two great stairways, which, at first confined by balustrading, broaden out near their bases and afford side as well as front descents. The stairways leave room for considerable plats of pavement at either end of the orangery, and these prevent the building having any appearance of being squeezed or trespassed upon by the high walls and the flights of steps which surround it on three sides.   Before it lies a terrace twenty feet wide, whereon the arrangement of the great plat of the main garden is repeated in so far as it is laid out in geometrically shaped grass patterns surrounded by flagging.   As an outlier, on the edge of the wild, the Dutch garden has an architectural treatment of the simplest type, enlivened only by the much-decorated Italian vases and the delicately modelled dancing amorini on the great posts (Fig. 259).

At Hestercombe resource and ingenuity have made the inorganic section—the architectural elements—exhibit greater variety than the organic section—the planting. The numberless forms, effects, surfaces and levels which have been produced with a very limited selection of materials and without sacrifice of unity of effect are very notable.   The really difficult problem of avoiding monotony without producing fussiness is here solved to perfection in the laying out.   Taking them altogether, the Hestercombe gardens are a creation wherein human imperfection of invention and of workmanship has been brought down to its minimum.   They will long stand as a work of art to be admired and an example to be followed. They prove that an architect can be in unison with Nature, that a formal garden can form part of a landscape.

FIG. 260.—LOOKING WESTWARDS ACROSS THE DUTCH GARDEN.
(From view-point T on plan.)

CHAPTER X.

ASHBY ST. LEDGERS, NORTHAMPTONSHIRE.

ADDITIONS TO MANOR HOUSE (1904) AND COTTAGES (1909).

ASHBY ST. LEDGERS takes its name from the dedication of the church to Saint Leodegarius, and is thus distinguished from other Ashbys in Northamptonshire. From the fourteenth century to the beginning of the seventeenth century it belonged to the Catesbys. It is unfortunate that Bridges' and Whalley's *History of Northamptonshire*, justly described in its Preface as "copious," is altogether silent about the house or its builders, and the only direct evidence afforded by the building itself is the date 1652, carved on

FIG. 261.—THE NEW WING ON GARDEN FRONT.

a stone in the south gable. There was a house on the site in Edward III's reign, and parts of it are probably embedded in the present building, which is Elizabethan in its main characteristics. It is difficult, however, to make any satisfactory guess as to who built it, and we are without any documentary evidence. Sir William Catesby, father of Robert, of "Gunpowder Plot" fame, was a stout supporter of the Roman Catholic party all through Elizabeth's reign. He suffered severely in person and substance from 1580 onwards. Robert followed in his steps, and his brilliant personal

FIG. 262.—ASHBY ST. LEDGERS : THE FORECOURT.

charms drew adherents to any wild and quixotic cause which he befriended. The lives of both these defenders of a lost cause were full and troublous, and it would seem unlikely that they concerned themselves with building. On historical grounds one would be inclined to attribute part of the work to the early years of James I's reign. The gatehouse, however, is certainly much earlier. Tradition has it that the " Gunpowder Plot," first hatched by Winter in 1604, was elaborated by him and Robert Catesby in the gatehouse room. When Guy Faux failed in his design, Winter rode north to

FIG. 263.—NEW ORIEL AND CHIMNEY OF WEST WING.

FIG. 264.—SOUTH SIDE OF KITCHEN COURT.

Ashby St. Ledgers, and Catesby followed. It is said that he reached there on the evening of November 5th, 1605, as Winter was sitting down to supper with Catesby's mother, who made her home at the manor house. They moved on quickly, and Catesby fell fighting a few days later at Holbeach. The manor passed a few years later, through Sir William Irwing, to Bryan I'Anson, whose descendants held it until 1703. It belonged to the Ashleys and their descendants, the Senhouses, from then until 1903, when it was bought by the Hon. Ivor Guest, now Lord Ashby St. Ledgers.

The plans of the manor house reproduced in Figs. 268 and 270, show by hatched lines the buildings which existed in 1903, and in solid black the additions made since that date. The ground-floor plan also indicates the position of the Tudor house, an old building of half-timber construction which was transported from East Anglia and re-erected by Lord Ashby St. Ledgers. The original accommodation of the manor house was small. It included a hall and common-room running north and south, which were connected by a staircase hall with what is now the study at the south-east corner. A block of servants' quarters existed at the north-west end of the forecourt. Mr. Lutyens' additions consisted of a new wing at the north end of the east front, matching the study wing, and a large music-room with a square bay, built on the east side of the hall and common-room, to connect the two wings. These additions are well shown in Fig. 261, and have resulted in the creation of a finely balanced garden front, which is the more beautiful by reason of the rich golden hue of

FIG. 265.—OLD GATEWAY TO NEW ARCHWAY AND BRIDGE.

FIG. 266.—DINING-ROOM BAY AND GALLERY ORIEL.

FIG. 267.—NEW ARCHWAY LEADING TO FORECOURT.

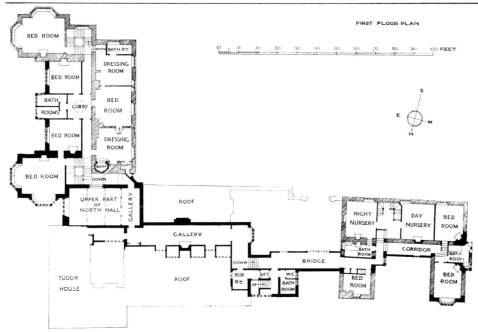

FIG. 268.—FIRST FLOOR PLAN OF MANOR HOUSE.

FIG. 269.—ASHBY ST. LEDGERS: THE NEW NORTH HALL.

the stone and the warm red of the tiled roofs. The stone of which the original house was built came from a quarry not far from Northampton. As, however, it had not proved very durable, the new work was built in a harder stone from Banbury, which is slightly less rich in tone owing to a hint of blue in it. Despite the extensive additions made on the north side of the forecourt, the original appearance of the house, as seen when it is approached from the west, has not been greatly changed. Through an old gateway a path leads to an archway, the north side of which is shown in Fig. 267. In the future this arch will take a more important place in the general building scheme than it does at present, because, as the plan (Fig. 270) indicates, it is proposed in the future to make very large additions on the north side. Meanwhile the arch is very attractive in its own right by reason of the curved steps on either side of it, which are set out on the lines of a complete circle. Above the archway is a bridge of half-timbered construction which connects the new gallery over the pantry with the nurseries in the old west building. This bridge appears in Fig. 265.

The photograph reproduced in Fig. 266 is taken from within the north gateway of the forecourt, and shows on the right the tall bay

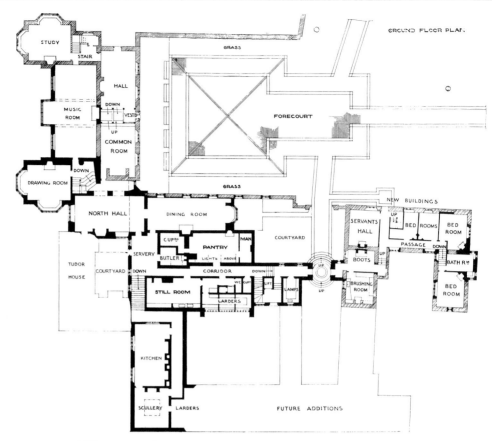

FIG. 270.—GROUND FLOOR PLAN OF MANOR HOUSE.

of the new dining-room and the oriel window of the gallery. When we have gone through the new archway we find the kitchen court and the building on its south side, which appear in Fig. 264. The openings near the ground between the two buttresses are coal-shoots. The nursery wing needed very little alteration, but Fig. 263 shows the new oriel window of the north-west bed-room and the big chimney-stack provided on the west side.

The most important interior created by the alterations is the north hall, which appears in Fig. 269. It runs up two storeys, and has not only a gallery at its western end, but an opening on its south side at the first-floor level, so that the main staircase is visible from the hall. It has been built with an open timber roof, which, though Gothic in its general outlines, shows delightful touches of personal fancy in its details. Its oak beams have a curious history. They were presented by Charles II. to the Church of All Saints, North-ampton, presumably as a store in case repairs were

FIG. 271.—GROUP OF SIX COTTAGES AT ASHBY ST. LEDGERS.

needed, but they were never used, and after having been stored in the belfry for over two centuries, were sold, and now form the roof at Ashby St. Ledgers.

A Group of Cottages.

Mr. Lutyens' activities were not confined, however, to the work at the manor house. He has designed an attractive group of thatched cottages in the village. Photographs of the block are reproduced in Figs. 271 and 272. The plan (Fig. 273) is broken up in the most delightful way, and produces a

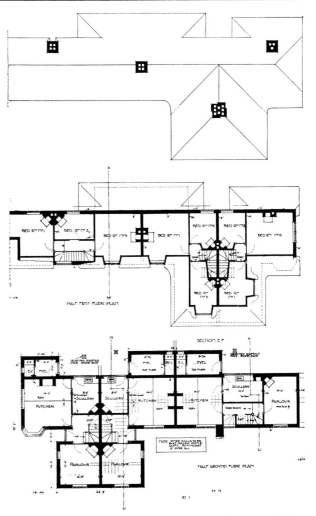

FIG. 273.—PLANS OF BOTH FLOORS AND ROOF OF HALF THE BLOCK OF COTTAGES.

FIG. 272.—A PROJECTING WING.

street picture of pleasant diversity, but the amount of accommodation is the same in all the cottages. Each boasts a kitchen, scullery, parlour and three bedrooms. There is a porch at the back which serves as a covered way from the cottage proper to the fuel-house, and the earth-closet is approached through the latter. This arrangement has the advantage of putting the earth-closet at a considerable distance from the living-rooms, while making it accessible under cover. A feature of the block is the arched passage-way through the middle of it, which leads from the village street to the cottage gardens at the back. A certain amount of old masonry was available, and use was made of this for the lower parts of the walls, as far as it would go, the upper parts of the walls being built of brick rough-cast. The thick thatched roof, with its admirable dormers and ridge, the unbroken roof-line and the stout brick chimneys produce an effect very picturesque and satisfactory. The cottages are large, but the planning of the chimneys has been so carefully thought out that only eight stacks were required for the six cottages, which form a very satisfactory example of what can be done by a landowner not only to preserve but to increase the amenities of a typical English village.

CHAPTER XI.

THREE SMALLER HOUSES (1905–7).

Millmead, Bramley ; The Dormy House, Walton Heath ; Barton St. Mary,
East Grinstead.

IN 1906, in the village of Bramley, near Guildford, there was a waste strip of ground some eighty
feet wide and four hundred feet deep, known as the " sordid half-acre." It stretched from road
to mill mead, and was the dumping-ground for the neighbours' potsherds and tin cans. A
year later a tile-coped wall, lifted at each end by a steep gabled outbuilding and pierced in the
centre by an arched doorway, shut out the view. Within the massive oak door is a charming
forecourt and a modest dwelling, thoughtful not only in its main outline, but also in its smallest
detail. A paved way cuts through the level grass and leads to the front doorway, with its architraves and pediment in dressed stone. This is the north side, and, in contrast with the south

FIG. 274.—MILLMEAD : THE FORECOURT.

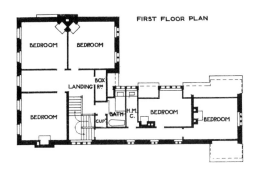

FIRST FLOOR PLAN

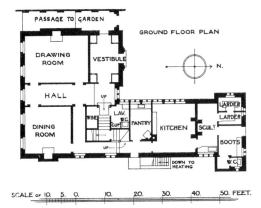

GROUND FLOOR PLAN

SCALE of 10. 5. 0.   10.   20.   30.   40.   50. FEET.

FIG. 275.—PLANS OF MILLMEAD.

FIG. 276.—MILLMEAD : ENTRANCE DOOR FROM THE WEST.

and west, the architecture is here serious and restrained, the main house or *corps de logis* being almost unwindowed, though the office wing, which fills the foreground of Fig. 274, is lit by a line of casements so long as to produce an effect of restfulness and to shed abundant light within. Above, the big hipped dormers spring out of the main roof in curves admirably adapted to throw off the rain. They also present that suavity of line to which we are more accustomed in t h a t c h . Millmead proves that it is as practicable and as pleasant to the eye in tiles. A vaulted vestibule, small but shapely, leads on one side to the garden passage, on the other to the inner hall. This is in effect a little gallery, ending in a south window facing the garden, and on each side a pair of doorways, the mouldings, overdoors

FIG. 277.—MILLMEAD : THE UPPER GARDEN HOUSE.

FIG. 278.—MILLMEAD: GARDEN FRONT.

and cornices of which, simple as they are, give architectural character to what in less able hands would have been a mere passage. The rooms, if few in number, are ample in size.

It was evidently Mr. Lutyens' idea to secure for Miss Jekyll, for whom Millmead was built, within narrow compass and with moderate expenditure, some modest

FIG. 279.—THE DORMY HOUSE, WALTON HEATH: ENTRANCE FRONT.   FIG. 280.—FROM THE EAST.

counterpart of the distinction of a great seventeenth century house. Convenience and comfort were, none the less, considered. The planning of the kitchen offices, of bathroom and lavatory, housemaid's closet and linen cupboard, is all effectively contrived. The whole of the little house gives the impression of being a happy unison of hygiene and good taste. Here, it would be thought, is not merely the house beautiful, but also the house healthy—an example to be praised openly by the public authority. On the contrary, it contravened bye-laws which cried for its mutilation. That sometimes comic element in our representative institutions, the district council, intervened. A blinding light streamed into an upstairs room, facing the sunny south-west and fully exposed to the open sky and the fresh air. It seemed rather over-windowed ; but the council ordered its enlargement. This is not the place to fulminate against the futility of bye-laws which are applied without intelligence and without reference to individual needs. When I saw the house, however, I was able to marvel at our patience in suffering such meddlesome regulations. Fortunately, they do not reach out to the garden, which is a standing example of what skilful design and good planting can effect on a very narrow site. As, however, considerable space is needed to do justice to Miss Jekyll's treatment of it, I must refer my readers to *Gardens for Small Country*

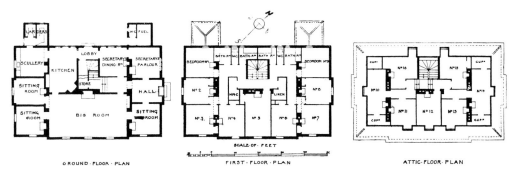

FIG. 281.—PLANS, DORMY HOUSE, WALTON HEATH.

FIG. 282.—DORMY HOUSE, WALTON HEATH : THE GARDEN FRONT.

Houses. In that book a chapter has been given to a full description of it, with photographs and planting plans.

There is a technical point in the roof construction of Millmead worthy of note. The cornice moulding beneath the eaves is made simply of pantiles, an ingenious use which was further developed at Lambay.

THE DORMY HOUSE, WALTON HEATH.

Probably it is because we like to play within easy reach of our work and homes that the residential country club, so popular in America, has taken no firm hold on English habit. The nearest things to it we have are the golf club, which by its ample bedroom accommodation takes on almost the character of a hotel, and the Dormy House that is an annexe of an ordinary golf club building. The planning of the hotel type of club-house is necessarily modelled to a large extent on hotel lines. A Dormy House pure and simple, however, is a building for which there is little precedent, for it is complementary to the golf club proper. The problem at Walton Heath was the provision of a large number of bedrooms and a limited number of sitting-rooms at a moderate cost. As the club-house, with its ample dining-room and kitchen, adjoins it, there was no need to provide in the Dormy House a members' dining-room. There is, therefore, only a kitchen of sufficient size to deal with casual refreshments for visitors and the needs of the staff. (The dining-room and parlour at the north corner of the ground floor are for the use

FIG. 283.—A SMALL SITTING-ROOM.

FIG. 284.—THE ENTRANCE HALL.

FIG. 285.—THE DORMY HOUSE : BIG ROOM.

of the house steward.) From the club a broad gravel path leads to the front door of the Dormy House, on its north-east side. We pass through a small entrance hall to the staircase hall, from which opens the big common room. Here on winter afternoons the interval between close of play and dinner may be spent in reading and smoking. Opening from it are three small sitting-rooms for writing, cards or private talk. One of these is illustrated (Fig. 283), also the entrance hall (Fig. 284) and the "big room" (Fig. 285). The latter looks out on the very attractive lawn on the south-east side,

FIG. 286.—GATE LODGE, BARTON ST. MARY: FROM THE ROAD.

FIG. 287.—SOUTH SIDE OF GATE LODGE, BARTON ST. MARY.

FIRST FLOOR

which is separated from the house by a broad path. Its paving with wide joints gives generous hospitality to saxifrages and the like. On the first floor are nine, and on the second seven, bedrooms, averaging about fourteen feet by twelve, and there are four bathrooms.

Of the treatment of the exterior Figs. 279, 280 and 282 speak clearly enough. The plan is a simple oblong, and the elevations are conceived in a spirit of symmetry and

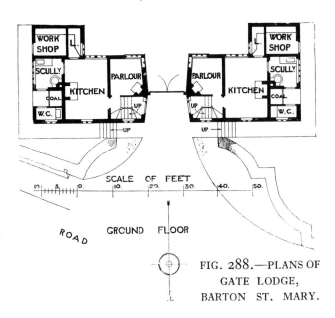

SCALE OF FEET

ROAD   GROUND FLOOR

FIG. 288.—PLANS OF GATE LODGE, BARTON ST. MARY.

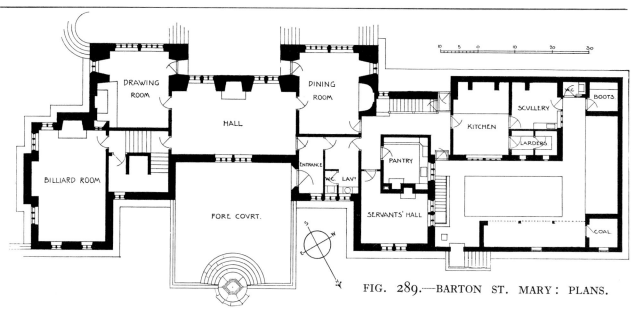

FIG. 289.—BARTON ST. MARY: PLANS.

unaffected reticence. The big pantiled roof, with strongly marked hips and little straight-topped dormers, the three bold chimneys, the whitewashed walls with base and quoins and string of red brick, the vigorous cornice and the green jalousies make up a composition that is at once simple and pleasantly diverse. The quiet formality of the house stretches to the garden, which is brilliant in summer with roses climbing richly over treillage pergolas of split oak.

BARTON ST. MARY, EAST GRINSTEAD.

This is one of the best, as it is also one of the latest, houses designed by Mr. Lutyens in a vernacular manner. The gate lodge first claims attention. A pair of lodges, one on

FIG. 290.—BARTON ST. MARY: ENTRANCE FRONT.

FIG. 291.—ENTRANCE FRONT FROM THE NORTH-WEST.

either side of the entrance gates to an estate, is a usual arrangement, but it would often be better to treat them as one building, the method employed at Barton St. Mary. This pair of cottages, with its central opening for the carriage-way to the main house, achieves a considerable dignity. The treatment follows the simple traditions of the neighbourhood—white walls for

FIG. 292.—BARTON ST. MARY : FROM THE SOUTH-WEST.

FIG. 293.– FROM THE SOUTH-EAST.

the ground storey and tile-hanging above. The inner walls of the carriage passage through the building are of half-timber work, but this construction has been used economically, and wisely so, because it becomes more and more an anachronism in modern work. The space in both halves of the lodge has been well utilised. The kitchens have windows to north and south, and the parlours to the south only. A practical provision is a workshop for each cottage. Upstairs, there are two bedrooms for one family and three for the other (Figs. 286 to 288).

The house itself is typically of the South Country, with white plastered walls and window dressings of red brick. An effect of simple richness is secured by the long ranges of narrow casements divided by bull-nose brick mullions. Despite the small height of the windows, they give full light to all the rooms. The elevations are the direct outcome of the plan, which is irregular, and demanded, therefore, an unsymmetrical treatment. Not the least charm of the house is the way the garden steals up to the walls. The little entrance forecourt is laid with rough

FIG. 294.—BARTON ST. MARY : THE HALL.

flagstones, their wide joints hospitable to poppies and snapdragons, daisies and stonecrop. On the south side of the house, retaining walls of yellow stone from Ashdown Forest, dry-built, hold up the terraces, and brilliant picotees give them the air of a rock garden.

The scale of Barton St. Mary is much helped by the size of the bricks used, which are only one inch and three-quarters thick. A good effect is secured within the house by brick

FIG. 295.—BARTON ST. MARY : IN THE DINING-ROOM.

vaulting, an example of which is seen in the staircase passage which leads up from the billiard-room to the hall (Fig. 296). Another interesting detail is the use of tiles set " hit-and-miss " fashion with thick mortar joints in the wall of this passage to make a ventilating grid for the wine-cellar. This is an example of how a purely utilitarian purpose may be turned to decorative ends. The interior treatment is of the simplest throughout. There are no cornices to any of the rooms, and little decorative emphasis anywhere save in the fireplaces, two of which are illustrated (Figs. 295 and 298). They are of the open type, and the canopies, built of thin tiles to match the backs of the fireplace openings, show Mr. Lutyens triumphing over adversity.

FIG. 296.—STAIR FROM BILLIARD-ROOM TO HALL.   FIG. 297.—FIRST FLOOR CORRIDOR.

These canopies were after-thoughts, made necessary by the smoke trouble which so often pursues the lover of open hearths. Both in the drawing-room, however, where the canopy is built square, and in the dining-room, where it is curved (Fig. 295), the additions have no air of being after-thoughts, but add instead to the decorative interest of the fireplaces. It was an ingenious idea to provide a little window in the left side of the drawing-room fireplace, whence it gives a peep into the billiard-room. The " surrounds " of the floors have been painted in the attractive cloudy colours which Mr. Lutyens uses so much, as, for example, in one room with dark blue, while the doors are of a lighter shade. The upstairs corridor (Fig. 297) is interesting by reason of its round plastered vault and unplastered brick walls on the staircase side. The timber-work is rather less marked by massiveness of material than in some of the earlier houses, such as Munstead Wood and The Deanery Garden.

This type of house gives the feeling of homeliness in marked degree. It is, perhaps, more instinct with an obvious air of comfort than houses designed in a graver and more formal manner. As Vivian says in that storehouse of paradoxes, *The Decay of Lying*, " If Nature had been comfortable, mankind would never have invented architecture, and I prefer houses to the open air. In a house we all feel of the proper proportions. Everything is subordinated to us, fashioned for our use and our pleasure." It is more true of a house designed on an unsymmetrical plan than of one that is planned to preserve a classical balance, that every detail of arrangement can be made subject to personal fancy. A symmetrical plan may demand some sacrifices of preconceived ideas as to the size and shape of certain rooms. It may be difficult, for example, to vary the heights of rooms on the same floor without disturbing the proportions and arrangement of the window openings. In a house of the less constrained type of Barton St. Mary such variations can be made the basis of attractive features that will add to the interest of the elevations and grouping. These facts go to show the need for a reasonable freedom in the choice of design, a freedom demanded as much by the variableness of personal taste as by the conditions of site and aspect and by local traditions of building.

FIG. 298.—IN THE DRAWING-ROOM.

CHAPTER XII.

NEW PLACE, SHEDFIELD, HANTS, 1906.

NEW PLACE, Shedfield, may be regarded as the apotheosis of modern English brick building, for no other materials, save red tiles, find any place in the fabric. Its interest is not confined, however, to the evidence it brings of the versatility of Mr. Lutyens. Some of its rooms take us back to the days of James I in so convincing a fashion that when the doors are shut the twentieth century fades from our minds. Many years ago John Langton's house on the Welsh Back, Bristol, fell from its high estate as the palace of a merchant prince, and it served for some time as a tobacco factory, until the tide of commerce overwhelmed it in destruction. Its owner, Mrs. A. S. Franklyn, determined to build a house worthy to enshrine its more splendid rooms, and New Place is the result. The task was no light one—to devise a shell worthy of so fine a kernel, while yet avoiding mere imitation, but the problem was admirably solved. The building is in accord with the imported glories of John Langton's home, but by its treatment stands confessed a modern house. As its very *raison d'etre* is the work of the craftsmen employed by that Langton, the interior shall first be described. The conditions of the cramped site by the river bank at Bristol drove Langton to a state room of irregular plan with consequent angles of some awkwardness. At New Place this has been corrected, and the room is rectangular, with an added bay

FIG. 299.—THE WEST FRONT.

overlooking the garden.   Its main features are the magnificent stone fireplace, the richly decorated
door and frame and the characteristic Jacobean plaster ceiling (Fig. 301).   The Bristol house
was building in 1623, for that year, with the initials J.L., appears on an overmantel, but the
state room door bears the date 1628, five years later.   Langton was then Mayor of Bristol, and
one may well believe this room was panelled and its great features wrought with intent to form
the main " chamber of delight " for the chief magistrate of England's second greatest city.   The
great mantel-piece is of freestone and richly treated.   While it is perhaps the better as a work
of art, the mahogany door is the more rich, and has a peculiar interest.   It is a hundred
years earlier than any other English use for fixtures such as doors of mahogany, which was
rare even for furniture as late as Queen Anne's day.   Not content with the great consoles on

FIG. 300.—THE DINING-ROOM.

the panel, the pierced obelisks above the cornice, Justice in the middle panel, and a general
profusion of strapwork and heads, the craftsman has inlaid the face of the columns and the plain
panels of the door with delicate mosaics of white and coloured ivory, ebony and engraved
mother-o'-pearl.   The effect altogether is one of undisciplined richness, the art that would
appeal to the pride and magnificence of the merchant whose ships unloaded at his very
door their store of gold and silver, ivory, apes and peacocks.   Yet the room does not lack
decorative reticence, for the panelling is plain, relieved only by the frieze, with shields of arms
and merchants' marks alternately breaking the flow of the scrollwork.   Not only has the ceiling
its own beauty to commend it, but we may well mark the skill and care which enabled both it
and the soft stone mantel to be removed from their original home, taken by road to Shedfield
and re-erected undamaged—a notable feat.   The dining-room shows panelling not less

FIG. 301.—THE OAK ROOM REMOVED FROM BRISTOL.

delightful, but the fireplace and ceiling,
though fine examples of Jacobean work, are
markedly simpler (Fig. 300). On the smoking-
room and drawing-room ceilings have been
fixed admirable oval plaster frames of rich leaf
and fruit work, while the latter is tied at
four points with flowing tasselled ribands
that give a great decorative gaiety. Last,
but not least, of the Bristol spoils is the oak
staircase (Fig. 308). So piously has the
old work been treated that the upper
floors are on two levels. To have fixed
levels that followed the turns of the stair
would have meant upper rooms unduly lofty,
for the state room occupied the first floor at
Bristol; so they were adjusted to keep the
main stairs intact. The stair treads are new,
but the newels, the handrails, the fifty-one
heavy balusters richly carved on both sides
with fruits in high relief and the heraldic
beasts are those that Langton set up at
Bristol. It is of interest to note that the
lion, unicorn and griffin are carved in elm,
not oak. At the top of the stairs the ceiling is also the original—an oval frame of fruits with
four heavy swags about it. When I first saw this ceiling it was in its original place at Bristol,
long before New Place was thought of. In those days it had a gaping hole, which was repaired
when it was transferred to New Place.

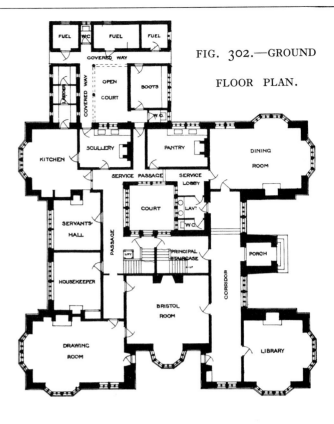

FIG. 302.—GROUND

FLOOR PLAN.

So much for the old work, and now for the house which Mr. Lutyens built to receive it.
In the internal treatment he did not attempt to compete with the sumptuous relics of the past,

FIG. 303.—THE GARDEN FRONT AT NEW PLACE.

FIG. 304.—THE ENTRANCE FRONT.

and wisely so.   The past is past, a simple fact that the designers of great houses of to-day are sometimes slow to learn.   Everywhere at New Place, save in the old work, there is a simplicity of treatment almost monastic in its severity.   The entrance hall has a long, low, barrel vault,

FIG. 305.—NEW PLACE, FROM THE NORTH-EAST : A STUDY IN BRICKWORK.

the brick mullions are plainly plastered on the inside and square edged, and the window-sills are of red brick, their surface enriched by the simple process of waxing them.   Upstairs the corridor walls are without cornices, and the walls are everywhere finished with a surface slightly rough and colour-washed.   Everything conspires to heighten the effect of the Bristol work,

FIG. 306.—THE NORTH FRONT.

and to proclaim that the building has its own character, instinct with the modern sense of decorative restraint and representative of its owners of to-day.

As to the outside, I began this chapter by saying that it is the apotheosis of modern English brick-building, and nothing less is true. It would be difficult to estimate too highly the value of well proportioned and well burnt English red hand-made bricks, a product of sound craftsmanship too little seen until very recent years. The moulded bricks of the mullions and the curved tiles that adorn the parapets are happy examples of how sleeping traditions can be rightly awakened. The prevailing effect of the whole, which it derives from the various forms of brick and tile which have gone to its building, is one of unity, a quality which cannot be over-valued. The walling is studiously plain, save where, as at the porch, a touch of gaiety and conscious texture is given by the open parapets and the projections of the quoins. The window treatment is restrained. The rounded faces of the minor mullions contrast with the more scholarly curves that mark the mouldings of the larger ones. The projecting courses above the window-heads make a

FIG. 307.—THE POWER-HOUSE.

pleasant line of shadow, besides having their practical use in throwing off the rain from the walls.   No elaboration of chimneys has been attempted.   They are unaffected and of a right mass and height.   The rain-water pipes have a wiry and meagre look, and the scraps of gutter which take the outflow from the parapet openings are mean.   Pipes of this sort are the poorer by reason of having no perceptible ears for fixing them to the wall.   They have the air of being gummed on.   The owner of New Place, however, was not concerned to finish New Place at one blow.   The time will come when bold square lead pipes with ears visibly securing them to the brickwork will carry the water down.   It was Viollet-le-Duc who wrote that the art of the leadworker was to do goldsmiths' work, but on a huge scale.

In nothing is this house more happy than in its great spaces of plain brickwork, untroubled by windows save where use demands them.   It needs a certain courage to leave big expanses of wall unpierced and unmoulded.   How well artistic gallantry can be rewarded the illustra- tions amply show.   If, however, the prevailing note is one of simplicity, there is a freshness and vivacity in the massing of the parts.   While the main bays and gables are severely plain, the tiled dormer windows which appear in Figs. 299 and 305 give a homely touch which is altogether valuable.   It is unfortunate that the smallness of the central court and of the open court on the north side make it difficult to secure satisfactory photographs, because the roofs and windows are contrived with singular charm.   Of the general arrangement of the house there is no need to write particularly, for it is as straightforward as the exterior is sober, and the ground plan (Fig. 302) is clear.   Perhaps especial praise should be given to the liberal quarters assigned to the servants and their work.

FIG. 308.—BRISTOL STAIRCASE REFIXED AT NEW PLACE, SHEDFIELD.

CHAPTER XIII.

HEATHCOTE, ILKLEY, 1906.

TO anyone who knew the work of Mr. Lutyens only from what he has achieved in the domain of traditional English architecture, the first sight of Heathcote, Ilkley, would bring a shock of surprise that could not fail, however, to turn swiftly to pleasure. It is not, of course, that he neglected in his earlier buildings to avail himself of classical motives, but in his domestic work at least the exteriors were conceived on vernacular lines. At Marshcourt the hall is of a stately sort, with columns and entablature. It is successful, but there is an air about it which suggests that the designer was at that date not entirely at home in this manner. At Little Thakeham the exterior relies for its charm on great mullioned windows and tall gables, while internally the air is Palladian, and one feels that Wren had walked that way. It is, indeed, one of Mr. Lutyens' happiest gifts

FIG. 309.—THE NORTH FRONT.

FIG. 310.—BILLIARD-ROOM—WEST END.

that he can mingle Gothic and classical motives with such skill that they seem to be rightly married. In the result there is unity instead of the jarring discord which is apt to come of such boldness in the hands of lesser men. Both those houses, however, are purely country homes with wide prospects and spacious grounds. They have no immediate architectural surroundings tending to influence their treatment, which thus proceeded on lines as normal and traditional as the individuality of their designer would allow. In the case of Heathcote the conditions were altogether different. The site is of four acres only and lies between two roads, while there are houses on each side of it. The greatest admirer

FIG. 311.—THE SOUTH TERRACE ASCENT.

FIG. 312.—THE GARDEN FRONT.

FIG. 313.—HEATHCOTE: THE SOUTH TERRACE.

FIG. 314.—THE EASTERN ASPECT.

FIG. 315.—THE SOUTH-EAST POOL.

of Ilkley and the splendid moors above it is unlikely to be able to say much for its architecture, though a church by Norman Shaw must not be forgotten. The local materials and traditions of building are not prepossessing, and the smoke of neighbouring towns settles down on the rough grey stone, to its great disfigurement. There is a tendency in all Yorkshire architecture in the direction of dourness, a natural expression of the sturdiness and bluntness which are so finely characteristic of Yorkshiremen. At all stages of development the rather harsh, unsympathetic nature and colour of the local masonry and the practice of laying low-pitched

FIG. 316.—HEATHCOTE: THE STAIRCASE HALL.

roofs with great slabs of stone, rather than with red tiles, have emphasised the bleak qualities of the stone architecture of the county. Respect for local tradition in building is always valuable, but special conditions demand particular treatment. To have followed a pure county tradition on what is practically a suburban site would have meant the sacrifice of an opportunity, and possibly a dreary house. The need was for a design which should stand by its own merit, without the aid of such a background as would bring it into relation with large surroundings of beauty. The problem was to lift the house by its own intrinsic distinction above the level of the buildings of the neighbourhood, while making it sufficiently akin to them not to give a sense of eclecticism and of conscious superiority. The situation was full of pitfalls; but in the result not only has it been solved to admiration, but it shows us the versatility and grasp of its creator in a fascinating light. It would not be right to say that Mr. Lutyens gave to his client, Mr. Hemingway, an Italian villa, for there are features distinctively English about it; nor can it be regarded simply as a development of our national variant of Palladianism. Men like Kent and Gibbs, and later Isaac Ware, who stereotyped for us in the eighteenth century the English translations of the Italian villa, neglected one of the finest features of the prototype when they eschewed the roof of red pantiles and showed above their parapets nothing, or, at most, a low line of lead or slate. It must ever be remembered to the honour of Sir Charles Barry that in the big villa which he built at Walton-on-Thames in the eighteen-thirties, he reintroduced the Roman pantiled roof, with which such skilful play has been made at Heathcote. Had the Yorkshire tradition of stone slates been slavishly followed, their great size would have killed the scale of the house, and the lack of colour-contrast would have shrouded it with a mantle of dulness. The entrance is through a forecourt with a round grass plat in the middle (Fig. 309). There are openings on the

FIG. 317.—THE STAIRCASE.

FIG. 318.—THE HALL.

left to the garden and on the right to another court with a low range of buildings, which includes garage and engine-house and is balanced on the east by cottages for outdoor servants. The general effect of the north front is one of extreme sobriety. On the garden front severity is relaxed, and there are touches, not of gaiety, but of a smiling graciousness, which befit the outdoor moments of the home. It is not too much to say that the entrance front is a *tour de force* in an exacting manner. It all looks so simple and easy, and is, in fact, so very difficult to do well. There are no graces in the materials, in the Guiseley stone walls, with grey dressings from the Morley quarries. In Somersetshire the Ham Hill stone, with its russet gold tints, and in Surrey the wonderful texture of Bargate, win half the battle. But here it is only by mastery of the material, by subtlety of moulding, boldness of mass and rightness of line, that the native hostility of the stone may be overcome. We enter by doors, painted the cloudy green which Mr. Lutyens understands so well, into a vestibule paved in white marble, with panels of red brick set in herringbone and waxed to a

FIG. 319.—A CORRIDOR ON THE FIRST FLOOR.

rich tone (Fig. 322). The walls here are of dressed grey Morley stone. The vaulted ceiling is not in rectangular compartments (the plan prevents it), but the wreathing is done with such skill that it passes unnoticed, the more easily perhaps because it is painted a dull, indefinite

FIG. 320.—STAIRWAY GALLERY.

FIG. 321.—IN THE BILLIARD ROOM.

blue, which gives a magical softness of effect. Doors lead from the vestibule to the kitchen quarters, to the staircase hall, and to a lobby, which opens both on to the latter and to the main hall on the south front. From the staircase hall we enter the billiard-room, a large apartment of considerable merit. The panelling, of unpolished walnut, gives to the room a singular breadth, and the dome over the billiard-table emphasises the general restfulness of the scheme. There is an air of " the grand manner " about the composition of the windows, and by a happy inspiration the hangings are of the cloth sacred to billiard-tables the world over. It is refreshing, after the chaos of yellow-greens and brown-greens that are confounded together in that name of reproach, " art-green," to find a green which

FIG. 322.—THE VESTIBULE.

is wholly green. The cover for the table is of the same cloth, with great panels of vivid purple, while the delicate outlines of the walnut electrolier are emphasised by the ordinary shape of the shades, which are in leather of an orange red. The staircase hall shows fertility in planning (Fig. 316). The doors to billiard-room and lavatory are pulled together into one composition by the carved tympana and the staircase arch, and the plan is further emphasised by the design of the marble pavement. By a happy boldness the black marble stairs and the black iron balustrade (Fig. 317) with its steel handrail contrast with the cream-coloured walls of Ancaster stone below and the plaster-work of the upper landing. The strong green of the carpet adds its note of richness.

The graceful lines of the ironwork afford relief to the large solidity of its surroundings, and the electrolier must not be overlooked. There is a general increase in richness as we go from vestibule to staircase hall, and from the latter to the main hall, which gives on to the terrace. The hall is notable both in its plan and

FIG. 323.—A CHINA CUPBOARD.

FIG. 324.—CUPBOARDS BY BEDROOM FIREPLACE.

FIG. 325—IN THE DINING-ROOM.

proportions (Fig. 318). Its middle space is divided from the sides (which serve as passage-ways to the terrace doors) by columns of a green Siberian marble, then for the first time used in England. The middle ceiling is treated as a great shaped panel with a rib of so heavy a section that nothing but the sure judgment of its designer has saved it from seeming clumsy. The middle space has an oak floor, but the sides are paved with white and *fleur de pêche* marbles. The purple bloom of peaches is, as the name suggests, the prevailing hue ; but in some pieces it is more blue than red. The windows are towards the outside of the walls, an arrangement which gives a deep-set look within, and the thickness of the walls prevents the afternoon sun from pouring directly into the room. Notable among the many little devices which add to the amenities of the house are the curtain blinds of embroidered brocade which open door-fashion on swinging rods, an improvement on ordinary forms of blind and curtain. At each end of the hall are glazed cabinets for china, which show that delicacy of detail combined with a prevailing simplicity which is characteristic of Mr. Lutyens' designs for furniture. It is rarely the case,

FIG. 326.—PLASTERWORK ON STAIRCASE LANDING.

as at Heathcote, that the architect has the opportunity of designing every piece of furniture for the house and choosing every hanging and carpet. The overruling unity which here prevails is not only a tribute to the skill of the designer, but to the unusual wisdom of the client. Mr. Hemingway had the judgment to value the policy of the free hand, with the results that all may see, and he is to be congratulated as much as Mr. Lutyens, who has risen to the occasion by devising every detail, obviously with delighted freedom and always with success. East of the hall is the dining-room, and at the other end the morning-room (Fig. 327), both charming. There are concealed lights above the cornice of the morning-room, which are reflected downwards by a big cove, and give a soft suffused light. The dining-room has a handsome mantel-piece in *fleur de pêche* and white marbles (Fig. 325). A subtle contrast has been secured here by polishing parts of the *fleur de pêche* and leaving the big slabs which surround the grate unpolished. So different do they look that they might almost be of different marbles. It will be noticed from the plan that the kitchen-quarters are somewhat restricted in size; but they were devised to suit exactly the requirements of Mr. Hemingway's household and are good in arrangement both in themselves and in relation to the dining-room. It may be said of some of Mr. Lutyens' early work, and with perfect fairness, that the planning is ill-considered; but this house is eminently workable and practical in every way. Upstairs the rooms are large, but call for no particular description. One of the bathrooms is attractive, with a vaulted ceiling and walls in green tiles with wide white joints. The outlines of the glazing bars in the doors of the cupboards in the corridor are good (Fig. 319) and the arrangement of a glazed screen which shuts off the back stairs is ingenious. Upstairs, as elsewhere, the colour schemes show subtlety of choice. In the chief bedroom hangings of old rose contrast with a carpet of cool grey. In another the grate is set in a sea of tiles of a blue which suggests no name.

FIG. 327.—IN THE MORNING ROOM.

In yet another the furniture is painted the cloudy blue which Mr. Lutyens likes so well to use.

It is when we come to the garden front that the full charm of the house is apparent (Figs. 311 to 315.) It is not beyond criticism, but few faults are to be found. It seems a pity that the simplicity of the roof has been broken to admit of the little central

FIG. 328.—SOUTH ENTRANCE FROM THE GARDEN.

window, and a more strict adherence to Palladian models would have suggested the crowning of the facade by some marked feature like a pediment, particularly in view of that window. But Mr. Lutyens is a law unto himself, and happily so. Instead of a central doorway, which would have ruined the hall plan, he has put one on either side. The cornice of the order is protected from the rain coming from the upper roof by a roofing of pantiles, which add warmth and bring the colour scheme downwards to the terrace, where it is picked up by the risers of the terrace steps and by great red pots for growing plants. The side pavilions are rather large (according to Italian precedents) as compared with the central block ; but here again there has been no attempt to distort the plan to suit any preconceived ideas of exterior treatment. It is perhaps only the expert in this most difficult architectural language who can appreciate the hard thinking and infinite patience that have gone into the detail of the garden front. The carving is well placed and good in itself, but the masculine proportions of the building are so independent of the prettinesses of the minor arts that the house would nowise suffer by their omission. The terrace pavement is ingenious in its scheme of panels done in slates on edge with margins of stone. It is from the lawn that the scheme of the design is presented in its entirety to the eye (Fig. 312). Note how the building piles itself up from the ground, the side chimneys with their heavy banding marking the break between the three middle elements and the low wings of billiard-room and kitchen. Observe, too, the solid base which is afforded by the terrace walls, with their sturdy bastions and the delightful sweep of the flights of steps. At each end of the terrace are gabled walls, which form a background to pergolas. There is a true

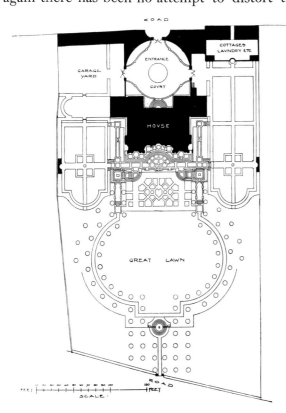

FIG. 329.—GARDEN PLAN.

Italian note in the lily ponds beneath the terrace (Figs. 312 and 315), and the very practical need of an air inlet for the heating system of the house adds a touch of interest to its middle opening (Fig. 311). The design of the balconets is blended of strength and pleasant line and yet lightens the prospect of the terrace. In the garden rhododendrons bloom vigorously, and the dry stone terrace walls confirm the name of wallflowers. There is something almost of a foreign air about this Yorkshire garden on a summer evening, for the terrace looks across a little valley to the moor, which rises there some eight hundred feet, and the lights of houses on the slope twinkle like glow-worms. Although the space to be dealt with was small, the great curves of the lawn have given an air of spaciousness. The style of architecture adopted is an inelastic one ; but it has this merit in competent hands, that, though in part foreign to English traditions, it has an essence that is acceptable to all cultivated Western minds. It is the outcome of fifteen centuries of trial and error. It possesses the elements of absolute permanence, and depends on its right handling for its success. Heathcote shows the blending of feeling with scholarship without which Palladianism becomes merely an historical husk. The effect is not merely the result of learning nor of an accepted style. A man may know ten languages and yet be unable to express an idea in one of them. Architectural museums have just such capitals as are here, and the mouldings, good as they are, have been done before. What is needed, and what Heathcote gives, is the just gift of selection and the courage to use the fit, the power to stay the hand and to eliminate the inessential.

FIG. 330.—GROUND FLOOR PLAN OF HEATHCOTE.

CHAPTER XIV.

THREE ALTERED HOUSES: 1906—1909.

Copse Hill, Gloucestershire ; Wittersham House, Kent ; Whalton Manor, Northumberland.

THE remodelling of houses is often enough a thankless task, demanding an amount of labour and contrivance which are hardly justified by the results. The most difficult type to handle is that which inspires no sort of enthusiasm, because it is neither old nor new, and lacks any character which needs to be preserved in the remodelling. Among such are the gabled houses in the Tudor manner built in the Cotswolds about the middle of the nineteenth century. Few architects of that day, if any, had captured the spirit of the old work, and their copies of it were dull and lifeless. Needful concessions to modern ideas of convenience involved new elements in plan, and consequently in elevation, which they failed to harmonise with the traditional aspect of Cotswold building. The texture of surfaces in various material, whether masonry, wood or plaster, was a by-way of the builder's craft of which, at that time, the importance was not even suspected. Copse Hill, Upper Slaughter, is just such a house, convenient and well built, but lifeless. Mr. Lutyens was called upon to remodel the hall and staircase, and to effect other minor alterations. He did not attempt to give to the hall any of the characteristics of the period which the original house had tried to suggest. The walls are covered with broad panelling which owes its idea to the end of the seventeenth century. The staircase is a modern translation of the Jacobean idiom, seen so well in the old

FIG. 331.—COPSE HILL : AT THE FOOT OF THE STAIR.

FIG. 332.—COPSE HILL : THE HALL.

FIG. 333.—COPSE HILL: NEW STAIRCASE—   FIG. 334.—UPPER FLIGHT.

manor house of Upper Slaughter, which now forms part of the Copse Hill estate. The two twisted wooden pillars at the foot of the stair are of a form which seems greatly to attract Mr. Lutyens, for he has employed it even in very recent houses of an austere Georgian type. They give a touch of gaiety, often of the greatest value in a composition which might otherwise lack something of vitality. Figs. 333 and 334 show well enough the delightful character of the woodwork on the staircase, which need not be described in detail. Attention may be drawn, however, to the sunk panelled treatment of the solid ends of the stair-treads, a device which appears in his early works, and always successfully.

WITTERSHAM HOUSE, KENT.

This was remodelled for the late Mr. Alfred Lyttelton, for whom also was built Grey Walls, Gullane, illustrated in Chapter VI. It was a plain square brick house, entirely

FIG. 335.—WITTERSHAM HOUSE: FROM THE GARDEN.   FIG. 336.—SUMMER-HOUSE.

FIG. 337.—WITTERSHAM HOUSE:
PERGOLA.

FIG. 338.—A GARDEN GATE.

FIG. 339.—WITTERSHAM HOUSE: ENTRANCE FRONT.

inoffensive, but lacking any definite character or interest. These were supplied by re-roofing it with pantiles laid to a low pitch, by making some round windows which contrast pleasantly with the old square openings, and by building a broad pedimented loggia-like porch on the entrance side. The alterations within were not of much importance, but some re-arrangements in the garden added greatly to the charm of the place. A little open air parlour was provided by paving an oblong space alongside an old wall, adding two pairs of pilasters crowned with trophies of fruit to the latter, and throwing out niches between them which are occupied by leaden boys bearing baskets. Old vases are set at the corners of the paved space, and the table, chairs and benches are of the simple heavy sort which is fitting out of doors (Fig. 340). From one side of the lawn near the house a pergola leads down a

FIG. 340.—WITTERSHAM HOUSE: AN OUTDOOR PARLOUR.

FIG. 341.—WHALTON MANOR : THE ROAD FRONT.   FIG. 342.—NORTH SIDE.

gentle slope to a long and narrow grass plat set between two wide herbaceous borders, at the end of which is a round pillared garden-house (Fig. 336). Facing it at the other end is a simple and very effective iron gateway framed in masonry piers (Fig. 338). Altogether Wittersham House and its garden show how a new i n t e r e s t can be given to a place, once of no charm, by simple additions devised with taste and judgment.

WHALTON MANOR, NORTHUMBERLAND.

There is no more searching test of an architect's i n g e n u i t y than his alteration of old buildings to make them suit new uses. The difficult conditions imposed often exhibit him in the light of a good man struggling with adversity. The mere addition of two

FIG. 343.—WHALTON MANOR : THE FOOT OF THE MAIN STAIR.

or three rooms may raise problems which sorely tax his invention ; but the case of Whalton Manor was far more complex, for it involved the welding together of the side of a village street into one house. Originally the rooms to the right of the new archway were two houses, which had been thrown into one, with the addition of the wing of kitchen offices running northwards. This was the state of the house when Mr. Lutyens was called in to enlarge it. To the left of what is now the new archway were a house and cottage, which had been turned into a single dwelling, the cottage being converted into a wash-house. The problem was to provide a new dining-room and hall, and to join up these oddly assorted elements

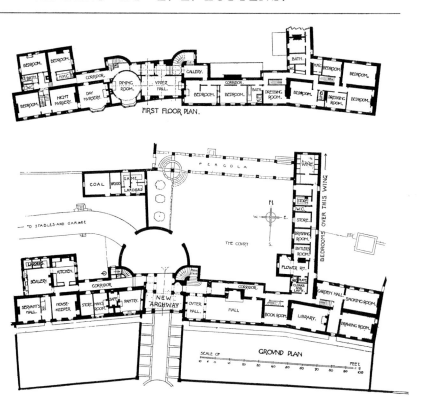

FIG. 344.—PLANS OF WHALTON MANOR HOUSE.

into a new home. Between the buildings to the left and right of the new archway there was no sort of connection, and the provision of one was no small part of the difficulty. The part of the old manor house that had been used for domestic offices was cleared out, and is now occupied by the hall, outer hall and main staircase. The drawing and smoking rooms and library which existed remained unchanged. The old house and cottage to the left of the archway were converted into kitchen premises, and other servants' quarters were

FIG. 345.—WEST END OF HALL.

arranged in the old north wing. The chief difficulty of the situation was solved, and admirably solved, by providing over the new archway an upper hall, which connects the head of the main staircase with the new r o u n d dining-room built on the walls of the old cottage. The requirements of service were met by building a service stair from the kitchen corridor to the dining-room corridor and providing a lift alongside it. In other respects the alterations were slight, and Figs. 341 to 348 reveal practically all the new work. Particularly attractive are the vaulted undercroft of the archway and the treatment of the stone hall on the g r o u n d floor. The charming feature of a round dining-room h a s b e e n secured without prejudicing the rest of the plan, for two of the cut-off corners serve as useful cupboards, and the others are absorbed quite naturally into the corridor. The e x t e r i o r treatment is simple and full of character. The staircases indicated the curved wings of the new north front, and the line is taken up by the enclosing walls of the little paved yard. The scheme was completed and the outbuildings related to the whole by the building of a stout stone pergola which forms a court on the north side. Though the extent of the new work outside is not great, it is enough to show that the spirit of Northumbrian building, masculine and strong, was justly assimilated.

FIG. 346.—DINING-ROOM.

FIG. 347.—HALL FIREPLACE.

FIG. 348.—WHALTON MANOR: THE NEW ARCHWAY.

CHAPTER XV.

LAMBAY, IRELAND, 1908—1912.

A SQUARE mile or so of rock and turf, washed by the waves of the Irish Sea and honeycombed with caverns which are the home of great grey seals, a castle unique in its plan, and made the more attractive by a new group added by Mr. Lutyens, an abandoned coastguard station, an enchanting animal population and a fascinating history—these are Lambay. The island lies about three miles from the coast of County Dublin. It is the last outcrop of the Wicklow Mountains, and owes its masses of porphyry and greenstone to volcanic energies, quieted unknown ages ago. Its early history is obscure, but it needs small stretch of imagination to look back and see it, like many another little island off British shores, as the home of early Irish saints and hermits. To just such a retreat would St. Patrick have loved to go when wearied by heathen enemies. On its slopes sheep might have been grazed by St. Brigit :

A beautiful ladder, for pagan folk
To climb to the kingdom of Mary's Son,

as an early hymn describes her. Perhaps on the site of the present castle was that theatre of

FIG. 349.—THE CASTLE AND WEST FORECOURT.

FIG. 350.—FROM THE SOUTH-EAST : OLD AND NEW.
Castle on left, new building on right.

FIG. 351.—CORNER OF THE NORTH COURT.
Showing on left (new wing), and (on right) reconstruction of north-east front of castle.

miracles, St. Brigit's cottage, where she hung her cloak across a sunbeam ; and her dog, left communing with visible bacon, showed a holy self-restraint. This, however, is conjecture. Before it can be shown with what skill Mr. Lutyens has turned an inconvenient little castle into a home of peculiar charm, the history of Lambay must be recited. And it is worth setting down in its own right. Except the vague references to the descent of Norsemen on Lambay in the Dark Ages, the first outstanding fact is the grant of the island by Prince John, then Earl

of Moreton, to John Comyn, Archbishop of Dublin, in 1184.

In 1337 the building of a chantry chapel was authorised, but no trace of it remains ; a retreat so suitable would be sure to attract the " religious." Their devotions, however, would be disturbed from time to time by the resort of shipmasters, pirates and other foes to the devout life. By 1467 this aspect of Lambay was so forcibly brought before Englishmen that it is described as " a receptacle for the King's enemies, as Britons, Spaniards, French and Scots, to the annoyance of the mainland." This brings us into touch with a very notable man, John Tiptoft, Earl of

FIG. 352.—SOUTH-EAST SIDE OF NEW WING FROM NORTH COURT.

Worcester, Lord-Deputy for Edward IV. He was commissioned to build a fortress on the island, which was granted to him by the Irish Parliament, and it may be that the present castle owes its first building to him, though it was certainly altered in later days. J. R. Green has said that Tiptoft exhibits " the ruthlessness of the Renascence, side by side with its intellectual vigour." He drew tears from Pope Pius II " by the Elegance of his Latinity." Caxton cannot praise him too warmly, yet he received in the Civil Wars the name of " butcher." It seems clear that Tiptoft was not able for long to prevent freebooters from using Lambay as a base. Although Sir Richard Edgcumbe, in the *Anne of Fowey,* touched there unopposed in 1488, about ten years later the Prior of St. Patrick's of Holmpatrick recites that in the havens and creeks on the shores of Lambay pirates were accustomed to shelter. We obtain glimpses of these brave doings. One Brode, a pirate, was chased from Lambay to Drogheda in 1534 by the ships of Sir William Skeffington, who " bowged him so that he ran his vessel a-land." The State Papers next give us a letter of 1536, written to Thomas Cromwell by Justice Aylmer to recommend the petition of John Garret, " whose things the army had for their relief in Lambay." This suggests that Garret was then occupying the island as tenant of the Archbishop of Dublin, to whom Lambay had reverted after Tiptoft's death. From this time onward Lambay was used as a base to assemble war-vessels and troopships going from England to Dublin, and on several occasions by the enemy's ships. In 1543 Lord-Deputy Sentleger complained to the King that " the fleet lying at Lambay does not intercept the communication between Scotland and France "; and two years later reported that there

FIG. 353.—LAMBAY CASTLE : THE NEW KITCHEN COURT.

were " four ships of war, supposed Scottish, off Lambay." In 1548 one Logan, a Scots pirate, hovered about Lambay " in his tall ballinger of fourscore tonne " and took several vessels. Later in the year the Lord Protector Somerset was warned how awkward it would be if the French landed at Skerries on the mainland opposite Lambay and fortified it.

In an inventory of 1541, the year the tithes of the island were taken over from the famous nunnery of Gracedieu by Sir Patrick Barnewell, Lambay is described as " waste." None the less, it clearly presented attractions to a purchaser. In 1551 John Chaloner secured from the Archbishop of Dublin a perpetual lease of the island *with the castles*, etc., at a rent of six pounds thirteen shillings and four pence. It was stipulated that within six years he should make a harbour and a place of refuge fortified with a wall or a mound and ditch for the protection of the colony he was about to introduce. This seems to show that Lambay was then uninhabited. One of the castles referred to as existing was possibly Tiptoft's building. The " place of refuge " may be identified with a ditch and mound which can still be traced in a field south of the castle. As to Chaloner himself, all students of seventeenth century England know of the Chaloners of Steeple Claydon, Bucks, friends of the Verneys of Middle Claydon. Roger Chaloner, a citizen of London, who died in 1521, had three sons—Sir Thomas of Steeple Claydon, father of another Sir Thomas, a famous traveller and writer ; John (of Lambay), who migrated to Dublin ; and Francis. Luke, the son of the last mentioned, was a famous divine, and had a daughter, Phœbe, who married James Ussher, the great Archbishop of Armagh. After Mary's accession, John Chaloner found it necessary to petition the Crown for confirmation of his new ownership of Lambay.

FIG. 354.—LOOKING INTO THE NEW KITCHEN COURT.

Probably Lord - Deputy Sussex was very willing to see Chaloner righted, because as Alderman and Mayor he had behaved well when Sussex arrived in Dublin in 1556. The city was raided by the Kavanaghs, and Chaloner obtained from Spain at his own cost arms for the civic force which beat back the assault. It is probable that he also superintended the usual sequel of such success, the hanging of seventy-four Kavanaghs. Sussex offered to knight Chaloner, but he replied : " It will be more to my credit and my posterity's to have it said that John Chaloner served the Queen upon occasion, than to say that Sir John Chaloner did it." From a letter of 1563 to Cecil we learn that Chaloner served three years as Secretary to Queen Elizabeth, was then ill and unfit for the office, desired to be discharged, and wished his young brother to obtain the post. Cecil received another letter the following year with a little grumble from Chaloner that he had lost three hundred pounds " by spoil of the French." It is possible that they had landed at Lambay and cleared his farmyard.

During this time he remained Secretary, and in July, 1564, asked Cecil to make him Master of the Rolls. Cecil's reply has not survived, but we can guess its nature, for Chaloner remained at his old post.   By 1566 he seems to have thought he would do better by word of mouth, so he persuaded the Lord-Deputy to send him to London with a letter to the Privy Council and a commendation of his service of six years.   Nothing came of the visit.   The next year Lord Justice Fitzwylliams writes sharply to Cecil about the " weakness of Mr. Chaloner's dealings," but in 1569 the Lord-Deputy reported well of him.   In the same year he pleads to have his " little Kingdom of Lambay " exempted from a wine-tax.   We get a

sidelight on Elizabethan methods from Chaloner's gift of falcons to Walsingham in November, 1579. Clearly he was wanting something done or left undone. Ten weeks later Waterhouse, his superior officer, wrote to Walsingham that Chaloner was old and a new secretary should be sent. In July of 1580 Chaloner sent Walsingham " two falcons and their tersel of this year's eiry in his rocks of Lambay, by his servant John Ayer, also sundry samples of the ' marbles ' of Lambay of rare beauty." However, the sands were running out, and on May 13th Burghley was informed of his death. On July 15th protection was granted by the Lord-Deputy and Council "to

FIG. 355.—THE NEW BUILDING FROM THE WEST.

Thomas Chaloner, Gent, son of John Chaloner of the Isle of Lambay, Esquire, deceased, the late secretary, for one whole year, while he may collect his father's property."   This was presumably protection from distraint, for John had left his affairs in a bad way and debts of a thousand pounds or more.   Thomas, the son, had some chance of making money out of Lambay, for Waterhouse reported to Walsingham in 1584 that there are quarries in Lambay yielding fair stones, but not long enough for pillars.   Presumably they were busy

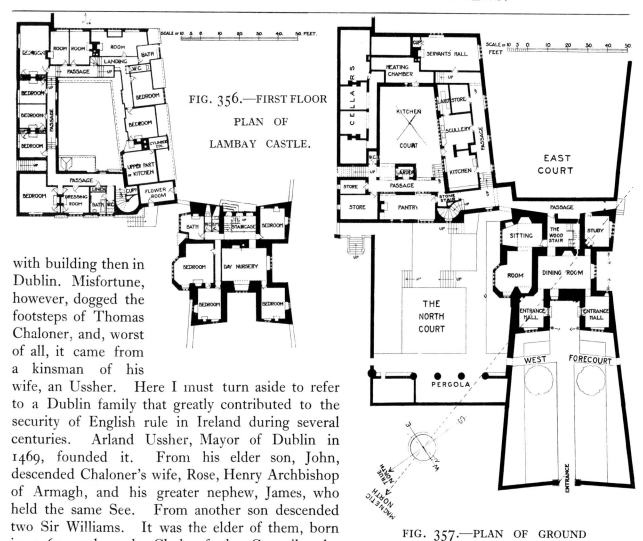

FIG. 356.—FIRST FLOOR
PLAN OF
LAMBAY CASTLE.

FIG. 357.—PLAN OF GROUND
FLOOR AND COURTS.

with building then in Dublin. Misfortune, however, dogged the footsteps of Thomas Chaloner, and, worst of all, it came from a kinsman of his wife, an Ussher. Here I must turn aside to refer to a Dublin family that greatly contributed to the security of English rule in Ireland during several centuries. Arland Ussher, Mayor of Dublin in 1469, founded it. From his elder son, John, descended Chaloner's wife, Rose, Henry Archbishop of Armagh, and his greater nephew, James, who held the same See. From another son descended two Sir Williams. It was the elder of them, born in 1561, and made Clerk of the Council, who served Chaloner so ill. He had married Beale, a daughter of Archbishop Loftus. Of this ecclesiastic we get a picture in an undated note in the State Papers, showing how he had " linked and allied himself in strong friendship and kindred by means of the marriages of his children, marriageable *and unmarriageable.*" We sympathise with those sons-in-law of His Grace who had to take the unmarriageable daughters ; but Beale Ussher was useful to her husband, who "obtained by colourable means of the Archbishop his father-in-law, whilst he was one of the late Lords Justices," various things not necessary to set out, " and also holds the island of

FIG. 358.—FROM THE SOUTH-WEST.

FIG. 359.—NORTH CORNER OF THE EAST COURT.

Showing (on left) new entrance to castle, and (on right) door to new building.

FIG. 360.—THE ENTRANCE FORECOURT, SHOWING RILL.

Lambaye, a goodly portion of living, whereof Mr. Chaloner, the Queen's Secretary, was possessed in his lifetime . . . since wrested away from his son Thomas the doing whereof merits due examination." Probably Thomas Chaloner found it of little use to fight the Archbishop and the Clerk of the Council, and let Lambay go; but it is a pleasant commentary on the ways of the great in sixteenth century Ireland. The island remained in the hands of Sir William Ussher the elder until his death in 1659. His grandson, also Sir William, succeeded, and died possessed of Lambay in 1671. These facts dispose of the legend, printed by Lewis in his *Topographical Dictionary of Ireland*, that Lambay was granted by Queen Elizabeth to James Ussher, Archbishop of Armagh and Primate of Ireland, "who resided there some time and there wrote part of his works." The Archbishop never owned the island; but we can see how the story arose. James Ussher, not only the greatest

FIG. 361.— ENTRANCE TO CASTLE GROUNDS THROUGH RAMPART WALL.

FIG. 362.—NEW BUILDING FROM NORTH-WEST OF NORTH COURT IN WINTER.

FIG. 363.—NORTH COURT FROM ITS NORTH-EAST ENTRANCE.

man that the Church of England bred in Ireland, but one of her greatest scholars of any place or time, married Phœbe Chaloner, daughter of his great friend, Dr. Luke Chaloner, who was first cousin of Thomas, the dispossessed of Lambay. In 1640 the hopeless state of affairs in the Church in Ireland drove him to England, and he never returned, dying four years before the Restoration of Charles II. This explodes the story that he fled to Lambay in 1650 to escape the plague on the mainland. An account of his only recorded visit to the island is to be found in the diary of a Dr. Arthur, who, in 1626, spent seven weeks with the Lord Primate on Lambay, and cured him of an obstinate disease. It thus appears that Sir William Ussher lent Lambay Castle to his cousin for a few weeks, but nothing more.

There were outbreaks in Ireland upon the relaxation of the policy of "Thorough" after Strafford's execution. One Derrick Huibarts, described as a Protestant gentleman, who lived on Lambay at that time, was killed. The insurgent army completed its control of the coast from Dublin to Drogheda in December, 1641, by the seizure of the island, but Cromwell's scourge did not descend upon it, and in 1659 it was almost deserted. In 1691 De Ginkel accepted the surrender of the forces of the deposed James II. at Ballymore. Colonel Toby Purcell was left in charge there, but prisoners to the number of seven hundred and eighty soldiers and two hundred and sixty rapparees were interned at Lambay.

The Usshers owned it until 1804, when it passed to Sir William Wolseley, Bart., and Mrs. Talbot, afterwards Lady Talbot

FIG. 364.—NEW BUILDING IN SUMMER FROM UPPER LAWN.

de Malahide, purchased it ten years later. In 1888 Count James Considine bought Lambay from Lord Talbot de Malahide, and in 1904 the present owners acquired it.

The castle itself is of peculiar architectural interest by reason of its original plan and treatment. The name "castle" does not strictly belong to it, for it has no defensive works beyond its own strong walls; it is, in fact, rather in the nature of a blockhouse. Reference to the plan shows that the house exists to-day as it was first built, except for additions on the north-east and south-east sides. These were made before it came into the present owner's possession. Originally the ground storey consisted of a central room with four apartments, all of identical shape and size, opening from it, and the arrangement on the upper storey was the same. The most striking elements of its design are the splays of the walls at each corner, which bring them to acute angles. This device gives colour to the view that the castle plan may owe its shape to John Tiptoft, Earl of Worcester. It marks a military refinement comparable only with the pentagonal bastions which the science of defensive architecture owes to Sanmicheli. It is altogether foreign to native Irish or British castle design during any period when the castle could have been built. As shot-holes were provided in the corners of the ground-floor rooms (in the direction shown

FIG. 365.—NORTH COURT FROM A BEDROOM WINDOW.

on the plan (p. 210) by dotted arrows) the defenders could shoot assailants as they came round the corners of the castle. Had the corners been square, the enemy could have reached the break in the wall before being seen. The castle has never been of more than two storeys. The ground floor has low vaulted ceilings, and the roof was of timber and covered with slates.

It is of importance to note that the records of the island and its owners give no specific information about the building of any castle, beyond the fact that Tiptoft was commissioned to construct a fortress. We have considerable knowledge of Chaloner and the Usshers, and it is difficult to believe that any serious works carried out by them would have escaped record. We know, moreover, that Chaloner found castles on the island when he acquired it. Although the roof must have been reconstructed, it is not impossible that the ground storey dates from

FIG. 366.—LAMBAY: THE FOOT OF THE STONE STAIR IN THE NEW WING.

the fifteenth century. Most antiquaries would hesitate to place it so early, and I make the suggestion with diffidence.

At the beginning of the twentieth century the island was in an almost derelict state, and only the outhouses of the old castle were used for such farming as was still done. In 1904 certain alterations and repairs were effected in the castle to make it habitable, such as the renewal of the fast-decaying roof. The sliding sash windows, which had replaced the original openings (possibly unglazed) of roughly chamfered stone, were replaced by teak casements. The rooms on the north side, then used as a dairy, were converted into living-rooms, and a new room added in what is now the north court. Some cowhouses and a cottage which abutted on the east side were turned into kitchen and offices. Defects in the masonry were made good —if good is the word—by liberal applications of Portland cement. This contrasted harshly

FIG. 367.—EASTERN HALF OF THE SITTING-ROOM, SHOWING NEW ARCH AND FIREPLACE.

with the lime-mortar and pebble-dashing with which the old walls had been clothed long before in the manner so familiar in the " harled " walls of Scottish castles.

It follows, therefore, that Mr. Lutyens, who made his first acquaintance with Lambay in 1905, found the castle somewhat battered by time, and its history and character obscured by restoration.   His first act was to remove the cement roof, which had proved inefficient, to substitute grey pantiles of delightful colour and texture, and to abolish the iron down-pipes and gutters.   In this connection attention may be drawn to the delightful cornices then formed simply of pantiles, a use of their curved outline which is as successful as it is fresh.   Not until

1907 was his complete scheme for renewal and enlargement elaborated, and indeed the need for careful deliberation was clear. The work was begun in 1908. The accommodation was very limited, and to enlarge the castle without destroying its character presented a difficult problem. The original castle was very primitive in its arrangements, but was left untouched except for slight internal re-arrangements and for the re-building of the north-east side, which had already been subjected to successive alterations. The ground-floor rooms were entered on the north-west side, and only one fireplace opening existed in the eastern end of the sitting-room. The

FIG. 368.—AT THE HEAD OF THE STONE STAIR IN NEW WING.

FIG. 369.—THE HEAD OF THE NEW STAIR IN THE OLD BUILDING.

arch stones of this were part of the original building, and were utilised for the new fireplace in the dining-room. Other fireplaces were provided in the north entrance hall, sitting-room and study. On the first floor there were originally four fireplaces. The old entrance was certainly where is now the door to the north entrance hall. It had been walled up, but was re-opened. The opposite door to the south entrance hall is new. The lime-mortar and pebble-dash on the outside of the castle walls was retained, for the masonry was very rough. In connection with the making of the new staircase in the castle proper, the middle part of the wall on the south-east front had to be reconstructed. In the course of the work it appeared that this front had been originally recessed like the entrance front on the north-west. It would seem, therefore, that the filling-in was done when the predecessor of the new stair was built. In that case the old castle would have either lacked a staircase altogether or had a trap-door and ladder to connect the ground and first floors. No trace of such a trap-door remains. Kitchen quarters and additional bedrooms were provided in a new quadrangular block at the east corner, connected with the old castle by an underground passage only. This was practicable because the ground slopes sharply upwards to the east. In order to give access from this passage to the upper level of the new quadrangular block an important staircase of stone was built in the south west corner of the latter. In the result the two buildings, old and new, are unconnected at the first-floor level, and the castle stands free to tell its own story. The determination to prevent the new roofs dominating the old meant carving a substantial piece out of the hillside. Although the island is of volcanic origin, the castle and its grounds occupy a small remnant of sedimentation in the shape of a bed of much-tilted and shaly Silurian slates which lend themselves, more or less reluctantly, to displacement by pick and shovel. This difficulty loomed large in the preparation of the ground for the new block and in the terracing of the north court. Among other causes obstructing the work were the absence on the island of any materials save stone and sea-sand. All other necessaries had to be brought by sailing boats, always a laborious and sometimes a risky process. It may also be guessed that the visits of supervision, extending over years, involved the architect in a peculiar and extensive acquaintance with the moods of the Irish Sea. In the building of the new wing and of the extensive range of garden walls, advantage was taken of the stone that the island affords, a splendid blue-green porphyry, shot with feldspar crystals. As this is rather refractory to work, the mullions and other dressings are of a cool blue-grey limestone that came from the Milverton quarries, near Skerries on the mainland, and were skilfully wrought by the local quarrymen. The new roofs are also covered with grey pantiles and the sides of the dormers are hung with flat tiles of the same colour. Very wisely Mr. Lutyens made no attempt to reproduce in the new block such characteristics of the old as the crow-step gables that are so delightful a feature of the castle. Moreover, in the necessary re-building of the north-east front he has not hesitated to mark its newness and relate it to the new wing by hipping the roof of the small corner bay and by parapetting the larger one (Fig. 351). It is especially to be noted that only on this north-east front has the symmetrical plan of the old castle been disturbed. Alterations had been made there, before Mr. Lutyens' advent, of so drastic a character that a restoration of the old plan would have been insincere. This abundantly justifies the new tower which adds greatly to the accommodation on both floors. The new wing is kept low and markedly domestic in character, so that it does not compete with the military note of the old castle.

The kitchen court is particularly attractive, with its broad sweep of pantiled roof, its demure dormers and its pavement, part of slabs and part cobbled (Figs. 353 and 354). Of the interiors little need be said, for the pictures explain them. The stone stair in the new wing has a fine dignity, and the oak landing and balustrade of the new stair in the castle proper, by its hint of Elizabethan feeling, is reminiscent of the John Chaloner whose life is so much interwoven with the story of the island. Considerable alteration was necessary to create the present sitting-room out of two small chambers, and the new pointed arches are very successful. On the first floor of the old castle are connecting bedrooms and a nursery suite, and one of the stone fire-places is now illustrated (Fig. 371). The wood casements were removed and iron casements, set in mullions of the Milverton limestone, were used throughout the building.

FIG. 370.—DINING ROOM.

The gardens are as yet not fully matured, but it can be seen how pleasantly they have been laid out. The scheme of planting was devised by Miss Jekyll with her usual skill, and has since been developed in a sympathetic way. Much excavation was necessary to produce the north court with its varied levels, and the shale thus removed was used to build, in 1909-10, a great rampart skirting the north-west side of the wood in which the castle is set. It is entertaining for the antiquary of to-day to guess what solemn theories his successor of A.D. 2913 will build on this imposing structure (Fig. 361). One feature in the new north court, namely, the pergola pillars (as yet unfurnished with roof beams) are a survival. They were the piers of an old farm shed. Other farm buildings to the north of this court have been remodelled and roofed anew with grey pantiles. A feature of the island growth is the profuse way in which fuchsias thrive. Here, as in Connemara, the soft sea air swiftly turns a low bush into a great hedge, brilliant with showers of crimson blossom.

The enclosing walls of both the east and west courts mark by their splay the unusual plan of the castle itself, and the western forecourt has an added interest from the stone runnels that intersect its paving. Not often can it be said of an old building that additions covering an even greater area have failed to take away the charm of the old, and still more rarely that they have increased it ; but no less is true of Lambay Castle. It is worthy of the island, which is to say much. The great grey seals which breed in the caverns are the most attractive of its indigenous animals ; but the fallow deer introduced by Count Considine, and the moufflon, chamois and rheas brought to the island by Mr. Baring, add to its attractions. Lambay is a paradise of birds, especially during the summer, and close on a hundred varieties make it their home. Among them are still breeding the descendants of the falcons, whose nestlings Chaloner sent to Walsingham in the sixteenth century. Lambay is an island of flowers. On the cliffs grow acres of scurvy-grass, with its creamy white flowers smelling like honey, and flooding the land with blossom. Grass, bracken, heath, rush and stony ground combine into a wild harmony. Rocks blazing with stonecrop and golden samphire, swards bright with the cool grey-blue of scilla verna enclosed by banks of sea pink, and great stretches of purple heather— these are the pictures framed by the margin of low water rocks black with fungus or brilliant with yellow lichen. We sail out of the little harbour of Lambay with the feeling that Prospero has been that way, and laid an enchantment on the island that history and Nature conspire to make real and abiding.

FIG. 371.—A BEDROOM FIREPLACE.

CHAPTER XVI.

TEMPLE DINSLEY, HERTS, 1909.

TEMPLE DINSLEY as it stands to-day is a seventeenth century house to which Mr. Lutyens has added on a large scale, but its name marks its relation with the Knights Templars. The atmosphere of the house will be the more real to the reader who has never seen it, if some account be given of the History of the place. It is in the fascinating power of some simple English manors to lead us abruptly from the parochial tale of carucates and pannage that we read of in the Domesday Survey, into the great fields of national and even of European history. In the case of Temple Dinsley it is the Temple which gives the cue. Dinsley, or, as they wrote it then, Deneslai, was part of the manor of Hitchin, and became interesting when Bernard de Balliol was its lord. He flourished between 1135 and 1167, and brought Dinsley into the current of European affairs, probably in 1147, with pleasant scenical accessories. Bernard gave to the Knights Templars land worth fifteen pounds a year, called Wedelee, at Hitchin, which gift was made to Pope Eugenius at Easter in Paris,

FIG. 372.—GATES AND FORECOURT.

FIG. 373.—THE ENTRANCE FRONT.

where the King of France and four archbishops and one hundred and thirty Knights Templars, clothed in their white vestments, were present.   Dinsley, thus formally made Temple Dinsley, was securely in the possession of the Knights of the Temple of Solomon in 1185, as a document of that year attests ; but Clement V suppressed this, the greatest of the military orders, and Temple Dinsley passed soon after into the possession of the Knights of the Hospital of St. John of Jerusalem, in whose hands it remained until the Dissolution.   It is

FIG. 374.—THE KITCHEN WING **AND** THE LOWER POOL.

FIG. 375.—NORTH FRONT : TERRACE AND PERGOLA.

impossible to do more than guess at the nature of the buildings which formed first the Preceptory of the Knights Templars, and afterwards the Commandery of the Hospitallers, at Temple Dinsley ; but there is the bare record of a castle there in 1278. It is improbable that in 1541, when the manor went to Sir Ralph Sadler as his share of the monastic spoils, there was a house of any importance, for he does not seem ever to have lived there. Of Sir Ralph it is not needful to say more here, than that he was a most faithful servant to Henry VIII, Edward VI and Elizabeth and the gaoler of Mary of Scotland at Tutbury. He died at Standon in 1587, and left Temple Dinsley to his second son, Edward. Leigh Sadler and Thomas Leigh Sadler in turn succeeded Edward, but it was Sir Ralph's great-great-grandson, Edwin, who seems to be more definitely associated with Temple Dinsley. By turns a barrister, a commander of a troop of horse in the Civil War (doubtless on the Royal side) and a J.P. for the County of Bedford, we find that " he removed from thence to Temple Dinesley, was created baronet in the second year of Charles II's reign and died in 1672."

In Chauncy's *History of Hertfordshire* there is a picture of the house as John Drapentier drew it some time before 1700, when the book was published. It is possible that it shows the house that the first Sir Edwin built for himself just after the Restoration, though the casement windows and the pedimented gables may be held to suggest a builder of some twenty years earlier. In 1712 Temple Dinsley was bought by Benedict Ithell. He was succeeded by his son, another Benedict, whose last surviving daughter bequeathed the estate in 1767 to Thomas Harwood. The later history of Temple Dinsley until it came into the possession of Mr. H. G. Fenwick we need not pursue, but its failure to continue in the Sadler family is typical of Hertfordshire estates. Returning to the house itself, it seems likely that Benedict Ithell found in 1712 that his newly acquired home had suffered with the declining fortunes of the Sadlers and was in ill repair. The middle of the front of the house as we see it now is absolutely different from the building shown in Drapentier's drawing, which was evidently pulled to the ground.

It is interesting to note that the old walls of the seventeenth century house were uncovered when the foundations for the walls of the present west wing were being excavated. When Mr. Lutyens was called in to make Temple Dinsley what the illustrations show it, its extent was small. The only part of merit, but it has great charm, was the block that now shows its symmetrical front through the gates (Fig. 372), with its central doorway and a trio of windows on either side. To the left was a drawing-room (an addition to the original house), occupying the site of the present boudoir and passage ; to the right were the kitchen offices, the south wall of which remains as part of the lavatory, but has been newly windowed. The interior of the old middle block has been remodelled. The present entrance hall was formerly two rooms, and the south end of the dining-room was cut off by a wooden partition which formed a passage-way from the staircase hall to the old kitchen offices. The main staircase is the old one, but its disposition has been a little altered. A good many years ago, but obviously long after the old house was built, there was added to the dining-room an unattractive bay window, which has been retained, and wisely. Not only would its destruction have interfered with the history of the building, but it plays its part in the pleasantness of the room within. It is true that it destroys the balance of the north front, but some owner of last century tried to retrieve it in very amusing fashion by growing and trimming yew trees on the other side of the garden door to match the bay window in shape exactly. This rather engaging conceit has also been retained. Many problems were involved in adding to the house so largely as was desired. First, and of most importance, as always in such cases, was the need to maintain with pious care the ancient fabric. Secondly came the addition of wings covering three or four times the area of the old house in such a fashion that they might not, on the one hand, look new and over-whelming, or, on the other, be a simple repetition of existing features. Both these questions are inevitable in all works of this kind, but it is rare that both yield such satisfactory answers. The old work has been respected in all faithfulness, and the new rhymes with it delightfully, but does not fail of showing the individuality of its creator. One odd characteristic of the old house is apparent from a glance at the plan (p. 228). The entrance front is to the south and the garden front to the north, instead of *vice versa*. In order to ensure sunny aspects for the new

FIG. 376.—LOOKING INTO FORECOURT FROM THE EAST.
A study in brick and iron.

FIG. 377.—GARDEN HOUSE FROM THE SOUTH—

FIG. 378.—AND FROM THE WEST.

FIG. 379.—THE SOUTH-WEST CORNER AND THE UPPER POOL.

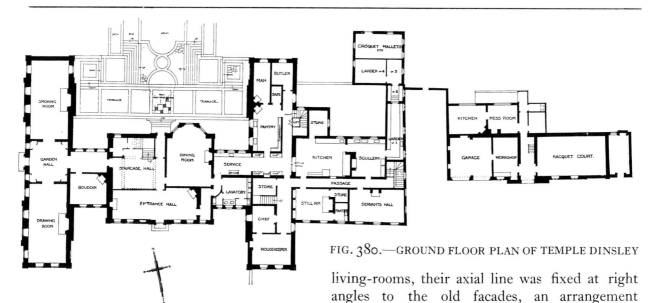

FIG. 380.—GROUND FLOOR PLAN OF TEMPLE DINSLEY

living-rooms, their axial line was fixed at right angles to the old facades, an arrangement which gives west windows to them all, and to the drawing-room a south aspect as well. The sharp fall of the land eastwards was a happy accident which has added greatly to the grouping of the east wing. Its principal part balances the drawing-room wing, but the rest of the kitchen quarters are at a much lower level, and lift their delightfully modelled roof in the modest fashion which becomes their use. So much by way of outline of the idea informing the new work, which clears the way for considering the house in detail. It is approached by a drive which brings the visitor to a spacious forecourt enclosed by a curved dwarf wall surmounted by simple railing

FIG. 381.—THE NEW WEST SIDE.

FIG. 382.—HALL AND STAIRCASE.

with ornamental panels at regular intervals. The gates in the middle are admirable examples of eighteenth century ironwork, and the brick piers at the end of the sweep bear engaging little leaden Cupids (Fig. 386). As the front door is neared, we notice on the right an opening towards the drive that skirts the lower pond, furnished with a gate which justifies the title of the picture, " A Study in Brick and Iron " (Fig. 376).

The entrance hall is panelled simply in white, and the walls of the inner stone-paved hall are treated in like fashion. We go by the doorway that appears in Fig. 382 into the garden hall. This is a white and enticingly cool-looking apartment, which turned into an octagon on two sides by corner cupboards, one of which is old and painted with cherubs, now much darkened by age. The outer corners are windowed and fitted as aviaries,

FIG. 383.—SMOKING-ROOM.

a pretty thought. Left and right of the garden hall are the drawing and smoking rooms. In the former is a fine mantel-piece of red and white marble. Below it big logs burn merrily, and, better still, without paying toll to the smoke fiend, who is apt to be busy with such big open hearths. Between the windows are glazed china cupboards with engaging wooden tracery, and the whole room takes on an air of

FIG. 384.—FROM DRAWING-ROOM TO SMOKING-ROOM.

breadth from the large simple white-painted panelling. Standing here and looking across the octagon hall into the smoking-room (Fig. 384) we note as a conspicuous feature the long range of hanging candelabra in clear glass lustre, which emphasise the vista. The smoking-room (Fig. 383) is interesting by reason of its unpainted panelling of pine, left clean and untouched from the tool and looking very fresh and pleasant. No little of the wall space is shelved and hospitable to books. Upstairs the bedrooms are planned on ample lines, and the treatment of one of the baths with white marble top and an ebony case of open fretwork, hung behind with a gay-coloured fabric, represents a new idea. (Fig. 385.) The bedrooms in the old part of the house have delightful little toilet rooms, which are simply the old powdering closets brought to a new use. We go downstairs again and make our way on to the big north terrace down the original garden steps. The ground here slopes away rapidly past the pergola to a garden-house. (Fig. 375.) The terrace enclosed by the new wings and the balustrade of open brickwork are sunless, but that is the fault of the old builders, who

FIG. 385.—IN A BATH-ROOM.

placed the house so oddly on its site. We walk round, therefore, by the north-west corner, past a rose garden, to seek the most gracious part of the garden, which stretches away from the new west front. (Fig. 381.) This elevation is gravely elegant. The general character of the old house is maintained, the keystones being based on the old work, but improved in their proportion. A modern note is struck by the treatment of the central door and the window above it as a single composition, relieved by the iron balcony. Facing it from the midst of a little paved rose garden is Father Time, an old leaden figure, silvery white and armed with scythe and hour-glass, the emblems of his sovereignty.   Running westwards from the north corner are a pair of garden-houses divided by a pillared loggia (Figs. 377 and 378), and the ground rises into a lawn and brilliant flower-beds flanked by raised terraces, which turn into paths under the trees and bring us to the upper pool. Fig. 379 shows the south-west corner clearly mirrored in it, and the graceful lead vases crowning the angles.   Some of these are original ornaments of the house; others are faithful copies.   One or two have been kept in the garden, which is fortunate, for their drums are gay with little classical scenes in clear relief.   In a quiet house like this, where the effects are won by sheer rightness of proportion, little incidents, like the dancing of garden gods on the side of a vase give a sense of pleasure altogether out of proportion to their intrinsic merit, which, as usually in such eighteenth century work, is not of a very lofty order.   In his roofing of the main parts of the building Mr. Lutyens followed the precedent he found, and has hidden his gutters behind a parapet ; but in the kitchen wing, which is seen reflected in the lower pool (Fig. 374), he has followed his more usual practice, and behind it from the kitchen court the hipped roofs pile up delightfully.

And so we finish our survey of this gracious country home, with its sober Georgian flavour enlivened within by pleasant refinements of design.   The great plain spaces of red brick that mark the sides of the new wings and the quiet line of the gables north and south are elements far removed from the boisterous days that saw Dinsley take what may rightly be called its Christian name.   There is, however, one more building we have not yet visited.   East of the kitchen wing is a range which includes not only garage and workshop, but, more interesting, a racquet court.   Are we tempted to set this down a too modern adjunct in a place which has rung with the tread of the mailed Knights Templars, who took their rights in Dinsley from Bernard de Balliol, in the presence of that Pope who called Bernard of Clairvaux friend ?   If so, we may remember Henry V as Shakespeare makes him speak in answer to the French Ambassadors, who brought him from the Dauphin a jesting gift of tennis balls :

> When we have matched our rackets to these balls
> We will, in France, by God's Grace, play a set,
> Shall strike his father's crown into the hazard.

FIG. 386.—THE FORECOURT RAILINGS.

CHAPTER XVII.

THREE SMALLER HOUSES : 1908-9.

MIDDLEFIELD, GREAT SHELFORD ; CHUSSEX, WALTON-ON-THE-HILL ;
KNEBWORTH GOLF CLUB HOUSE.

THIS chapter is devoted to three houses which show Mr. Lutyens' art in its most recent and, as it seems to me, a very satisfactory development. Heathcote, Ilkley, was conceived, within and without, wholly in the Palladian spirit, with a savour of Italy in its handling. It marked a break in his affection for national traditions which was abundantly justified by its intrinsic success. Middlefield, finished later than Heathcote, is an example of purely country architecture, and it cannot be imagined anywhere but on English soil. It stands on a site which looks southwards down a gentle slope and over a characteristic but, it must be confessed, not highly attractive stretch of Cambridgeshire farm lands. When the accompanying photographs were taken the gardens were on paper only, and the building, therefore, owes nothing in its pictures to the charm which Nature adds with a setting of tree, shrub and flower. The house sits starkly on the ground, but pergolas will be built from the loggia and from the other end of the south front to enclose a garden, if, indeed, they have not been added since I visited the house in 1910.

If it is an ordeal to show Middlefield without the framing which is its due, the success which it achieves is at least owed to no external aids. When it was built Mr. Lutyens had done nothing more austere, or any building which relied so entirely on the qualities of mass, symmetry and

FIG. 387.—MIDDLEFIELD, GREAT SHELFORD : ENTRANCE FRONT FROM NORTH-WEST.

proportion. There is nowhere an external moulding but in the windows and doors, and they are of extreme simplicity, except only the subtle line of brickwork which marks the slight recessing of the lower part of the projecting wings on the north front. Perhaps an observer will look for relief in a carved tympanum here or a keystone there, and missing it will bring against Middlefield a charge of baldness. With such a criticism it is difficult to argue, but it would be based on a large misunderstanding of a prin-ciple which seems to have inspired the design. Were it made, it could best be met as Pope Julius II was answered when he complained that there was no gold on the painted figures of the Sistine Chapel. "Simple persons," said the painter, "simple persons, who wore no gold on their garments." It has been always the finest types of small domestic architecture which disappoint the unthinking critic by lacking gold on their garments, buildings which have won their place in our affections by the very fact

FIG. 388.—GROUND FLOOR PLAN OF MIDDLEFIELD.

FIG. 389.—THE ENTRANCE DOOR.

of being "simple persons." Such houses, like the people whom they represent, have the gift of repose, and it is precisely in that sense that Middlefield will impress the thoughtful. The perfect suavity of the lines of the roofs, which are kept in harmonious and unbroken planes, the masculine tower-like bulk of the three chimneys, the windows few but large, the dormers with their angles swept in generous curves so that they grow organically out of the roof, all these things produce an effect of extraordinary repose.

Fig. 389 gives some hint of how the mass and outline are helped by the texture of the bricks and tiles. The house is not large, and its scale is made the greater by the smallness of the bricks. They are hand-made, and only seven inches long by one and three-quarter inches thick. There is a charm about these bricks which it is difficult to explain. Though they are well made and hard, their faces have that hint of cushion shape which lets the play of light send a ripple of colour over the wall. The wide white joints, more

FIG. 390.—MIDDLEFIELD FROM SOUTH-WEST.

plentiful than in normal brickwork, help to give a roughness of texture which adds vitality to the surface. This is another example of the effects which are to be got simply by wise choice of materials; for some part of the charm of Middlefield would be lacking had the bricks been of ordinary size and inferior texture.

Now as to the plan of the house. (Fig. 395.) It is often supposed that there is some special cleverness

FIGS. 391 AND 392.—FIREPLACE AND STAIR PILLAR AT MIDDLEFIELD.

in houses that are broken up into odd nooks and corners, features that are externally emphasised by turrets, chimneys and gables of queer shapes placed in an irregular fashion, that such exercises, in fact, serve best to exhibit an architect's ability. Nothing is further from the truth. The combination of symmetry outside with well shaped rooms conveniently disposed within needs far more thought and skill. Middlefield is an example of large success in this direction. The entrance on the north front opens into a long hall, which has no pretensions to being more than a convenient passage-way. From it is entered the whole suite of ground-floor rooms. The kitchen quarters are to the east, the study and garden room to the west, while the dining, drawing and school rooms face due south. Particular

FIG. 393.—CHUSSEX, WALTON HEATH: GARDEN FRONT FROM THE SOUTH-WEST.

FIG. 394.—CHUSSEX : ENTRANCE FRONT FROM THE EAST.

attention must be drawn to the hygienic virtue of the plan, a quality to which far too little attention is ordinarily given. By opening at once a few doors and windows perfect cross-ventilation is secured and the free air will blow through the house. This is an advantage often lacking where rooms are grouped round a main hall. The same simplicity which informs the exterior is carried into the treatment of the rooms. The fittings throughout are of the plainest and least expensive. In the drawing-room a little more elaboration has been allowed in the mantelpiece (Fig. 391), but even that maintains the prevailing note of gravity. The doors are all of two panels only, and the lock handles are very small round knobs. The windows in all the rooms except the attics are sliding sashes, for the site is so windswept that casements would have been unsatisfactory. The sash-bars are half round in section, and their stoutness adds no little to the general effect. Some people have the idea that heavy bars cut off too much light, and this may be true of town houses with little windows.

At Middlefield, however, there is not a room in the house but is lit not only well, but brilliantly. The loggia is conveniently placed with doors from the dining-room and from the kitchen quarters, and makes a fine open-air meal-place. The day nursery is above the dining-room, and has a casement door opening on to the flat roof of the loggia, which was designed to have railings, so that it might serve as an outdoor nursery.

Not the least of the difficulties involved in a symmetrical plan is the adequate lighting of the main staircase without interference with the balance of the windows. This has been accomplished by placing the bathroom window in the corresponding projection on the other side of the front entrance. The gaiety of the main staircase is a brilliant foil to the gravity that rules everywhere else. There is a touch of wayward fancy about the use of a single twisted pillar (Fig. 392) that sends my mind back to a letter that Charles Lamb wrote to Coleridge in 1800. He had received from Cottle a copy of that worthy bookseller's epic " Alfred."

FIG. 395.—GROUND FLOOR PLAN OF CHUSSEX.

FIG. 396.—CHUSSEX : GARDEN FRONT.

" When he is original," writes Elia, " it is in a most original way indeed. . . . Serpents, asps, spiders, ghosts, dead bodies, *staircases made of nothing, with adders' tongues for bannisters.* What a brain he must have ! "

Now, it would be a libel to liken Mr. Lutyens' delicately turned balusters to adders' tongues, but the pillar suggests just that delightful hint of extravagance in design which brings Lamb's criticism to the memory. That is not to say that tradition has been flouted, for a doorway at King's Lynn of 1708, attributed to Henry Bell, has a pair of twisted Corinthian columns which strike the same attractive note. In a house notable for

FIG. 397. – CHUSSEX : THE STAIRCASE.

breadth and sobriety Mr. Lutyens has given rein to his fancy and produced a feature which offends against no rule of reasonableness and yet entertains us hugely.

CHUSSEX.

Chussex, Walton-on-the-Hill, is another, but rather smaller, house in the same manner. That golfer must indeed be an unobservant soul who can play over Walton Heath without noting this austere yet fascinating house which lifts its front to the links. I have heard descriptions of it from many mouths, and they vary mightily. Of hostile criticism there is no lack, mostly directed to the undoubted fact that Chussex is not " pretty." That is true, and happily so, for what is wanted

FIG. 398.—KNEBWORTH GOLF CLUB : GROUND FLOOR PLAN.

FIG. 399.—KNEBWORTH GOLF CLUB : FROM THE NORTH-EAST.

from architects is not prettiness but character ; and this gift is better expressed by mass, proportion, texture and colour than by arrangements of trivial features, however ingenious. The tendency in modern work which is represented at Chussex is the apotheosis of architectural common-sense. It starts with a basis of absolute simplicity and continues to the chimney-tops in the same spirit. The house resembles Middlefield in its general conception, but there are notable differences that serve to mark the invention which has gone to the design of both. At Chussex the hipped roof, with its little dormer windows, finishes in a flat, from which the two massive chimneys rise at right angles to the main line of the building. On the south side the middle part of the front rises some feet above the eaves, and the ends are marked by admirable stone vases. A vigorous rhythm is afforded by the plain brick pilasters, and they further give a vertical emphasis to a wall that might be dull without them. The entrance front is ripe and scholarly in its balance, and the woodwork of the door-frame, continued up to the roof-line, gives a quiet relief by its slight projection and mouldings. The garden, under the able hand of Mr. Herbert Fowler, has taken good shape, and Fig. 396 shows the generous lines on which borders and paths have been planned. We are accustomed to regard the maturing of a garden as necessarily a lengthy process, involving infinite patience ; but the results at Chussex show how markedly it may be accelerated when methods are inspired by experience and good judgment. Within the house all is simply and sanely devised. The arrangement of the rooms is as practical as can be, and the spacious loggia which opens out of the drawing-room is a pleasant place. Of conscious decorative effect there is little, but in the open screen which divides the staircase from the passage to the garden lobby Mr. Lutyens has employed irregular trellising with his usual skill. (Fig. 397.) Chussex is a house that grows on the observer. When its plan (Fig. 395) is examined, it is seen how practical it all is, and how the elevations grow out of it. Yet they express, in subtle fashion, an idea evolved by sheer power of design, and show what large experience and skill go to the making of successful architecture.

THE KNEBWORTH GOLF CLUB HOUSE.

This is a good example of perfectly symmetrical treatment in a type of building which usually is conceived on irregular lines. Its plain brick walls and pantiled roof show none of those prettinesses which are too often thought the needful equipment of a building consecrated to play. The dignified planning of the forecourt has the advantage of pulling together into a coherent scheme the outbuildings which are so important an element in the working of the place. Often these are mere hutches scattered about without any definite relation to the club-house. Here they are an added attraction instead of an eyesore. The disposition of the rooms in the club-house is straightforward and convenient, and ample floor area is provided for the dressing-room.

FIG. 400.—KNEBWORTH GOLF CLUB : ENTRANCE FRONT.

CHAPTER XVIII.

NASHDOM, TAPLOW, BUCKS, 1909.

THE lower reaches of the Thames are not rich in houses that have a history. It is a country too near London to have been friendly to long ownerships, and frequent change brings with it the risk of rebuilding to suit the passing fashion of the day. By the same token, the modern houses in the district are many, and Nashdom is one of the most interesting. The site was small, and the contour of the ground determined that the house should stand by the roadside. The elements which went to its design were of the simplest—whitewashed brick walls, red-tiled roof and green shutters. The conscious austerity of the mass is relieved by no ornament save the conventions of the Doric porch (Fig. 403), the quiet mouldings round doors and windows, and a cartouche of arms. On the south-east side two curved bays break the line (Fig. 407), but otherwise Nashdom is almost nakedly severe. In the hands of a less skilled designer than Mr. Lutyens, such a conception would have

FIG. 401.—NASHDOM: FROM THE WEST. THE WAY TO THE PORCH.

taken shape as a barrack. As it is, the house has a character of distinction which marks it as an English variant of eighteenth century Italian and French mansions, yet without a mark of foreign detail. Nashdom is a *tour de force* in whitewashed brick. Its nearness to the road has impressed on the plan the character of a town mansion rather than of a country house. From the pillared porch there is a glimpse through an iron gate of a paved court, which lights staircase and service rooms (Fig. 402). From the entrance door we ascend twelve steps to get to the ground

FIG. 403.—THE PORCH : FROM THE ROAD—

FIG. 402.—LOOKING INTO COURT.

floor, which is level with the garden front. On this side is the range of reception-rooms, of which the dining-room is typical. It is decorated in white and a delicate grey-blue, and the walls are hung with abrocade of blue and silver (Fig. 414). The round dining table has been equipped by Princess Alexis Dolgorouki in an entertaining way, with a hint of the garden. Its middle is occupied by a round pool, and amidst miniature rock work there bloom forget-me-nots and other delicate flowers in their seasons. A tiny

FIG. 404.—AND FROM WITHIN.

FIG. 405.—THE GREAT GARDEN STAIR.

fountain tinkles, and electric lamps, secretly disposed, add brilliance to the goldfish which inhabit the pool. The winter garden hall is carried up two storeys to a dome. At the east end a recess for billiards forms part of a big sitting-room, and the round drawing-room and vaulted loggia (Fig. 409) open from the latter. An effective and unusual feature is the treatment of the landing of the main staircase as a writing-room (Fig. 413). The fireplace here deserves a word. Over a hundred and fifty years ago Isaac Ware suggested that the blank space in the panel of an overmantel might be filled with a wind-indicating dial. The author of a recent book devoted wholly to fireplaces and their history quoted Ware with the wish that such a device might be tried nowadays. He was evidently unaware that Mr. Lutyens has been doing it for some years. The dial, round which the wind-pointer swings, is decorated with a map of the district, so that the compass lettering on the outer ring serves to mark both the direction of the wind and the position of the surrounding

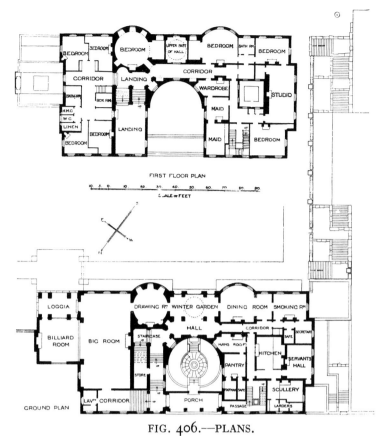

FIG. 406.—PLANS.

FIG. 407.—THE SOUTH-EAST FRONT.

landmarks. The mechanism of the pointer is simple. A small additional flue is provided in the chimney, down which runs a rod connected by cogwheels both with the weather-cock outside and the pointer on the dial. It would be difficult to find a more interesting or more decorative treatment for the broad panel of an overmantel (Fig. 412).

At the south corner the ground drops suddenly, and has given opportunity for a retaining wall and great stairway, devised with a fine realisation of the possibilities of the site. There is a largeness of idea in the treatment of the stairway, which is altogether admirable. Like the house, it is of simple brick and tile, with its retaining walls white-washed. It is laid out without any artfulness of curve, and relies wholly on the masculine disposition of its platforms and walls. Its severe line is in accord with the angular mass of the house, the latter but slightly relieved by inconspicuous roof and chimneys, and by two bays of flat curve on the garden front. The white mass of brickwork seems to furnish the house with an inviolable buttress, but garden needs are not forgotten. Treillage with creeping plants robs the outer wall of any hint of crudity, and the growth of the wide border beneath the terrace wall is continued on the broad platforms that flank the stairway. Returning to the upper level, we note at the north-east end of the garden a delightful temple-like front that looks down on a round paved garden (Fig. 408.) It masks the power-house where electricity is generated, and is at the same time a telling piece of garden design. A house of the character of Nashdom demands that its surroundings shall be treated in a purely architectural fashion. " Natural " gardening may have its own charms and prettinesses, but their function is not to make the setting for so austere and masculine a conception as this.

To most observers it will appear that Nashdom is invested with the quality which, for want of a better name, is known as originality. Hackneyed in use and idea as this word is, it may be accepted as reasonably descriptive if it carries the limitations of meaning which Coventry Patmore laid down. He claimed that originality, in art as in manners, " consists simply in a man's being upon his own line ; in his advancing with a single mind towards his unique apprehension of good, and in his doing so in harmony with the universal laws." The sort of sham originality which finds its issue in antics, oddities and crudities of architectural expression is,

FIG. 408.—TEMPLE, SCREENING POWER-HOUSE.

FIG. 409.—IN THE LOGGIA.

FIG. 410.—FROM THE LOWER LAWN.

FIG. 411.—GARDEN FRONT FROM THE EAST.

in fact, violating those reasonable laws which have crystallised as traditions of design and building. True originality finds its outlet " in upholding those laws and illustrating them and making them unprecedentedly attractive by its own peculiar emphases and modulations." It is precisely in this fashion that Mr. Lutyens succeeds in giving a personal character and distinction to his work. In some of his earliest buildings there are conceits that cannot justly resist the harsh name of quaint, but, as his art has matured, they have dropped away. He has been content in his later work to follow the narrow path of tradition, but always with emphases and modulations of his own. Adherence to the main outlines of any tradition lies open, in the judgments of some minds, to the charge of narrowness, but the swift phrase of Henry James meets this objection. " We must be narrow to penetrate." It is precisely in its penetrative quality that such a building as Nashdom makes its appeal. There is a sense of restrained harmony, expressed in the simplest materials and outlines, which could hardly have been expressed in a more forcible way. Patmore quoted with just approval a dictum of Coleridge,

FIG. 412.—A WIND-DIAL.

" All harmony is founded on a relation to rest—on relative rest," and built on it an ingenious essay about the point of rest and its functions in all the arts. Though he did not expand the

FIG. 413.—THE LANDING ROOM.

idea in relation to architecture, his reference to the recurring burthen of old ballads suggests an analogy in building. The repetition of features like the ranks of shutters on the south front of Nashdom, strengthened by the emphatic balance of the two curved bays, bring to the whole conception a marked atmosphere of repose. It has already been said that the exigencies of the site have impressed on it some of the characteristics of a town house. Town manners have given to the word urbanity its significant shade of meaning, and, despite the severity of mass and outline that marks the design of Nashdom, the repose with which it is instinct gives it an over-veiling sense of the urbane and makes it soundly domestic. Without that urbanity, without the hint of the spirit of Versailles in its great garden stair, without, in fact, the originality which brings personal emphases and modulations to give vitality to the usual, Nashdom would have looked like an institution instead of a dignified country house.

For a basis of comparison in this austerity of character we must look to Italian examples, such as the great Roman palaces. They are little known to readers, for the illustrator of books has passed them by in disgust at the lack of those moulded details which well employ deft pencils. There is a hint of Roman largeness of idea in the Doric porch, which masks the open court between the two wings and forms so effective a link in the dual design of the house. Mr. Lutyens has shown elsewhere a leaning towards the Italian internal stair, rising between walls, which is always successful when done on an adequate scale. It is, however, a type that is likely to be disastrous to convenience, when carried out on the miniature scale of the ordinary English staircase. The dual disposition of the plan explains and justifies the somewhat freakish dip in the southern façade, so startling in its unexpectedness. When all is said, the singular interest of the house is its uncompromising assertion of the right of whitewashed brick to a place among the materials of right use in a great mansion no less than in a wayside cottage. It is a claim of the humble to pride of place, and the claim must be allowed.

Nashdom, with its atmosphere of mingled opulence and austerity, is a fine exercise in that simplicity which has in it a hint of arrogance. It is the more interesting to the student of Mr. Lutyens' work because its character is remote from the tender qualities which inform his smaller vernacular work in what may be called a farmhouse manner, and from the broad humanism that marks his most mature work in the spirit of the early eighteenth century.

FIG. 414.—THE DINING-ROOM.

CHAPTER XIX.

GREAT MAYTHAM, KENT, 1910.

AND THE SALUTATION, SANDWICH, 1912.

GREAT MAYTHAM is one of the many houses which it has fallen to Mr. Lutyens' lot to build on a historic site. The early history of the manor is but slenderly supported by documents, but a lease of the fourteenth century throws an interesting light on the condition of the neighbouring lands. Nicholas Carew, when leasing the manor for seven years, stipulated that the tenants should "at their proper cost well and competently maintain and when necessary repair all the houses, walls and hedges belonging to the said manor, except the chapel and the sea wall and the great ditch." Another lease of marsh lands in the parish shows by its reference to "water-scots" that the land-owners of that day in the Rother Valley were active in the operations of damming and draining, which began perhaps even before the Roman invasion. Nowhere, it may be, has the "Law of Eastward Drift" changed the face of a country more markedly. The

FIG. 415.—THE ENTRANCE.

south-east winds steadily piled up banks of shingle about the harbours. Though this ruined the maritime fortunes of the Cinque Ports, it turned miles of impassable marsh into smiling pastures. Carew's mention of a sea wall emphasises the fact that in the Middle Ages the estuary of the Rother ran up to Bodiam, Northiam and Maytham, and possibly it was navigable for small vessels at high tide. It was not until 1661 that Guildford Marshes and Romney Haven became dry land and that Oxney ceased to be an isle except in name. At the end of the thirteenth century Arabel de Maytham and her sister Elwisa held the manor, which belonged to John de Malmains and his family in the reigns of Edward II and III, and passed to the Carews of Beddington at the end of the fourteenth century. Somewhere on the estate, perhaps hidden under the foundations of the present house, there must be fragments of the mansion and its chapel which existed in the fourteenth century, but no definite record of them remains, nor is it known who built them.

A Nicholas was the last as well as the first of the name of Carew to hold Maytham, and on his attainder in 1539 the manor went to the Crown. Sir Nicholas Carew was a picturesque

FIG. 416.—FROM THE NORTH-WEST.

member of an attractive race of men. He suffered with many another from his inability to steer his course safely through the shifting shoals of Henry VIII's changing tempers. As a young man he had attended the King in his invasion of France, and received a " coat of rivet " as a mark of the Royal favour. He served the King as squire of the body and cup-bearer in turn. So intimate a part did he play in Henry's life that he was banished from Court by the Council on the ground of too great familiarity with the King. Despite this, his name constantly appears among those who took a prominent place in jousts and revels. In 1518 he was made Sheriff of Surrey and Sussex, but the year after he was again driven from Court, only slightly consoled by securing an honourable and lucrative post at Calais. At the Field of the Cloth of Gold in 1520 his knightly skill stood him in good stead, and all manner of public employment followed. Carew must have been a great friend of Francis I, for twice the French King wrote to Henry, begging that the Garter might be conferred on Carew, and soon after the second plea Sir Nicholas was duly invested at a Chapter held

FIG. 417.—THE GARDEN FRONT.

at Greenwich.   Two years later his fortunes
began to fail.   He was accused of being
concerned in the treasonable behaviour of
the Marquis of Exeter, and in 1539 closed a
brilliant career at the block on Tower Hill.
Although Beddington returned to the Carew
family, Great Maytham seems to have been
alienated permanently.   Its next holder,
Thomas C r o m w e l l,   only
possessed it for a year, and
on his attainder it returned
to the Crown.   It went next
to Sir Thomas Wyatt, who
promptly alienated it to
Walter H e n d l e y.   H i s
daughter married one of the
Colepeppers, w h o   owned
Maytham until 1714, when
it was bought by James

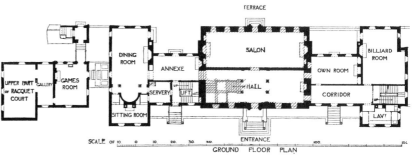

FIG. 418.—PLANS OF GREAT MAYTHAM.

Monypenny.   It is only to this ownership that we can ascribe any definite architectural
history of the place.   On the site of the present house he built in 1721 a seat in the
Georgian manner, which was altered in 1763 and partly destroyed by fire in 1893.   The

FIG. 419.—THE TERRACE LOOKING WESTWARD.

FIG. 420.—FROM THE SOUTH-EAST.

restorations and additions then effected wholly destroyed the character of the house, and when Mr. H. J. Tennant purchased the property a few years ago he wisely decided to disregard what he found. Some of the original cellars have been incorporated in the existing house, but to all intents the house is new. Mr. Lutyens has picked up the thread of early eighteenth century design where Mony-penny dropped it in 1721. The string-course on the garden front at

FIG. 421.—EAST STAIRWAY ON SOUTH TERRACE.

the second floor level marks the position of the eaves of the old house, and the south terrace is the same as before, but enlarged and beautified by great stairways. One or two old trees give an air

FIG. 422.—THE HOUSE FROM THE TERRACE BASTION.

FIG. 423.—IN THE WALLED GARDEN: GARDEN HOUSE—   FIG. 424.—AND GATE.

of maturity to the terrace, as may be seen in Fig. 419. On the east side of the house the old laundry has been retained, but turned into a squash-racket court. The bricks of which Great Maytham is built are particularly attractive. The mass of the walling is of mingled blue-grey and purple, and the quoins are a brilliant red. Green shutters add a charming contrast, which is emphasised by the cool cream colour of the stone used sparingly for the two main doorways on the north and south fronts. The terrace is paved with plain rectangular stone slabs which carry on the grave character of the fronts. " Crazy " paving has become such a fashion of late that it is a relief to see slabs laid in a quiet and reasonable way. Stones of random shapes are well enough in the outlying parts of gardens, where they are not close to the house, and when the quarry naturally yields pieces of irregular form. To lay them near a house of austere design, as is too often done, amounts simply to affectation, and seems the more foolish when rectangular slabs are solemnly broken up to give the " crazy " effect. South-

west of the house is a walled garden with two iron gates (Figs. 424 and 425).

The rooms, both in disposition and decorative treatment, are simple and unaffected. The dining-room fireplace, made of white and *fleur de pêche* marble, is particularly successful, and Mr. Tennant was lucky in getting two delightful French marble vases of a deeper purple to set on the shelf. Electric

FIG. 425.—SOUTH GATE INTO THE WALLED GARDEN.

FIG. 426.—THE HALL.

FIG. 427.—IN THE DINING-ROOM.

FIG. 428.—THE DINING-ROOM FIREPLACE.

FIG. 429.—THE STABLES, GREAT MAYTHAM : SOUTH SIDE.

lamps in the two porcelain baskets are an admirable lighting device. The end of the dining-room, behind the screen of columns, is also ingeniously lit by little gilt hanging baskets concealing lamps which reflect to the ceiling. We leave Great Maytham through the opening in the stable block, which stands on the main road, with the feeling that Mr. Lutyens has done no better house in this manner.

THE SALUTATION, SANDWICH.

This house takes its name from an inn which stood on the site. It is a younger sister of Great Maytham, but with such differences in treatment and, in particular, with so attractive a

plan as to make it no repetition to illustrate it here. The buildings are wholly new, except that an old cottage by the roadside has been remodelled and enlarged to serve as a gate-house. As The Salutation stands in the town, this gatehouse forms, when the gates are shut, a fitting screen for the house. The great cornice, above the gate opening, dies at either end into a pair of flanking dormers, and has a delightful effect, which reminds the student of Philip Webb's not dissimilar boldness in sweep of moulding (Fig. 438). The gatehouse forms a picturesque group from within the forecourt (Fig. 437) in contrast with the severe outlines and symmetry of the main building which it serves. The house is of red brick with stone quoins, and the entrance front, facing north-west, is treated with absolute simplicity, relieved only by the curved iron balustrading of the steps and the carving in the pediment of the main entrance (Figs. 431 and 433). Walls, segmental on plan, connect this front with two pairs of gate piers, one of which gives

FIG. 430.—GREAT MAYTHAM : SEEN FROM THE ROAD THROUGH STABLES.

FIG. 431.—THE ENTRANCE DOOR.

FIG. 432.—SALON DOOR ON SOUTH-WEST SIDE.

access to the kitchen yard and the other (seen in Fig. 433) leads to the garden. The south-east front is buttressed by a broad terrace (Fig. 435), from the middle of

FIG. 433.—THE SALUTATION, SANDWICH: ENTRANCE FRONT FROM THE WEST.

which an ample flight of
steps descends to a grass walk
dividing two flower - borders
(Fig. 439).

Unlike the entrance front,
the middle third of which
breaks forward about eighteen
inches, the south-east elevation is flat save for the
enriched architraves of the
dining - room windows, and
the same is true of the
south - west front with its
outer door of the *salon*.
Kitchen quarters, including
servants' bedrooms, are provided on the north-east side
in a single - storey annexe,
which is scarcely noticed
because its floor is some feet
below the ground level of the
main part of the house.

The plan is original and
fascinating, but lacking in no
element of convenience. From
the entrance hall, with its
two great black twisted

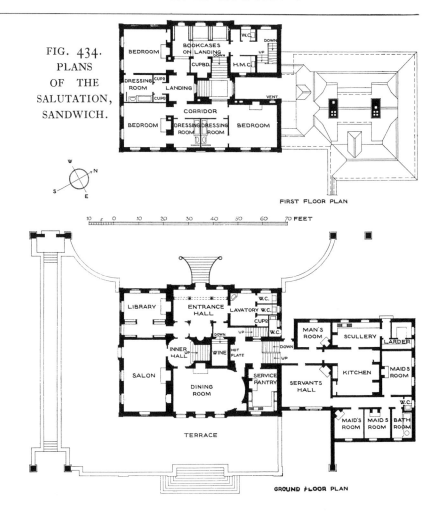

FIG. 434.
PLANS
OF THE
SALUTATION,
SANDWICH.

FIRST FLOOR PLAN

GROUND FLOOR PLAN

FIG. 435.—GARDEN FRONT FROM THE EAST.

pillars, a little lobby gives access to the library and to an inner hall with a low dome painted white and green. From this the *salon* and dining-room open, and the staircase rises and winds to the first-floor landing. Although it is carried up wholly between walls, a flood of light is secured by a tall north-east window. This staircase is altogether a success, and if the criticism be made that it occupies a lot of space, the answer is that the house contains all the accommodation required, and that an economy of cubic content in the staircase would have served no purpose.* The hollow core of the stair is utilised as a large cupboard at the first-floor level. This storey is occupied by three bedroom suites, and there are more bedrooms on the attic floor.

In giving great praise to the distinguished design of Great Maytham and The Salutation, it is proper to remember that some may prefer Mr. Lutyens' art when it is busy with Tudor fancies, such as he has used with such brilliant effect at Marshcourt. It would be foolish to claim that one type of house is better than another : each is admirable in its own kind, but at least it may be said that the quiet rhythm and masculine repose of the two houses illustrated in this chapter, are qualities of which it is impossible to tire. Many feel that the atmosphere of Tudor architecture, to the modern interpretation of which Mr. Lutyens has brought so much freshness and invention, lacks the quietude which seems the best corrective of the hurried conditions of modern life. It is probably for this reason, as much as because the æsthetic pendulum

* *Photographs of the staircase and of other interiors are omitted by the wish of the owner.*

FIG. 436.—SOUTH CORNER OF THE SALUTATION.

FIG. 437.—GATE HOUSE FROM FORECOURT.

FIG. 438.—GATE HOUSE FROM ROAD.

FIG. 439.—GRASS WALK LEADING TO SOUTH-EAST FRONT.

has swung back to the ideals of the eighteenth century, that those who care to be beautifully housed take especial pleasure in the more severe manifestation of Mr. Lutyens' art as it is seen in these two houses.

CHAPTER XX.

GREAT DIXTER, SUSSEX, 1910,

AND HOWTH CASTLE, CO. DUBLIN.

SOUTHERN KENT and East Sussex are peculiarly rich in early timber houses which reveal the simple plan that contented our mediæval forbears. Though all of them have been altered to fit them for less simple conditions of life, their general arrangement can be disentangled. Most of them were yeomen's houses, and the only one in that district which can claim to be a manor house of dignity is Great Dixter, near Northiam. In nearly all of these timber houses the alterations made by succeeding owners have been so drastic that their general appearance no longer represents with any faithfulness the work of their builders. It is, therefore, the more interesting to examine the successful way in which Mr. Lutyens has repaired the broken architectural fortunes of Great Dixter.

It is necessary to enter into the early ownership of the manor in some detail, because of the light thrown thereby on the date of what must be regarded as one of the most important and perhaps the earliest timber house in Sussex. There was an Adam de Dyksters in 1295, and in

FIG. 440.—ENTRANCE FRONT FROM THE NORTH-WEST.

1340 one Hamo at Gate was liable to find one man-of-arms in respect of his land in Dicksterve. Hamo's daughter Joan married Robert Echingham, and on their death, Dixter passed to the descendants of Robert's younger brother, Richard. Another Robert Echingham was in possession in 1411. His daughter, Elizabeth, married Richard Wakehurst, who died in 1454, leaving his widow in possession until her death in 1464. Their son had died young, leaving two daughters, under the guardianship of their grandmother, Elizabeth Wakehurst, and of Richard's brother-in-law, John Gaynesford. The two girls were entrusted to Gaynesford's sister Agnes, wife of Sir John Culpeper, who quite probably was privy to their abduction and marriage by his two brothers, Richard and Nicholas. This exploit was doubtless inspired by the intent to secure Dixter for the girls when their grandmother died ; but by Richard Wakehurst's marriage settlement the manor was to go back to the Echingham family in default of male

FIG. 441.—A CORNER OF THE SOUTH TERRACE.

Wakehurst heirs. Sir Thomas Echingham accordingly succeeded, and was followed by his daughter Margaret, whose second husband was Sir John Elrington. We know that Sir John was in possession of Dixter in 1479, because he was granted licence to crenellate and fortify the manor in that year, and he died in 1483, leaving to Margaret his household stuff at Dixter. Shortly afterwards the two Culpepers who had married the two Wakehursts claimed the manor from the widow, but she had powerful friends. One of her daughters by her first marriage had married Andrew Windsor, who afterwards became Lord Windsor, and he stood by her. The lawyers were busy with the quarrel for several years, but the Culpepers failed in their suits. When Dame Margaret Elrington died the property passed to the Windsor family, with whom it remained until 1595. It was then purchased by John Glydd, but in 1640 his family ended in three heiresses, who subdivided the property.

FIG. 442.—PORCH FROM THE NORTH-EAST.

A few years ago Mr. J. E. Ray wrote a most interesting paper on Great Dixter, which was then disfigured by modern accretions, such as the two floors which had been inserted across the great hall. His analysis of the building is a valuable contribution to the development of timber " hall houses." Judged merely by the architectural evidence of its fabric, the house can safely be placed between 1440 and 1480, but the heraldic devices on the hall roof enable us to narrow this down considerably. Among the shields of arms is that of the Gaynesfords. Mr. Ray points out that one of them became interested in the manor after the death, in 1464, of Elizabeth Wakehurst. He suggests that it is unlikely that the Gaynesford arms could have been carved long after the building was finished, and decides on 1464 as the earliest date for the hall. This theory, however, requires examination. On the death of Elizabeth Wakehurst the manor returned to Sir Thomas Echingham, but there seems no reason why,

FIG. 443.—THE STAIRWAY TO THE TERRACE.

FIG. 444.—FROM THE SOUTH-EAST.

FIG. 445.—THE SOUTH SIDE WITH BENENDEN HOUSE IN FOREGROUND.
(Detail drawings of these steps are reproduced in the Appendix.)

if he built the house, he should have carved on the roof the arms of John Gaynesford, with whom, as the guardian of the two girls who were claiming the estate against him, he can scarcely have been on good terms. On the other hand, if Richard Wakehurst, who married Elizabeth Echingham, the heiress of Dixter, built the hall, it would have been a very natural thing for him to set up the arms of his brother-in-law, who belonged to a family distinguished in the locality. It seems reasonable, therefore, to attribute the hall to some date between 1440 and 1454. It is a noble apartment, and runs up three storeys in height. It measures forty feet by twenty-five feet—about double the size of the hall of a yeoman's house—and the construction is particularly interesting. It is divided into four bays by great oak posts, which extend from the ground to the eaves, and form the vertical framework of the building. On top of them, and running through the length of the house, are big timbers, which form the wall plate. The unusual feature at Dixter is that, while these uprights are connected across the hall at its lower end, and also in the middle, by tie-beams, the intermediate

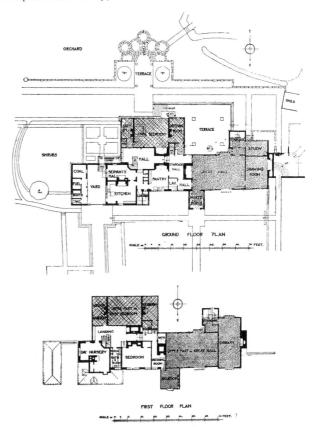

FIG. 446.—GROUND AND FIRST FLOOR PLANS.
The area of the original house of Great Dixter is covered with a dotted tint. The Benenden house on the south side is cross-hatched, and the new work is left white.

posts dividing the solar from the first bay, the first from the second, and the third from the fourth, are furnished only with three pairs of short hammer-beams. This construction is certainly rare, and possibly unique, in a large building wholly of timber, as it is much better adapted for use with stone walls. On the ends of these hammer-beams, and fixed at a slope, so that they look down to the hall at an angle of forty-five degrees, are shields of arms bearing the cognisances of the Echinghams, the Dalyngrugges and the Gaynes-fords. When the hall was built there was an open hearth on the floor from which the smoke found its way out by the windows or through chinks in the roof, or by a louvre, just as it did in the notable case of Penshurst. The roof timbers show by their blackened surfaces the inconvenience that fifteenth century folk were ready to suffer. At the upper or west end of the hall

FIG. 447.—THE HALL: LOOKING EASTWARDS.

FIG. 448.—THE HALL : WEST END.

there was a dais, on which stood the dining-table for the owner and his family.　Mortice holes in the posts at the end of the wall remain to show that the dais floor was about fifteen inches above the general level of the hall, which in those days was sometimes known as the " marsh." As it was usually of beaten earth, strewn with rushes, and mingled with scraps of food and bones, this name seems to be apt enough.　The apartment opening out of the west of the hall, with the room above it, and the porch are of later date.　The ground floor room in houses of this type is ordinarily called the " cellar," but this is a misleading description at Dixter, because there is a real cellar beneath it.　The room on the upper floor is the solar and runs up two storeys. These two west rooms were the private and sleeping apartments of the family, to which they

FIG. 449.—THE SOLAR.

retired after eating in hall.   At the south end of the hall dais was a doorway to the staircase, which led up to the solar, but, unhappily, all traces of the original staircase work have disappeared. The solar itself had originally two fine tie-beams, which supported the king-posts of its hand-some open roof.   One of these has been cut away, but the other remained intact.   Both the solar and the parlour below had big stone fireplaces.   The one in the solar remains in an admirable condition, but is rather puzzling, as it reveals on the spandrels of its carved mantel-piece the hawk's lure of the Lewknor family, who were associated with Bodiam Castle, and the antlered head of the Windsor family.   Unhappily, the fireplace in the room below has been hopelessly mutilated.

FIG. 450.—THE NEW UPPER STAIRCASE.

That the rooms were in full use during the sixteenth century is shown by the legend scratched on the beam of the parlour, which runs as follows :

" JOHN HARRISON DWELLT ATT DIXTERN XXXVI YERS AN VI MONTHES.

CAME YE FERST OF ELISABETHE RAIN."

It is probable that when Lord Windsor and his wife entered into their inheritance they did something which added to the amenities of Dixter. The first baron died in 1543 and his successor in 1558. The Windsors leased Dixter to the father of the John Harrison who, in

1595, or thereabouts, scratched the inscription already quoted.

A glance at the plan will show that nothing remains of the old house of Dixter but the hall, solar and porch already described, but there are clear evidences as to how the east end was treated. Crossing the hall there was a screen, perhaps with a gallery over, and into this entry, commonly called " the screens," the porch would have given. Two doors would open into the hall and two to the left into buttery and pantry. Servants' rooms would be provided over the latter, and probably the room above the porch had a door from the screen gallery. By the end of the sixteenth century people were getting tired of

FIG. 451.—ON THE STAIRS.

being smoke-dried in the hall, and were building fireplaces at the lower or buttery end of it. It is a probable theory that when John Harrison died or left Dixter in 1595 the new owner, John Glydd, remodelled the house, built the great chimney and divided the open hall into three storeys. The mantel-beam of the similar but smaller house at Benenden was dated 1595, which marks the time at which other places in the neighbourhood were being converted. From the beginning of the seventeenth century and

FIG. 452.—THE HALL OF THE BENENDEN HOUSE, NOW PART OF GREAT DIXTER.

for three hundred years the main fabric suffered little, save by the usual insertion of sliding sashes and other minor alterations. When Mr. Lloyd acquired Dixter it presented in some ways a rather woeful appearance, but it was sound in its bones. In one respect the task of restoration was easy, for there was no work of later than the fifteenth century which had any intrinsic merit entitling it to continued existence. All the additions to the original house were sheer defacements. Mr. Lutyens handled the work in an admirable way. It is obvious that when the two added floors which cut up the hall, and that which divided the solar, and all the cross partitions had been cleared out, the rooms available, though large, were few, and it was necessary to decide how the needful accommodation should be provided. Mr. Nathaniel Lloyd, the owner of Great Dixter, and Mr. Lutyens made visits to many of the yeoman's hall houses in the neighbourhood in order to mark the local peculiarities of treatment, and among them was the typical house at Benenden in Kent, which was known as " The Old House at Home." It was very dilapidated, and the great chimney-stack had lately collapsed and broken down the floors and partitions in its fall. Its owner was then arranging to demolish the framework, and Mr. Lloyd bought it. The transplanting of houses from their original site is generally a meaningless proceeding, greatly to be deprecated ; but in this case it was amply justified. Indeed, in no other way could a valuable example of timber building have been spared. It was accordingly rebuilt to the south-east of the Dixter house. All the timbers were numbered and photographed before being taken down and carried to the new site, and the Benenden house was connected with the Hall of Dixter by a wholly new eastern wing. In designing the latter, Mr. Lutyens has made no sort of attempt to imitate the timber construction of the two old houses, but has built in brick and weather-tiling.

Nor were any alterations or restorations made in the old work save where absolutely necessary. Neither dais nor screen was set up afresh in the great hall. The big fireplace in the hall was built against its east wall, but in the new wing. Adjoining it in the north-east corner was provided an internal wind-porch to keep the hall warm and comfortable. The parlour at the west end had been divided by a partition into two rooms, and this convenient arrangement was retained. As the unlovely additions of the nineteenth century, mostly of lath and plaster, were one by one removed, a window here and a moulding there came to light, damaged sometimes, but not so far that renewal could not be done with certainty rather than conjecture to guide it. Some of the windows had originally been filled, not with glass, but with shutters sliding in grooves, and the latter remained. By great good fortune one of the ancient shutters of the Benenden house had survived, and new ones were made from it for use in two pairs of pointed windows in the porch room.

In the Benenden hall, now the chief bedroom at Dixter, the upright bars, which were provided as a protection to the shuttered openings, have survived, and the openings have been glazed behind them on one side, but boarded up on the other, as seen in Fig. 452. This yeoman's hall never boasted a screen, but the crenellated beam which crossed the hall at the upper end was returned two feet into the room to screen the master of the house from the neighbouring door as he sat at meat. This interesting feature remains. The warming of a mediæval house is rather a problem. Radiators strike an unduly modern note, but they are a necessity, especially in rooms with open roofs. At Dixter, their cases are mainly old oak chests with chases suitably contrived to allow free circulation of the warmed air. In one example the radiator case serves as a wash-stand.

The planning of the new wing is ingenious, as the two old houses are perfectly connected, but they are yet allowed to stand out freely from each other and from the connecting wing. The north or entrance front is Dixter, the south or garden side Dixter and Benenden. As the ground sloped rapidly to the south, the yeoman's house had to be set up on a brick substructure, with which is linked a delightful scheme of terrace and stairways. The group of steps, round on plan, which appears in Fig. 445, is very characteristic of Mr. Lutyens' invention. In the

FIG. 453.—HOWTH CASTLE: THE NEW TOWER.

treatment of the garden the same conservatism which informed the repair of the house has been the keynote. All the old farm buildings have been retained. The orchard comes up to the lower terrace with its flagged walk over a hundred yards

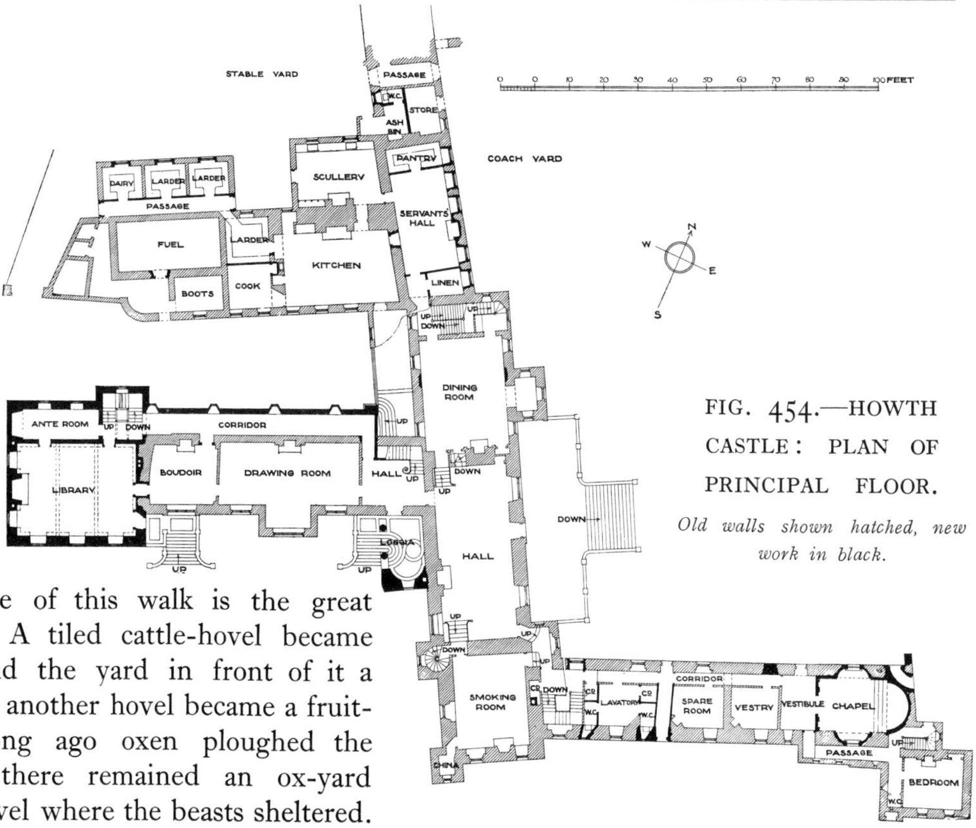

FIG. 454.—HOWTH CASTLE: PLAN OF PRINCIPAL FLOOR.

Old walls shown hatched, new work in black.

long. On one side of this walk is the great herbaceous border. A tiled cattle-hovel became a garden shelter and the yard in front of it a formal rose garden ; another hovel became a fruit-house. Not so long ago oxen ploughed the Dixter land, and there remained an ox-yard with its thatched hovel where the beasts sheltered.

FIG. 455.—HOWTH CASTLE: THE LOGGIA.

This yard is another garden, and the shed makes a children's play-house. Another great thatched barn serves as a garage and generating station. All these farm buildings had been added from time to time regardless of right angles or of any relation to each other or to the house. Yet so skilfully has Mr. Lutyens linked them up by various features which mask the riot of contending lines that the combined effect is wholly restful and coherent. As time goes on, doubtless many more such houses as Great Dixter will be rescued from neglect and will reveal again the delightful craftsmanship of later mediæval times. It will be fortunate if they are restored by an owner so sympathetic and by an architect who so justly combines the antiquary with the artist.

HOWTH CASTLE.

Howth Castle is a scattered range of buildings, of which the oldest part is the mediæval gatehouse. Considerable remodelling was done at the beginning of the eighteenth century. More than one owner during the nineteenth century made additions, in which the gothic character of the old work was imitated with such amount of skill as was available at the time.

Mr. Lutyens' work consisted of building a new tower at the southwest end, a new loggia in the angle formed by the south and west wings, new corridors on the north side of the west wing, and the remodelling of some of the rooms. Fig. 453 shows the new tower as seen across the new walled garden from the south-west. The design necessarily is lacking in the personal touch

FIG. 456.—HOWTH CASTLE: HALL FIREPLACE.

for which we are accustomed to look in Mr. Lutyens' work, because he was tied down to follow the character of the rest of the castle; but he has at least given a better emphasis to the sash windows by providing them with very stout bars. In the loggia (Fig. 455) he has been more free to strike out in a new line, and he has done so with success. The plain pillars without capitals or bases and the simply worked stones of the arch show his usual keen appreciation of the value of material. The local granite is a somewhat refractory material, and does not lend itself readily to being moulded. An illustration at the end of the introductory chapter shows in the treatment of corbel and mullion the maximum of detail which is permissible and effective. In the loggia Mr. Lutyens has been content with far less, and the design loses nothing by its greater austerity.

One of the most interesting alterations within the house was concerned with the hall fireplace. The hall had been furnished with a new plaster ceiling frieze early in the nineteenth century, and, as can be seen at the top corner of Fig. 456, the detail was conceived in the least attractive kind of early nineteenth century gothic. When the recent alterations were being made, and the fireplace of the same period was taken down, the early stone arch, which appears in the illustration, was uncovered. The old mantelpiece, saved from the wreck of Killester House, on the Howth Estate, was fixed here. The space between its entablature and the fire arch has been utilised in delightful fashion for a wind dial, such as we have already seen at Whalton Manor and Nashdom. The rest of the space has been occupied by a map of the estate, including the neighbouring sea, which gave Mr. Macdonald Gill the opportunity to paint some pleasantly archaic galleons. Other internal work of interest is the new panelling of the library and the conversion of three rooms into a spacious dining-room. A less usual piece of interior treatment, namely, the conversion of some ordinary rooms into a private chapel, is illustrated in Fig. 457. The rooms of two storeys at the end of the east wing were taken for this purpose, and the first floor removed in order to give a lofty and dignified interior. The walls are painted white, and the barrel-vaulted ceiling a dark cloudy blue. The chapel has an apsidal end covered by a half dome.

FIG. 457.—HOWTH CASTLE : INTERIOR OF CHAPEL.

CHAPTER XXI.

FOLLY FARM.

FIRST ADDITIONS, 1901. SECOND ADDITIONS, 1912.

FOLLY FARM has so enchanting a name that it prepares us for a building of unusual charm. Farm, too, is not merely a pretty word, but tells of the use the place served for many generations. Sulhampstead is buried in typical rich Berkshire lands a couple of miles south of Theale ; and while the new parts of the house are set in a new garden, there are old orchard trees which bring into the picture an air of maturity and long well-being. The house and garden, as they appear in the accompanying pictures, are the outcome of two additions, both made by Mr. Lutyens, one in 1906 and the other and larger in 1912. Folly Farm may first be described as it was left after the enlargement of 1906. Its plans at that stage are shown in Fig. 459, and the extent of the building by the photographs reproduced in Figs. 458 to 464. The original farmhouse was little more than a cottage, and was represented in the 1906 house by the kitchen offices, barn and store. The wing then added appears in Fig. 460. The house stands close to the road, but a forecourt, with

FIG. 458.—WING OF 1906 FROM SOUTH-WEST.

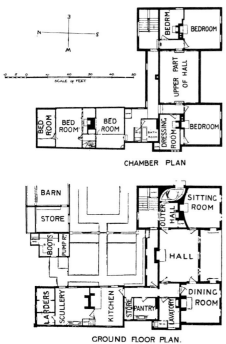

CHAMBER PLAN

GROUND FLOOR PLAN.

FIG. 459.—PLANS AS ENLARGED 1906.

FIG. 460.—FROM THE SOUTH, BEFORE THE 1912 ADDITIONS.

FIG. 461.—FORECOURT WALL AND 1906 WING
FROM EAST.

FIG. 462.—ENTRANCE GATE FROM ROAD.

its wall pierced by a round-headed arch, gives privacy (Fig. 462). When the passer-by sees the east side framed in the entrance arch (Fig. 463), no more is revealed than the front door with a single window above it, an architectural reticence very well conceived. The walls which

FIG. 463.—ENTRANCE FRONT THROUGH GATEWAY.

FIG. 464.—SOUTH-WEST CORNER OF 1906 WING.

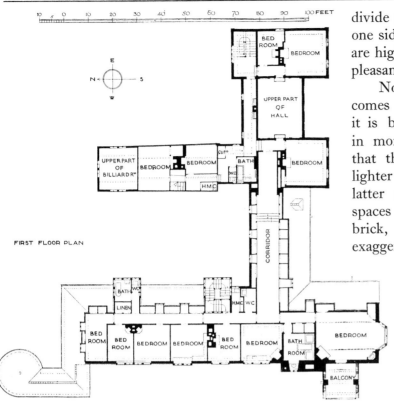

FIRST FLOOR PLAN

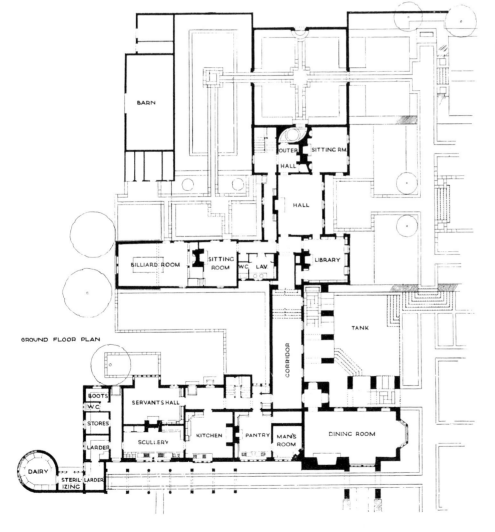

GROUND FLOOR PLAN

FIG. 465.—GROUND AND FIRST FLOOR PLANS.

divide the forecourt from the garden on one side and the stable-yard on the other are high and solid, with tiled copings of pleasant pitch.

No little of the quality of this wing comes from the unusual bricks of which it is built. Unfortunately, photographs in monochrome can tell no more than that the greater part of the walling is lighter in colour than the quoins. The latter are a strong red, but the main spaces are of a soft blue-grey Reading brick, with a surface which (it is no exaggeration to say it) suggests by its softness of tone the bloom on a peach. The beautiful wall-texture throughout is made possible largely by the small size of the bricks themselves.

The plan of the 1906 wing of Folly Farm is very straight-forward. The living-rooms were grouped round a main hall, which runs up two storeys (Fig. 474). At each end are engaging little balconies, opening from the first-floor corridors. The colour treatment is charac-teristically daring, even dramatic, but altogether successful. The walls are a dull black, the balconies Venetian red and the general woodwork and ceiling white. Facing the windows is a fine open fireplace. The sight of it makes one rather irritable with the vain imagin-ings of those folk who want to warm us and to cook for us wholly by electricity, or in some other ingenious fashion, and speak urgently of the wickedness of open fires. For radiators and other auxiliaries in a great cause one may have a respectful affection, and yet believe, with *Henry Ryecroft,* that "a fire is a delightful thing, a companion and an inspiration." There is a large common-sense in what is written in *The Private Papers:* "They tell me we are burning all our coal, and with wicked wastefulness. I am sorry for it, but I cannot on that account make cheerless perhaps the last winter of my life. . . . Use common-sense, by all means, in the construction of grates; that more than one half the heat of the kindly coal should be blown up the chimney is desired by no one; but hold

FIG. 466.—DINING-ROOM LOGGIA AND TANK.

by the open fire as you hold by whatever else is best in England. Because, in the course of nature, it will be some day a thing of the past (like most things that are worth living for), is that a reason why it should not be enjoyed as long as possible?" Most people who are not hypnotised by the desire to order their lives on scientific lines will cordially agree with

FIG. 467.—UNDER THE LOGGIA.

FIG. 468.—SOUTH SIDE: 1906 WING AT END OF LONG CANAL. 1912 WING ON THE LEFT.

FIG. 469.—WEST FRONT: SEEN ACROSS SUNK POOL GARDEN.

FIG. 470.—BALCONY AND DINING-ROOM BAY FROM THE SOUTH.

FIG. 471.—BALCONY FROM THE WEST.

the essayist that nothing can be the same (assuming we have imagination) as a beautiful core of glowing fuel. There may be added, however, a word of practical warning from the same source, especially as so many country cottages are built with big open hearths. " I tried fires of wood, having had my hearth arranged for the purpose, but that was a mistake. One cannot burn logs successfully in a small room ; either the fire being kept moderate, needs constant attention, or its triumphant blaze makes the room too hot."

George Gissing might have made his Ryecroft add a word about the smoke of wood fires in a little room. Even if the chimney works well and cannot be accused of smoking in the ordinary sense, a wood fire to which a new log has been added will nearly always throw out little whorls of smoke that eddy into the room. I have lively memories of a week-end at a little old country cottage, its low - beamed parlour gay with a wood fire. It was impossible to detect the smoke escaping into the room ; but escape it did, and its scent, half sweet, half pungent, and the slight blue haze through which the carven caryatides of the mantel-piece leered and quivered, were hardly compensation enough for red and smarting eyes. A wood fire for a large room —like that at Folly Farm— yes ; but in a low and little one, it is doubtful if the discomfort will not outweigh the pleasant elements. After this digression I must return to the great changes made in the building and the garden in 1912 for a new owner. The entrance forecourt and 1906 wing were left untouched, but the original cottage, which had become kitchen offices, was altered to billiard-room and sitting-room, and a large new block, with new dining-room and kitchens, was added on the west side. The house thus created and the garden near it are shown fully by plans in Fig. 465, and by photographs in Figs. 466 to 473, and 475 to 477.

It is characteristic of Mr. Lutyens' gift of unexpectedness that he should, after adding a symmetrical little house to the old cottage in 1906, make the 1912 extensions in an unsymmetrical manner. An examination of the problem shows him to have been right in his solution of it. The 1906 building as seen from the south is so complete in itself that a western wing in the same manner might have looked like a separate house instead of an addition, and its size would have destroyed the scale of the 1906 wing. As it is, the complete scheme tells its own story, and it does more. It shows that the many houses which Mr. Lutyens has built of late years in an austere Georgian manner, such as Great Maytham and The Salutation, have not lessened his skill in the use of earlier and more traditional motifs. I am inclined to feel, indeed, that in freshness of detail and ingenuity in the play of materials, he has done nothing better than the 1912 wing of Folly Farm. It bears his personal impress in a very marked way, and every detail has been perfected so fully that even the vegetable racks in the scullery are more interesting than the fittings of many a great library.

FIG. 472.—ORIGINAL COTTAGE NOW BILLIARD-ROOM.

FIG. 473.—DINING-ROOM FIREPLACE.

FIG. 474.—THE HALL.

The new west wing is connected with the 1906 house by a wide passage. On the south side of this is a loggia-like corridor with heavy brick buttresses holding up a great slope of roof. This corridor returns along the east side of the new dining-room, and half encloses a pool (Figs. 466 and 467 and a picture in Introduction). The dining-room has a bay window and the fireplace (Fig. 473) is attractively moulded. The new west staircase (Figs. 475 and 476) leads up to the principal bedrooms. The south-west room is the largest and has a delightful roofed balcony which forms so striking a feature in Figs. 470 and 471. The corner fireplace, with its shelves, is also a most interesting bit of detail, reminiscent of Wren's work at Hampton Court. Returning along the corridor to the original cottage we find that the billiard-room (Fig. 492) has been formed by carrying half of it up to the roof—a device which reveals the old timber construction.

The garden scheme has been well contrived, and water plays a large part in the design. The pool by the dining corridor has already been mentioned. To the south-west of the west wing is a sunk garden enclosed by yew hedges, not yet fully matured, and an octagonal pool with a shaped bed for heaths set in the middle (Fig. 469). Stretching southwards from the 1906

FIG. 475.—FOOT OF WEST STAIR.   FIG. 476.—HEAD OF WEST STAIR.

wing is a broad canal in which the building is happily mirrored (Fig. 468). Still further to the south is a great walled kitchen garden.

A stoutly built garden wall is a desirable thing always, not only because it is economical in the long run, through needing no repair, but because the uses to which it will be put cannot always be prophesied. If the temptation comes to have the bricks laid loosely and carelessly, there should be remembered the experience of Lady Mary Wortley Montagu. Writing to Mrs. Hewet when a girl of only twenty-two, she relates the following engaging story : " The lady has made acquaintance with me after the manner of Pyramus and Thisbe : I mean over a wall three yards high, which separates our garden from Lady Guildford's. The young ladies had found out a way to pull out two or three bricks, and so climb up and hang their chins over the wall, where we, mounted on chairs, used to have many *conversations à la dérobée* for fear of the old mother. This trade continued several days ; but fortune seldom permits long pleasures. By long standing on the wall the bricks loosened ; and one fatal morning, down drops Miss Nelly ; and to complete this misfortune, she fell into a little sink, and bruised her poor ——

self to that terrible degree, she is forced to have surgeons and plaisters **and** God knows **what,** which discovered the whole intrigue." It is to be feared that the two **centuries** which have gone since this letter was written have not greatly modified the will of the Miss Nellies to climb for sufficient cause shown, and it is a kindness, therefore, to provide walls which shall not behave thus treacherously.

FIG. 477.—CORNER FIREPLACE IN CHIEF BEDROOM.

CHAPTER XXII.

WORK AT THE HAMPSTEAD GARDEN SUBURB.

St. Jude's Church; The Free Church; The Institute; The Vicarage;
Houses in North Square.

WITH the general plan of the Hampstead Garden Suburb Mr. Lutyens had nothing to do, but the design of the Central Square, with its buildings, was entrusted to him, and the whole scheme achieves a simple dignity which makes it well worthy of examination. The rest of the suburb shows an attempt to reproduce the casual irregularities of an English village. While no one can be insensible to the charms of an old village street, winding, perhaps, round the side of a hill to secure the easiest gradient, or to the medley of jutting fronts and broken roofs that enshrine the history of a village community, these effects cannot be manufactured anew, and such an attempt is almost certain to produce a sense of affectation. It may be at once explained that the Central Square at Hampstead is not yet completed in accordance with the plan, which appears in Fig. 480, but enough has been done to indicate how admirable is the scheme. The intellectual and religious life of the new suburb is focussed in the square. The garden space is bordered on one side by the Institute, on another by St. Jude's Church, and on the third by the Free Church, while the

FIG. 478.—St. Jude's Church, the Free Church (*on left*) and the Vicarage (*on right*):
FROM THE SOUTH.

FIG. 479.—ST. JUDE'S CHURCH: A DORMER WINDOW.

fourth side is left open. Adjoining St. Jude's is the Vicarage (Fig. 493), and next to the Free Church is the Manse for its minister. To the west of the Free Church there have already been built two groups of houses, seen in Figs. 494 to 496. By the side of the road which leads north-west to existing parts of the suburb is a series of detached and grouped houses, also designed by Mr. Lutyens, which serve as an architectural connection between the Central Square and the rest of the suburb. The particular points to be noted are that the square and its surroundings are laid out strictly on axial lines, and that the site is a large plateau which commands the whole suburb. There is a subtle excellence in the principle which has governed the design both of the Established Church and the Free Church. The idea has clearly been to establish a definite relationship between these ecclesiastical buildings and the homes which surround them. Churches sometimes give the impression, by their design, that they are remote from the life of the people. At Hampstead they seem

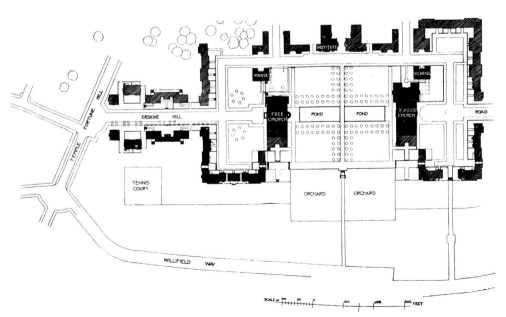

FIG. 480.—PLAN OF THE CENTRAL SQUARE.

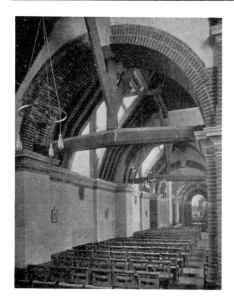

embedded in it. In the days of the Gothic Revival an attempt was made to give to houses an ecclesiastical air; the converse has been done at Hampstead. Though both churches possess a large dignity, they have a somewhat domestic character. This has been emphasised by fixing the cornice level of the churches at the same height from the ground as it is in the houses. Their monumental character is secured by the treatment of their great roofs, also by a dome in the case of the Free Church, and by the leaded spire of St. Jude's. A further note of homeliness is created by the lighting of both buildings by great dormer windows instead of by the more usual clerestory.

FIG. 481.—ST. JUDE'S: AN AISLE. FIG. 482.—ST. JUDE'S: THE PULPIT.

In general character the design of all the buildings, both secular and ecclesiastical, is based on Renaissance *motifs*. St. Jude's Church (Figs. 478 to 485) may first be described. We are impressed on entering it by the skill with which Mr. Lutyens has given to a building, with details chosen largely from domestic work of the Renaissance, something of the sense of mystery which belongs to Gothic art. Though from the outside the great roof sweeps almost to the ground, reaching down, as it were, to the stature of the houses near it, the predominant impression within

FIG. 483.—ST. JUDE'S: THE NAVE. FIG. 484.—ST. JUDE'S: ARCH TO CHAPEL.

is one of great height, for the nave arcade masks the low pitch of the aisles. Very effective is the shallow saucer dome at the crossing, its circle and the arcs of the supporting arches marked out from the prevailing whiteness by rings of vivid red brick. Both east and west ends are far from finished, and the dossal behind the altar is merely a temporary expedient, though its great height makes it extremely effective. A word must be given to the cross and candlesticks on the altar. The former is a daring design, the cross being fixed to a tall twisted pillar, while the latter are exquisitely moulded. No less successful in every way is the Lady Chapel to the north of the sanctuary. Mr. Lutyens is not, of course, responsible for the pictures which hang there. I confess I cannot bring myself to admire the timber roofs of the aisles (Fig. 481). They give me the impression of being only half thought out, and of forcing on our attention, somewhat aggressively, a rather clumsy construction.

FIG. 485.—ST. JUDE'S CHURCH: THE QUIRE.

The openings in the tower look rather large when seen from some points of view. The spire is sixteen-sided, an unusual treatment, and rests on an octagonal stage of brickwork

FIG. 486.—THE FREE CHURCH: NORTH-WEST SIDE.

FIG. 487.—THE DOOR.

rising from the square tower. This is an original treatment and has much to commend it. The sixteen sides
of the spire connect with the eight sides of this stage by
little broaches.

We pass now to the Free Church. Its dome, when
compared with the spire of St. Jude's, marks very aptly
the difference of spiritual outlook between the Free
Churches and the Established Church, just as Wren's
dome of St. Paul's marked the change that the English
church had undergone since the destruction of the lofty
spire of old St. Paul's. Except for this main difference,
the exteriors of the two buildings are conceived on the
same lines, and much the same details are employed.
Figs. 486 and 488 show how magnificently the elements

FIG. 488.—FREE CHURCH: NORTH-
EAST END.

of the Free Church pile up in
harmonious sequence from
ground to dome. The general
likeness of the two churches
emphasises the underlying

FIG. 489.—THE INSTITUTE: SOUTH CORNER.

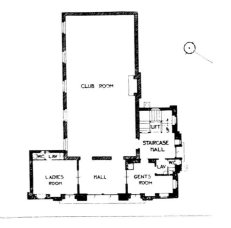

GROUND FLOOR PLAN

FIG. 490.—INSTITUTE:
GROUND FLOOR PLAN.

unity which in-
creased toleration
has brought to
light and the
improved rela-
tionship between
bodies professing
different phases of
Christianity.
There was a time,
not long past,
when differences
of creed were
thrown into relief
by differences in
the architecture
that expressed
those beliefs,
however imper-
fectly. It is a
pleasant sign of
widening charity
that the authori-
ties both of

FIG. 491.—THE INSTITUTE.

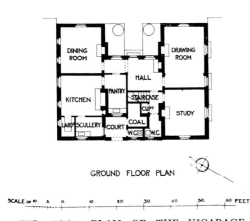

GROUND FLOOR PLAN

SCALE OF 10. 5. 0. 10. 20. 30. 40. 50. 60 FEET.

FIG. 492.—PLAN OF THE VICARAGE.

FIG. 493.—THE VICARAGE.

FIG. 494.—NORTH SQUARE FROM THE EAST.

Established and Free Churches at Hampstead agreed to come into a common architectural scheme, which thus forms a material symbol of their friendship. When we go inside the Free Church, however, the difference in outlook becomes more apparent. It is treated in altogether a simpler fashion than is St. Jude's.

The Institute, standing between the two churches but to the north-east of them, is a delightfully grave and balanced composition, made the more effective by the niches and the rich treatment of the brick pilasters. The arrangement of the ground floor is shown in Fig. 490. Most of the space is occupied by a large room for concerts, public meetings and the like. Upstairs are subsidiary rooms for various educational purposes, a library, etc.

FIG. 495. —NORTH SQUARE: FROM ERSKINE HILL.

The particular charm of this work at Hampstead is the combination of a robust austerity in the greater matters with gaiety in colour and texture. A good example of this appears in Fig. 496, showing a detail of part of the block of houses to the west of the Free Church. The niches and cornice are simple enough, but the richness of the brickwork and the happy combination of red bricks with others of a soft blue along the whole frontage gives a vitality to the whole which nothing in the Regent's Park manner can ever accomplish. It is easy, of course, to put an exaggerated value on materials and their textures. When all is said, success follows the right use of them. Among all the sounding phrases that Sir Henry Wotton wove into his discourse on architecture, there is nothing more abounding in good sense than one that bears on this question—" in truth wee want rather Art than Stuffe, to satisfie our greatest Fancies." At Hampstead we get the Art employed on the Stuff, and the result is eminently satisfying. As an example of sober and dignified town-planning, the Central Square of the suburb ought to have a good and increasing influence.

FIG. 496.—DETAIL OF HOUSE IN NORTH SQUARE.

CHAPTER XXIII.

TOWN BUILDINGS.

Houses in Westminster; Parliament Chamber, Inner Temple; Interiors at 16, Lower Berkeley Street and 28 and 15, Queen Anne's Gate; A Garden in Chelsea; St. John's Institute; "Country Life" Building; Theosophical Headquarters; Art Gallery, Johannesburg; Designs for Dublin Art Gallery.

IN the designing of town houses and office buildings a set of problems is involved altogether different from those which confront the architect of country houses. The limitations are generally severe. In most cases the frontage to the street is narrow, and the designing of the elevation is, or should be, conditioned by the adjoining fronts. For lack of some beneficent dictation in æsthetic matters, floor lines, cornice lines, and the modelling of the front, are rarely constrained within the bands of a reasonable uniformity. Everyone is free to strike a new note in a new building except in those rare cases where a ground landlord uses his powers to influence the design of a house in the right direction. It is unfortunate that his control is usually limited to ensuring that the building shall cost as large a sum of money as the leaseholder can be induced to expend.

After the Great Fire of London an ordinance was promulgated laying down rules for the "lining-up" of cornices and even for the technique of the brickwork used for window dressings and the like. It does not sound unreasonable to suggest that what was wise in the reign of Charles II would be no less valuable in our day. It is safe to say, nevertheless, that much water will run under London Bridge before ground landlords and building owners see that it is in their own interests, as well as in the interest of architectural decency, that some check shall

FIG. 497.—8, LITTLE COLLEGE STREET, AND THE CORNER HOUSE, COWLEY STREET, WESTMINSTER.

be put on the present state of individualism run mad. Meanwhile, as far as London is concerned, the chief door of hope now open is through the restraint due to that return to eighteenth century ideals, which is becoming manifest in town house design. Gothic and Tudor fancies are going out of fashion, and we are returning to a demure and balanced idea in the treatment of elevations. The houses in Westminster, shown in Figs 497 and

FIG. 498.—36, SMITH SQUARE, WESTMINSTER.

498, are good types of what Mr. Lutyens has done in this direction. The two forming one composition between Little College Street and Cowley Street (Fig. 497) are examples of

FIG. 499.—PORCH, 7, ST. JAMES'S SQUARE.

FIG. 500.—36, SMITH SQUARE: STAIRCASE.

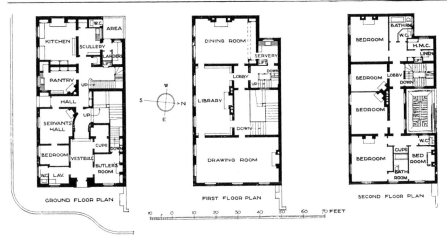

FIG. 501.—PLANS : 36, SMITH SQUARE.

FIG. 502.—36, SMITH SQUARE : VESTIBULE.

simple work in a straight-forward Georgian manner, and are built in bluish brick with some admixture of red and with an economical employment of stone for the cornices and door and window jambs on the ground floors. The general treatment is the most practical for London, as there are no delicate carvings to get blurred and choked with soot. Although the Little College Street block is six storeys in height, the provision of the two top floors as practicable and well-lit attics prevents an appearance of undue height and gives a roof of interesting outline. The plans of 36, Smith Square (Fig. 501) show a very interesting treatment of the corner site. The entrance door opens on a simply treated hall, and the staircase is an attractive feature with its stone walls and admirable iron handrail. Another brick house in the same manner is 7, St. James's Square, the stone porch of which appears in Fig. 499.

Among the interiors of old buildings in London remodelled by Mr. Lutyens must be described the work done at the Inner Temple. It consisted of altering the Parliament Chamber

FIG. 503.—PARLIAMENT CHAMBER, INNER TEMPLE.   FIG. 504.—A FIREPLACE.

FIGS. 505 AND 506.—THE LIBRARY AT 16, LOWER BERKELEY STREET.

by panelling it throughout anew, and by providing new fire places (Figs. 503 and 504). The bay window in the nineteenth century Tudor manner (which was already there) does not improve the shape of that side of the room, but the new oak panelling, which is conceived in the

FIG. 507.—LIBRARY AT 28, QUEEN ANNE'S GATE.

FIG. 508.—APSIDAL END OF DINING-ROOM: 15, QUEEN ANNE'S GATE.

spirit of the work of Charles I's reign, is simple and dignified. At the same time very satisfactory work was done in the Benchers' Reading Room. This was panelled in 1705, and some carvings, said to be by Grinling Gibbons, adorned the overmantel. Some time in the last century the panel or picture below the carving was taken out, and a mirror substituted. Mirrors also filled some of the panel openings on the wall facing the windows. These unsightly additions were removed, oak panels took their place, and the varnish which disfigured the whole room has been cleaned off.

Figs. 505 to 508 show various rooms in old London houses rearranged and decorated by Mr. Lutyens. The Library at 16, Lower Berkeley Street (Figs. 505 and 506) is attractive. It is panelled in bass-wood left untouched from the tool, and on the plain wooden filling above the books on one side of the room are three charming pictures of amorini, painted by Mr. T. M. Rooke. The long panel in the middle shows them playing among the flowers, while in the octagonal panels at the sides they act as supporters of coats-of-arms. The feeling of the room is at once graceful and scholarly. Not unlike it, but with books playing a more solid part in the wall treatment,

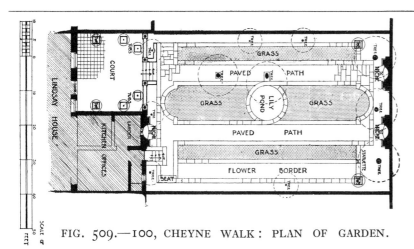

FIG. 509.—100, CHEYNE WALK : PLAN OF GARDEN.

is Viscount Haldane's library at 28, Queen Anne's Gate (Fig. 507). The panelling and bookcases here are of untreated cedar, which still sheds its thin fragrance.

Fig. 508 shows a good example of the remodelling of a room to suit a notable piece of furniture. Mr. Edward Hudson acquired a fine sideboard of Sheraton type, which had obviously been made to suit

the apsidal end of some late eighteenth century dining-room such as Robert Adam liked to design. When the planning of the reception-rooms at 15, Queen Anne's Gate was revised by Mr. Lutyens, he made an apse in the dining-room to suit the sideboard, with what pleasant results Fig. 508 shows.

Opportunities to design town gardens do not come often, but the garden at 100, Cheyne Walk, Chelsea, is a good example of what may be done in a limited space (Figs. 509 to 511). It is divided from the space at the back of the house by a simple colonnade of stone. Fortunately, there existed two fine trees, one a mulberry of noble growth, and these make brave features. A sense of length is given to the garden by the wide parallel stone paths, the middle one of which is interrupted by a round pool. At the far end the old, uninteresting wall has been transformed by the building

FIG. 510.—100, CHEYNE WALK, CHELSEA : THE SCREEN.

FIG. 511.—POOL AND STATUES.

of two niches, which shelter statues in the classical manner. Reference to the plan (Fig. 509) shows a practical point in the provision of a narrow flagged path up the east side, which gives access to the flower-beds on either side. The whole scheme is simple and unlaboured. Too often the makers of town gardens try to make up for the absence of a fine show of plants by an excess of sculpture, which raises visions of a monument mason's yard. Mr. Lutyens has shown a wise restraint, and the garden has a refined classical flavour without being stiff. When

FIG. 513.—" COUNTRY LIFE " BUILDING :
VESTIBULE.

FIG. 512.—" COUNTRY LIFE " BUILDING :
COVENT GARDEN.

the borders are furnished at their proper seasons with such things as arabis, spreading its bloom and leafage over the paving, and later with carnations that will bring their brilliant array of colour, the garden will be complete.

St. John's Institute in Tufton Street, Westminster, occupies a modest site in a narrow street, and is of so delightful a character that it is unfortunate it cannot be better seen. Fig. 514, however, gives a fairly good idea of the stately character with which Mr. Lutyens has invested this simple front.

FIG. 514.—ST. JOHN'S INSTITUTE, TUFTON
STREET, S.W.

FIG. 515.—"COUNTRY LIFE" BUILDING, COVENT GARDEN: ENTRANCE DOOR.

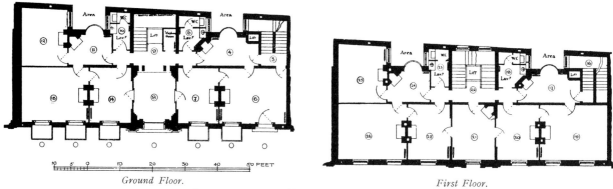

FIG. 516.—PLANS OF "COUNTRY LIFE" BUILDING.

Of office buildings Mr. Lutyens has not done many, but there is a house on the east side of Kingsway, now partly occupied by the Women's Social and Political Union, which gives interest to a street otherwise rather disappointing. No attempt has been made, however, to deal with the great difficulties involved in providing a shop front. In the interests of London street architecture it may be regretted that Mr. Lutyens was not called upon to try a solution of this difficult problem.

The offices of COUNTRY LIFE in Tavistock Street, Covent Garden, are generally held to be a more successful, if less monumental, treatment of a street front. It is unfortunate that no photograph can do it justice owing to the high palisading of the Foreign Flower Market, which is immediately

FIG. 517.—HEADQUARTERS, THEOSOPHICAL SOCIETY, TAVISTOCK SQUARE.

FIG. 518.—THE ART GALLERY, JOHANNESBURG.

opposite and is seen in the photograph reproduced in Fig. 512. The plan of the building provides rooms of a moderate height on the ground floor, and a low mezzanine storey above it, with windows curved at the heads and sills. On the first floor are the principal editorial offices, which consist of a suite of five lofty rooms with very tall sash windows facing the street. Above it is another suite of comparatively low rooms, and the big attic is occupied by printing offices, which are lit from the back. As the plans reproduced in Fig. 516 show, the problems of planning were considerably complicated by the small depth of the site, but the most has been made of the possible floor areas, consistent with the air of dignity which the proprietors of COUNTRY LIFE wished to give to the home of the paper.

Among the public buildings now being erected to Mr. Lutyens' designs is the Johannesburg Art Gallery, of which no photographs are yet available. It is therefore shown only by a

FIG. 519.—ONE OF THE DESIGNS FOR DUBLIN ART GALLERY.

perspective drawing (Fig. 518), which indicates its sober classical character. Even more interesting is the drawing of the Tavistock Square front of the fine building Mr. Lutyens has designed for the Theosophical Society (Fig. 517). The architect shows himself wholly untouched by the prevailing fashion for Neo-grec proportion and detail. He seems to take his stand on the broad traditions of Wren. The drawing reveals only the two five-storeyed blocks that flank the small entrance court and the dignified tower with its domed lantern, the archway in which gives access to the Cour d'Honneur. This quadrangle gives the scheme a collegiate character, and its building will be awaited with the liveliest interest.

A melancholy interest attaches to the designs shown in Figs. 519 and 520. Sir Hugh Lane offered to the City Corporation of Dublin a fine collection of pictures which was to form the nucleus of a great Art Gallery. He made the condition that the building to house them should

FIG. 520.—BRIDGE DESIGN FOR DUBLIN ART GALLERY.

be designed by Mr. Lutyens. Two schemes were prepared, of which the finer provided that the gallery should be built across the River Liffey. Sir Hugh Lane rightly felt that this was so much the more striking that his offer took the form of " No bridge, no pictures ! " The Corporation was divided on the question, and a strong local opposition was raised against the bridge site. Dublin feared to follow the example of Florence, where the Uffizzi and Pitti Palaces are connected by a gallery built on the bridge crossing the Arno. Mr. Lutyens' plan was like the letter H. The down strokes represent two main galleries, one on either quay, and the cross stroke a minor connecting gallery surmounted by a colonnaded footbridge. The suggested site is now occupied by a metal footbridge of peculiar ugliness. Cost presented no difficulty. Powers already existed to provide £22,000 from the municipal purse, a Citizens' Committee guaranteed £14,000, and Sir Hugh Lane promised to find anything needed above £43,000. The citizens could not, therefore, say that they were accepting an unknown liability. Dublin, however, was blind to the fine character of the design, which would have been an extraordinary addition to the amenities of the city at a point where it was most wanted. The Corporation vetoed the scheme. The citizens of Dublin have lost, therefore, not only a noble and monumental piece of architecture but a fine collection of pictures, and it would be difficult to find moderate language in which to describe the situation.

CHAPTER XXIV.

DESIGNS FOR PUBLIC MONUMENTS.

The Rand Regiments' Memorial; Two Schemes for Edward VII Memorial on
  Piccadilly Site; Scheme for Edward VII Memorial in Trafalgar Square.

PERHAPS there is no branch of architecture in which England lags so deplorably behind the Continent as in worthy memorials to great personages in parks and squares and streets. If we walk along the Victoria Embankment, bearing with us the remembrance of what Paris has done on the banks of the Seine, the comparison becomes painfully acute. Similar reflections in Trafalgar Square, accompanied by memories of the Place de la Concorde, are also humiliating, but not less so than a contemplation of the monuments in St. James' Park when compared with the treatment of the Gardens of the Tuileries. Our grievous failure compared with French success is due in part, no doubt, to a difference in temperament. The English character does not happily consort with visions of the Grand Manner. We are so desperately afraid of being pompous that our schemes generally issue in a small banality. Much, however, is due to a difference in general attitude towards the fine arts, and to a desperate unwillingness to spend money freely and gracefully on any object which is not utilitarian. Even when a big effort is made, it is generally spoilt for lack of courage to provide the extra amount of money which would save a monument from mediocrity by the comparatively simple process of giving it adequate size. Differences of method are also, no doubt, responsible for much of the lack of spirit which informs our monumental schemes. We lack any directing authority such as is afforded in France by the Ministry of Fine Arts. The choice of designs usually rests with a committee, representative partly of official interests, and partly of the worthy people who subscribe the necessary funds. It is quite common for such a committee to number among its members no representative of the arts of architecture and sculpture, and it is consequently guided by no informed opinion beyond that of the more or less (but generally less) cultivated amateur. Another fruitful source of failure is the common practice of entrusting the monument solely to a sculptor, instead of committing the problem of producing a satisfactory design to the joint efforts of architect and sculptor. It is in no spirit of disrespect to the many sculptors of high ability whom England has produced during the last half century to point out that their training, however adequate for the purposes of their particular art, does not necessarily fit them to solve architectural problems in the best way. The right placing of public monuments with reference to their surroundings, and the use of vistas, are factors of high importance. Too often the result of their neglect is that the architectural aspect of the monument is wholly misunderstood, and the sculptured figure or group achieves an air of unrelated isolation.

These considerations help to explain why some of the designs for public monuments prepared by Mr. Lutyens have not been carried out. It would seem, however, that South Africa has a more favourable atmosphere in this respect than we enjoy in England. Fig. 521 shows a perspective sketch made by Mr. Walcot of the memorial to the Rand Regiments, which is now nearly complete. It is being raised in Eckstein Park, Johannesburg, to the memory of the men of those regiments who fell in the South African War. The site is at the intersection of two great avenues of eucalyptus trees. Its central feature is a fine pavilion with four intersecting arches, on the imposts of which are being carved the names of the men commemorated. Surmounting this dignified structure is a bronze figure of Peace. Flanking the memorial

FIG. 521.—THE RAND REGIMENTS' MEMORIAL, JOHANNESBURG.

FIGS. 522 AND 523.—EDWARD VII MEMORIAL.   FIRST SCHEME FOR PICCADILLY SITE.
Two views of the model.

itself are some minor groups of allegorical sculptures and four ponds, which have not yet been made for lack of funds.   It may be hoped that the promoters of the memorial will not lose interest in the scheme, and leave these very necessary accessories undone.

The history of the memorial to King Edward VII is more typically English.   The commission for the monument was entrusted to Mr. Lutyens as architect, and to Mr. Bertram MacKennal as sculptor.   The first scheme which they devised provided for a stately monument to be set at the Piccadilly end of the Broad Walk, which leads up from the forecourt of Buckingham Palace. Figs. 522 and 523 reproduce photographs of the model which was prepared for the Memorial Committee.   The great colonnaded screen was to have been of

FIG. 524.—EDWARD VII MEMORIAL.   FIRST SCHEME FOR PICCADILLY SITE.

Portland stone, with a statue of King Edward on the south side looking towards Buckingham Palace. This screen would have been over one hundred feet long, and set back from Piccadilly far enough to leave a square space to be enclosed by trees and furnished with seats. Had this design been carried out, its fine architectural character would have done something to take away the reproach which lies on the English attitude to monumental design. It proved, however, to be too strong meat for the committee, and Mr. Lutyens was requested to make a fresh design on lines more in accordance with the habitual treatment of such things.

Figs. 525 and 526 show photographs of the model next prepared. Mr. MacKennal's statue of the King was practically the same as in the earlier scheme, and was to have been placed facing

FIGS. 525 AND 526.—EDWARD VII. MEMORIAL. SECOND SCHEME FOR PICCADILLY SITE.
Two views of model.

Buckingham Palace. On the Piccadilly side an allegorical group, representing "Arbitration Quelling Strife," was to have been set, and the monument included figures on either side representing Peace and the Hospitals, with St. George and the Dragon on the summit. Regarded merely as a base for statues the design has large merit, but it is, of course, lacking in the large and unusual character which Mr. Lutyens gave to the earlier design. Public opinion, however, with its curious terror of fine architecture, regarded the smaller alternative with little more favour than the first scheme, and King George, naturally anxious that the monument to his father should not be a cause of contention, intimated to the committee his readiness that the Piccadilly site in Green Park should not be used for the purpose. It is now proposed that a statue, with a very modest pedestal, shall be placed in the space between the top of the Duke

FIG. 527.—TRAFALGAR SQUARE SCHEME: ELEVATIONS.

of York's Steps and the bottom of Waterloo Place, an arrangement which closes a story very typical of the results obtained by the committee system.

At the time when various projects were put forward for placing the King's memorial on a more public site, Mr. Lutyens was privately commissioned to prepare, for the consideration of

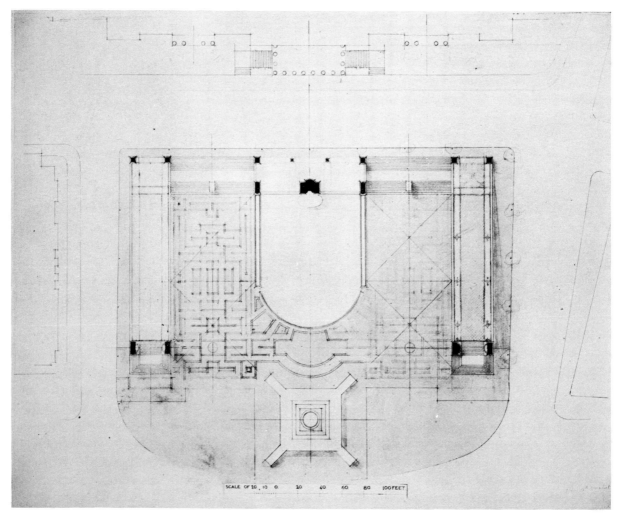

FIG. 528.—TRAFALGAR SQUARE SCHEME: PLAN.

the Committee, a scheme for remodelling Trafalgar Square, and for placing the King's statue on the north side of it, facing the Nelson column. The square owes its present shape to Sir Charles Barry, but the warmest admirer of that great architect cannot regard his work there as being among his more notable achievements. The design illustrated in Figs. 527 to 529 shows that Mr. Lutyens proposed to substitute, for the present high retaining wall next the National Gallery on the north side of the square, a great flight of steps, broken in the middle by the statue of the King, with its attendant sculptures, and in front of it a large fountain. On the east and west sides of the square two great bastions were to be formed, with their pavements at the level of the north roadway of the square, and finishing at their southern end with big stairways leading down to the present level of the south side. The existing statues were to have been rearranged, as shown in Fig. 527. The design has a fine monumental character, and would not have prejudiced the use of the square for public meetings. Indeed, the removal of the present pools and the substitution for them of one big pool at the foot of the King's statue would have left a more convenient and unimpeded space than now exists. The design did not find favour, and, indeed, would have been costly, but it is worthy of study.

FIG. 529.—SCHEME FOR PLACING EDWARD VII. MEMORIAL IN TRAFALGAR SQUARE.

CHAPTER XXV.

EXHIBITION BUILDINGS.

Paris, 1900 ; Rome, 1911 ; " Shakespeare's England," 1912.

EXHIBITION buildings are generally of a very unsubstantial and fleeting nature, and represent little of architectural interest. When good, however, they are of enough importance to be recorded among the other works of an architect, because they exercise an educational influence on the crowds which flock to them. The first work of this kind undertaken by Mr. Lutyens was the English Pavilion at the Paris Exhibition of 1900. He reproduced in the Rue des Nations on the banks of the Seine a typical English manor house of the early part of the seventeenth century, Kingston House, Bradford-on-Avon, and

nothing could have been more appropriate. It had the great advantage (not shared by any other replicas of national buildings at Paris) that the house was reproduced full size instead of to some smaller scale. As Mr. Frederick Harrison wrote at the time: " It is the best and most truly artistic in the whole of the street of nations, the only one, indeed, that a man of taste could view without a smile or a groan." It is enough to reproduce a photograph of the exterior of the pavilion as it was seen from the banks of the Seine (Fig. 530). The interiors were reproductions of various historical examples. The drawing-room, for instance, had a ceiling taken from the famous example at Broughton Castle, and the moulds for it were provided by the Victoria and Albert Museum. The chimney-piece was reproduced

FIG. 530.—PARIS EXHIBITION
OF 1900.

from the Cartoon Gallery at Knole Park (Fig. 532). The doorway to the saloon, with strapwork decoration on its flanking pilasters, is also a good example of Elizabethan treatment.

Rome, 1911.

The International Exhibition promoted by Italy in 1911 was in two parts: The industrial

FIG. 531.—PARIS EXHIBITION OF 1900 : SOUTH BEDROOM.

FIG. 532.—PARIS EXHIBITION OF 1903 : DRAWING-ROOM.   FIG. 533.—DOORWAY TO SALOON.

sections were assembled in Turin, and those devoted to the fine arts at Rome. The designing of the English Pavilion at Rome was entrusted to Mr. Lutyens, and a somewhat heavy responsibility lay on him to devise something that should be rightly typical of the Mistress Art in England. The domestic character of the British Pavilion at the Paris Exhibition of 1900 was obviously not the right note for Rome, where some more majestic motive seemed to be needed. It was desirable that the Rome building should follow in its character some representative historical example of English work. I believe that consideration was given in this connection to Hengrave Hall, and also to Dance's magnificent work, Newgate Prison, now destroyed. The latter would have been in many respects ideal, for it was a work of genius. Certainly no building in England was so directly due to the inspiration of Rome, for Dance caught with peculiar exactness the feeling that we take from Piranesi's famous drawings. Finally, however, it was decided that the design in its basis should do honour to the commanding genius of Sir Christopher Wren. Figs. 534 to 537 show that Mr. Lutyens went direct to Wren's masterpiece, St. Paul's Cathedral. Despite the fact that the British Pavilion was thus reminiscent of our greatest architect—and rightly so—it was none the less an original design, and a most interesting exercise in the

FIG. 534.—ROME EXHIBITION OF 1911 : THE MAIN FACADE.

Grand Manner. Incidentally, it served as a charming acknowledgment made by modern English architecture of the debt that we owe to the " Eternal City." In Wren's judgment he could claim no higher meed of praise for his own work than that it was designed and built in the Roman manner. While posterity recognises that it was by Wren's original genius that the elements of Roman building were rearranged to form compositions intrinsically English, the fact of the inspiration remains, and Mr. Lutyens could certainly have done nothing better than return to the original source of inspiration for a British building in Rome. Charm was added to the dignified front by the two interesting groups of figures modelled by Sir Thomas Brock, R.A. (Figs. 536 and 537). As planned

FIG. 535.—ROME, 1911 : THE PORTICO.

FIG. 536.—ROME, 1911.

FIG. 537.—ROME, 1911.

FIG. 538.—STREET WITH HOLBORN BARS (*on the right*).

FIG. 539.—COURTYARD OF FORD'S HOSPITAL, COVENTRY.

for its purpose as an exhibition pavilion the building comprised twelve galleries. It is now being remodelled to serve as the home of the British School at Rome, an institution devoted to advanced studies in the Fine Arts and Archæology. The rearrangement of the building provides rooms for lectures and exhibitions, a library and map-room, and studios for the holders of the scholarships instituted by the Royal Commission of the 1851 Exhibition and other public bodies. The main front has been reproduced in durable

FIG. 540.—STREET LEADING TO THE GLOBE THEATRE.

FIG. 541.—FORD'S HOSPITAL (*on left*) AND FOUNTAIN OF TRINITY COLLEGE, CAMBRIDGE.

FIG. 542.—ASHBY ST. LEDGERS; MARKET HALL,
LEDBURY; PORCH HOUSE, POTTERNE; DIXTER.

FIG. 543.—A PRIEST'S HOUSE AT END
OF STREET.

materials, and will form a striking example in Rome of the high standard of modern English
civil architecture.

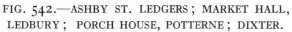

" SHAKESPEARE'S ENGLAND," 1912.

The most recent of Mr. Lutyens' adventures in the field of reconstituting ancient architecture
was at the Exhibition of Shakespeare's England at Earl's Court in 1912.   In this case the

FIG. 544.—TOWN GATE AND HARBOUR
WITH STERN OF " REVENGE."

FIG. 545.—ST. JOHN'S COLLEGE, OXFORD (*in foreground*) AND THE GUILDHALL, EXETER (*beyond*).

limiting conditions of the site and of the permanent roofs under which some of the buildings had to be set up prevented the houses being built to their full scale, but as this reduction was observed uniformly throughout, the street pictures secured by ingenious planning were very convincing. Under the series of eight illustrations reproduced here (Figs. 538 to 545) are noted the names of the historical buildings, which, in some instances, were copied. The absence of such names indicates that the picturesque effects were the outcome of more or less original design. One of the most effective and picturesque corners was the harbour in which was moored the replica of that gallant ship, the *Revenge*. The design of the ship itself was due to the collaboration of Mr. Seymour Lucas, R.A., with Mr. Lutyens. The regrettable feature of such exhibitions is that usually they vanish away and leave not a wrack behind. Some day, perhaps, a permanent Folk Museum will be established in England on a site large enough to allow old buildings, that must be moved from their original sites, to be set up again and recall street scenes which have passed from our ken for ever.

CHAPTER XXVI.

DESIGNS FOR FURNITURE.

REFERENCE has been made in some of the preceding chapters to furniture designed for various houses, and particularly in Chapter XIII to the fitted furniture at Heathcote. It seems desirable, however, to illustrate a few pieces separately in order to emphasise the importance which is now rightly attached to the investment of furniture design with architectural quality. Among the problems which confront a furniture designer none is more serious than that presented by the grand piano. The tendency of late years has

FIG. 546.—AT MARSHCOURT.

FIG. 547.—MADE FOR PARIS EXHIBITION OF 1900.

been to shorten the length of the case, and this has only added to the difficulty of giving a seemly shape to the instrument. Mr. Halsey Ricardo has said that " it has the size without the handiness of an African elephant, and the elegance of a mammoth toad." This is due in part to the practice which prevailed throughout the nineteenth century of fitting the great case with three fat and unconnected legs. As long ago as 1900 Mr. Lutyens made an interesting essay in the return to the type of design employed for the harpsichord. That instrument was usually treated as a separate box raised upon an underframe, the legs of which were connected by rails and stretchers. Fig. 547 which shows the instrument made for the Paris Exhibition, indicates how successfully this idea has been carried out, but in one respect the piano follows modern practice. The legs are framed directly into the case, instead of forming a separate structure upon which the case rests. For a smaller piano at Marshcourt a simpler case was designed with detail of a rather more classical character (Fig. 546). These two examples have shown a better way, and have not been without their influence on the stock patterns now produced by manufacturers on a commercial scale. We may be grateful for this, because the type with bulbous turned legs, which held full sway for about a century, was as bad a solution of a difficult problem as could have been devised.

Among other pieces of furniture which have felt the influence of the period of William and Mary is the four-post bedstead with more or less elaborate upholstery. Two

FIG. 548.—UPHOLSTERED BED AT GREAT MAYTHAM.

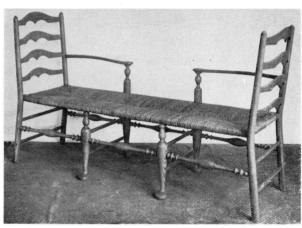

FIG. 550.—RUSH-BOTTOMED CHAIR.

FIG. 552.—A GARDEN SEAT.

examples are shown in Figs. 548 and 549. The former was made for Great Maytham, and shows a very interesting treatment of the valance, which is carried in one piece along the top of the window opening and round the bedstead. The design of the bedstead is thus tied to the general scheme of the room. Fig. 549 shows a bed at Temple Dinsley, which has a more elaborate cornice treatment, and the upper frame on the long side of the bed is arched. Two seats are illustrated, one (Fig. 550) in bent ash with

FIG. 549.—AT TEMPLE DINSLEY.

FIG. 551.—A BOOKCASE.

a rush bottom, and the other (Fig. 552) a garden seat of simple outline. Fig. 551 shows a painted bookcase with glass doors, the glazing bars of which are of admirable thickness. For buildings of a Tudor type Mr. Lutyens has designed several simple and stout oak tables, of which Fig. 553 shows a satisfactory example.

FIG. 553.—OAK TABLE.

FIG. 554.—TABLE WITH CABRIOLE LEGS.

More interesting, however, is the dining-table at Lindisfarne Castle, Holy Island, with four baluster legs, of which detail drawings to the scale of one inch to the foot are given in Fig. 558. Figs. 555 and 556 show two other

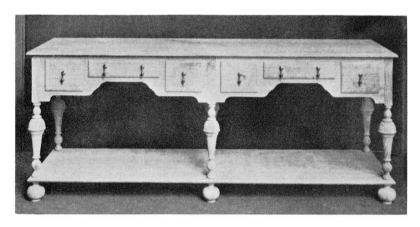

FIG. 555.—A SIDE TABLE.

FIG. 556.—A WRITING TABLE.

types of table, which rely successfully on the delicacy of their turned legs for a marked freshness and vitality of treatment. Of more definitely classical type is the little table shown in Fig. 554 with cabriole legs and shell patterns carved on the knees.

The outdoor bracket clock (Fig. 557) which is to be seen in Southampton Street, Strand, is a delightful echo of the street clocks of the early eighteenth century, of which some good examples are still to be seen in the City of London. Mr. Lutyens is usually very sparing of carved ornament, but in this case he has used it freely. The general impression which one takes from a survey of these designs is of a rigid adherence to the spirit of traditional work combined with such personal variation in mouldings as are enough to proclaim the modern provenance of the furniture. We are too prone to be satisfied with lifeless copies of antique pieces, as though the last word had been said on the subject of furniture design.

That such an attitude is unreasonable is shown clearly enough, not only by the work now illustrated, but by the admirable pieces made by such craftsmen as Mr. Ernest Gimson. We have gone some distance since the Exhibition of 1851, through which William Morris refused to go, finding the furniture so "wonderfully ugly." There is still room for an increase in the improvement which we owe largely to architects.

FIG. 557.—AN OUTDOOR BRACKET CLOCK.

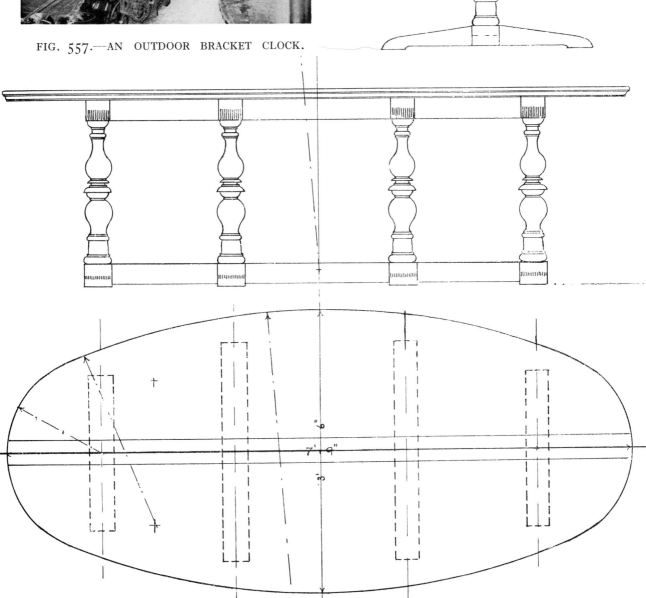

FIG. 558.—END AND SIDE ELEVATIONS AND PLAN OF OAK TABLE AT LINDISFARNE CASTLE.
Scale one inch to one foot.

LIST OF WORKS BY E. L. LUTYENS FROM 1888 TO 1913.

The buildings are given approximately in their chronological order, but definite dates are omitted because in some cases there was an interval between the preparation of designs and the beginning of the work. The works marked * are illustrated in the preceding pages.

Additions to The Corner, Thursley—*Mr. Edmund Gray.*
Cottage at Crooksbury—*Mr. A. W. Chapman.*
Cottage, Littleworth, Tongham—*Mr. H. A. Mangles.*
The Corner, Munstead—*Mr. C. D. Heatley.*
Stables at Little Tangley—*Mr. Cowley Lambert.*
*Crooksbury House—*Mr. A. W. Chapman.*
Cottages at Munstead.
Cottage at Shere (for barber's shop)—*Mr. (now Sir) Reginald Bray.*
Lodges at Park Hatch and Hoe Farm, Hascombe—*Mr. Joseph Godman.*
Chinthurst, Surrey—*Miss Guthrie.*
*Garden at Woodside, Chenies, Bucks—*Adeline, Duchess of Bedford.*
*Ruckmans, Oakwood Park—*Miss Lyell.*
Lascombe, Puttenham, Sussex—*Colonel Spencer.*
*Sullingstead—*Mr. C. A. Cook.*
Woodend, Witley—*Lady Stewart.*
Winkworth Farm—*Mrs. Lushington.*
Cottage and wheelwright's shop at Apsley End, Hemel Hempstead—*Mr. Longman.*
*Munstead Wood, Godalming—*Miss Jekyll.*
Liberal Club, Farnham.
Additions to inn at Roseneath—*Princess Louise, Duchess of Argyll.*
Burrows Cross—*Hon. Emily Lawless.*
Tower House, Mayfield—*Rev. A. Wickham.*
Berry Down, Hampshire—*Mr. Archibald Grove.*
Binfield Lodge, Newbury—*Captain Ernest Rhodes.*
Alterations to Stoke College—*The late Lord Loch.*
*Fulbrook, Surrey—*Mr. G. Streatfeild.*
House at Charterhouse, Godalming—*Rev. W. H. Evans.*
Holmwood, Dorking—*Mr. Wildman Catley.*
House at Sunningdale—*Major Crawford.*
Cottages at Milford and Thursley—*Mr. R. W. Webb.*
*Le Bois de Moutiers, Varengeville—*M. Guillaume Mallet.*
Additions to Crooksbury—*Mr. A. W. Chapman.*
*The Pleasaunce, Cromer—*The late Lord Battersea.*
*Nonconformist Chapel, Overstrand.
*Goddards—*Sir Frederick Mirrielees, Bart.*
*Orchards, Godalming—*Sir William Chance, Bart.*
*Tigbourne, Witley, Surrey—*Mr. Edgar Horne.*
*Overstrand Hall, near Cromer—*The Lord Hillingdon.*
*Littlecroft, Guildford—*Mrs. Bowes Watson.*
Alterations to 94, Eaton Place—*Mrs. Cavan Irving.*
*Royal Pavilion, Paris Exhibition of 1900.
Cottages at Knebworth—*The Earl of Lytton.*
Thursley Institute.
*Deanery Garden, Sonning—*Mr. Edward Hudson.*
*Grey Walls, Gullane—*The late Right Hon. Alfred Lyttelton.*
*Abbotswood, Gloucestershire—*Mr. Mark Fenwick.*
Lych Gate, Kelmersden, Somersetshire—*The Lord Hylton.*
*Fishers Hill, Woking—*The Right Hon. Gerald Balfour.*
*Homewood, Knebworth—*The Dowager Countess of Lytton.*
*Marshcourt, Hampshire—*Mr. Herbert Johnston.*
Gardens at Ammerdown—*The Lord Hylton.*

Additions to Rake House, Milford—*Mrs. Cavan Irving.*
Cottages, Old Basing—*Mr. Walter Hoare.*
St. Peter's Home, Ipswich—*Mr. C. Berners.*
Cottages at Thursley—*Mr. R. W. Webb.*
*Little Thakeham—*Mr. Ernest Blackburn.*
Dorking Church Room—*Miss Mayo.*
*Monkton, Singleton—*The late Mr. William James.*
Lych Gate, Shere—*Sir Reginald Bray.*
*The Hoo, Willingdon, Sussex.—*Mr. Alexander Wedderburn, K.C.*
*Ruckmans, addition of music-room—*The late Miss Lyell.*
*Sullingstead, addition of music-room—*Mr. C. A. Cook.*
Alterations and gardens at Buckhurst, Withyham, Sussex—*Mr. Robert Benson.*
*Lindisfarne Castle, Holy Island, restoration—*Mr. Edward Hudson.*
*Daneshill—*Mr. Walter Hoare.*
School at Hindhead.
*Papillon Hall, Market Harborough—*Mr. Frank Belville.*
Dalham Hall, entrance lodge—*Captain Ernest Rhodes.*
*Hestercombe Gardens and Orangery—*Hon. E. W. Portman.*
*Country Life Offices.
*Additions to Ashby Manor House—*The Lord Ashby St. Ledgers.*
Decoration of " Queen of Scots " Yacht—*Mr. George Coats.*
*St. John's Institute, Tufton Street, Westminster—*Archdeacon Wilberforce.*
*Dormy House, Walton Heath Golf Club.
*Millmead, Bramley—*Miss Jekyll.*
*New Place, Shedfield, Hants—*Mrs. Franklyn.*
*Folly Farm, first additions—*Mr. Cochrane.*
*Heathcote, Ilkley—*Mr. Hemingway.*
*Library, 28, Queen Anne's Gate—*The Viscount Haldane.*
Additions to Eartham House, Sussex—*Mr. William Bird.*
*Alterations to Copse Hill House, Gloucestershire—*Captain Harold Brassey.*
Alterations to house at Forest Row—*Miss Hale.*
Stonehouse Court, Gloucester—*Mr. A. S. Winterbotham.*
Columbaria, Wargrave.
*Barton St. Mary—*Mr. Munro Miller.*
House at Repton School—*Mr. L. A. Burd.*
Gardens at Angerton, Northumberland—*Mr. F. Straker.*
*Alterations to house at Wittersham—*The late Right Hon. Alfred Lyttelton.*
*St. Jude's Church, Hampstead.
*Middlefield, Great Shelford, Cambridge—*Mr. Henry Bond, LL.D.*
Office buildings, Kingsway, London—*Mr. William Robinson.*
*Whalton Manor House, Northumberland—*Mrs. Eustace Smith.*
Alterations at Mells Manor—*Lady Horner.*
*Lambay Castle, Ireland—*Hon. Cecil Baring.*
*Temple Dinsley, Hitchin, Herts—*Mr. H. G. Fenwick.*
*Chussex, Walton Heath—*Mr. W. H. Fowler.*
Remodelling of Knebworth House—*The Earl of Lytton.*

*Golf clubhouse and secretary's house, Knebworth.

Copse Hill Cottages, Upper Slaughter—*Captain Harold Brassey.*

*Cottages at Ashby St. Ledgers—*The Lord Ashby St. Ledgers.*

Les Communes, Varengeville—*M. Guillaume Mallet.*

*Taplow, Nashdom—*H.H. Princess Alexis Dolgorouki.*

*Great Maytham, Kent—*Mr. H. J. Tennant, M.P.*

*Houses, South Square, Hampstead Garden Suburb.

House at Tavistock—*Major Gallie.*

Gardens at Heywood, Abbeyleix, Queen's County—*Sir E. Hucheson Poë, Bart.*

Cottage at Knebworth—*Miss Plowden.*

*Additions to Howth Castle—*Mr. J. Gaisford St. Lawrence.*

Alterations and additions to Ranguin, near Grasse—*M. Guillaume Mallet.*

*Rome Exhibition Buildings, 1911.

Additions to Renishaw Hall, near Chesterfield—*Sir George Sitwell, Bart.*

Additions to Lowesby Hall, near Leicester—*Captain Harold Brassey.*

Drewsteignton, Devonshire, drive and first part of house —*Mr. J. C. Drewe.*

*St. Jude's Vicarage, Hampstead—*Rev. B. G. Bourchier.*

*Great Dixter, Northiam, Sussex—*Mr. N. Lloyd.*

Garden, White House, Balcombe—*Mrs. Hermon.*

Additions to Hanover Lodge, Regent's Park—*Admiral David Beatty.*

Alterations to 10, Connaught Place, Hyde Park—*The Lady Battersea.*

*Alterations to Goddards, Abinger Common—*Sir Frederick Mirrielees, Bart.*

Panelled room at Frankfort—*Mme. Grunelius.*

Alterations to 26A, Bryanston Square—*Hon. Cecil Baring.*

*Drawings for King Edward Memorial, Green Park (not carried out).

*The Free Church, Hampstead Garden Suburb.

*The Institute, Hampstead Garden Suburb.

*7, St. James' Square, London—*Mr. Gaspard Farrer.*

*The Salutation, Sandwich—*Mr. Gaspard Farrer.*

*Rand Regiments' Memorial, Johannesburg.

*The Art Gallery, Johannesburg—*The Corporation of Johannesburg.*

La Mascot, Holmwood, new billiard-room—*Mr. F. Pethick Lawrence.*

Coronation Ball at Albert Hall (decoration), 1911.

*" Shakespeare's England " Exhibition Buildings, Earl's Court, 1912.

*Inner Temple, panelling in Parliament Chamber and other alterations.

*100, Cheyne Walk, garden—*Sir Hugh Lane.*

Small house at Knebworth—*Mr. C. Reed.*

*36, Smith Square—*The Right Hon. R. McKenna, M.P.*

*Alteration and additions to Roehampton House—*Mr. Arthur Grenfell.*

Milton Abbot Village, Devon—*The Duke of Bedford, K.G.*

Ednaston Farm Buildings, near Derby—*Mr. W. G. Player.*

Chalfont Park, near Gerrards Cross, cottage and gardens—*Mrs. Edgar.*

*Further alterations and additions to Folly Farm, Sulhampstead—*Mr. Z. Merton.*

Additions to Renishaw Golf Club—*Sir George Sitwell, Bart.*

Additions to Barham Court, Kent—*Mr. E. Stainton.*

*Knowlton Court, near Canterbury, panelled room and lodge—*Mr. E. Speed.*

*Lindisfarne Castle, new bedrooms and entrance hall—*Mr. Edward Hudson.*

*8, Little College Street, Westminster—*The Hon. Francis McLaren, M.P.*

*The Corner House, Cowley Street, Westminster—*The Hon. Lady Norman.*

Alterations to 22, Bruton Street—*Mr. Mark Fenwick.*

*Theosophical Headquarters, Tavistock Square.

Additions to Frog's Island, Walton-on-the-Hill — *The Countess of Londesborough.*

28, Portman Square, new library—*Mr. A. Mildmay.*

Shenley Hill, Shenley, billiard-room—*Mr. S. de la Rue.*

Additions to The Deanery, Sonning, Berks—*Mr. C. W Christie-Miller.*

*The British School at Rome.

*Designs for Dublin Art Gallery.

Plans for the New City of Delhi.

APPENDIX OF SCALE DETAILS

OF

TYPICAL INTERIORS AND EXTERIORS.

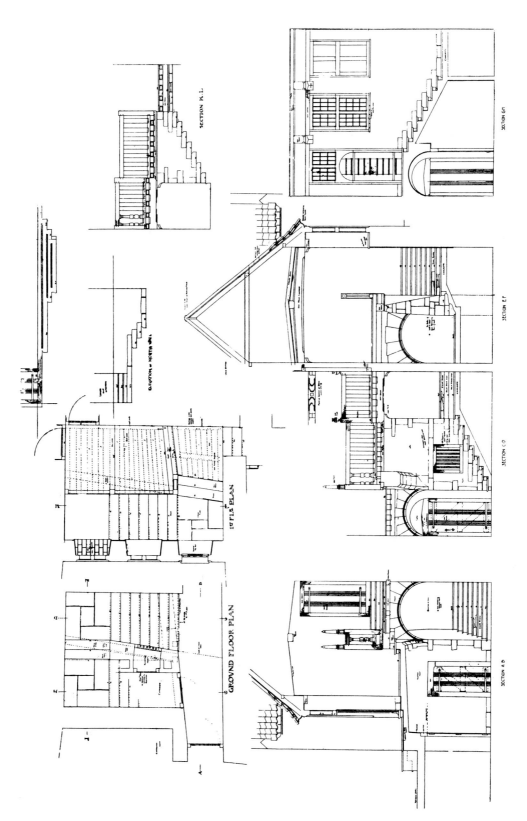

FIG. 559.—LAMBAY: DETAILS ON NEW STAIRCASE IN THE OLD BUILDING.

Scale one-eighth of an inch to one foot. A photograph of the head of this staircase is reproduced on page 218.

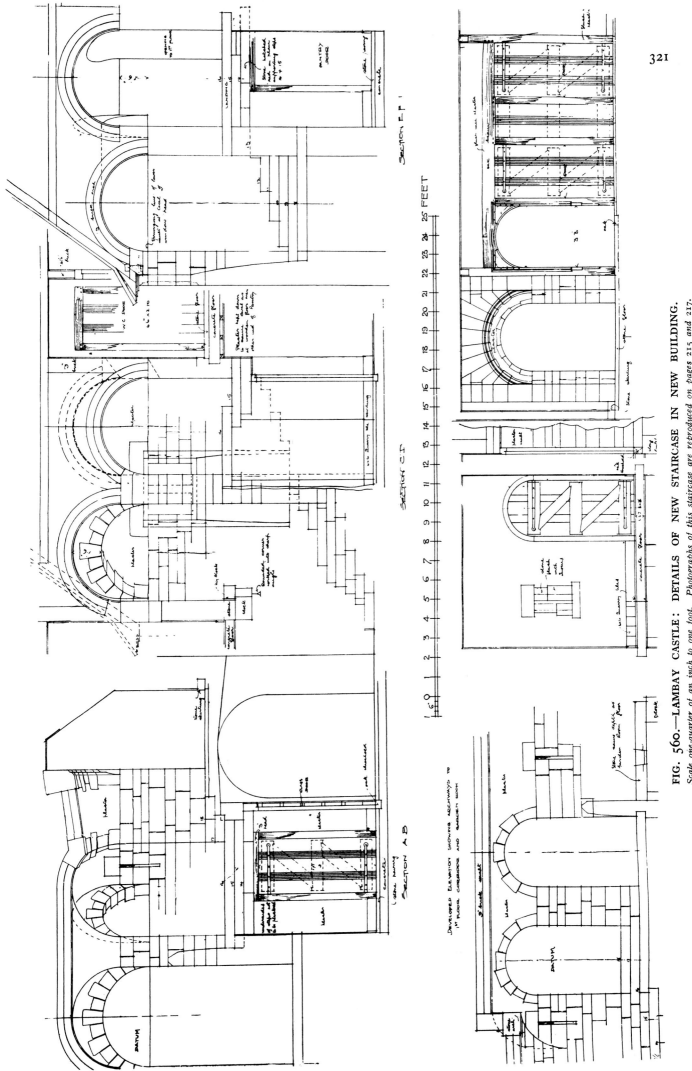

321

FIG. 560.—LAMBAY CASTLE : DETAILS OF NEW STAIRCASE IN NEW BUILDING.
Scale one-quarter of an inch to one foot. Photographs of this staircase are reproduced on pages 215 and 217.

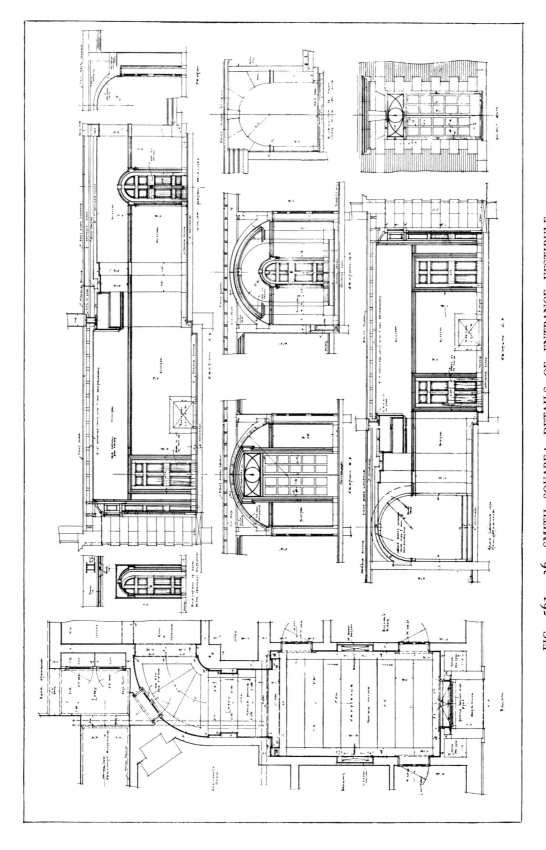

FIG. 561.—36, SMITH SQUARE : DETAILS OF ENTRANCE VESTIBULE.

Scale one-eighth of an inch to one foot. A photograph of this vestibule is reproduced on page 293.

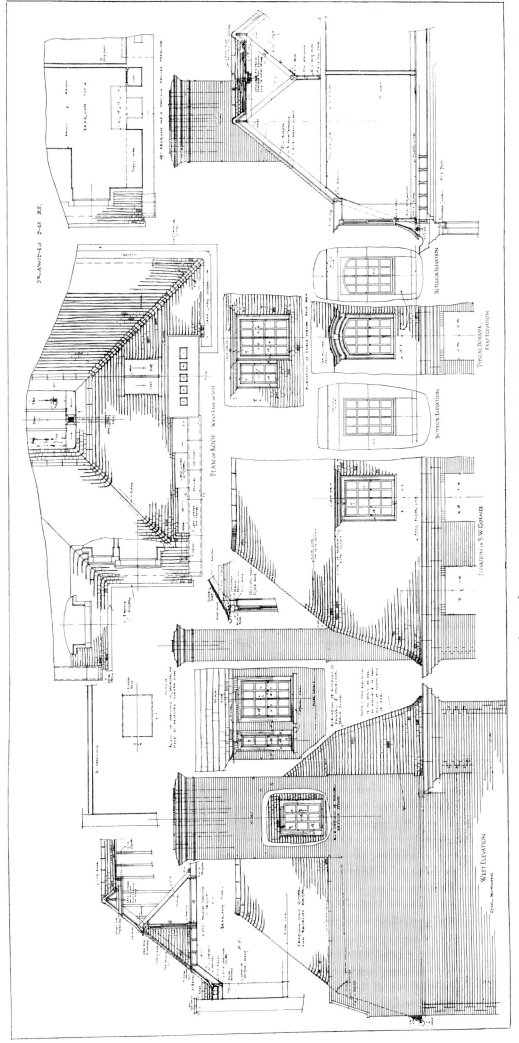

FIG. 562.—36, SMITH SQUARE: DETAILS OF ROOF.

Scale one-eighth of an inch to one foot. A photograph of this roof is reproduced on page 292.

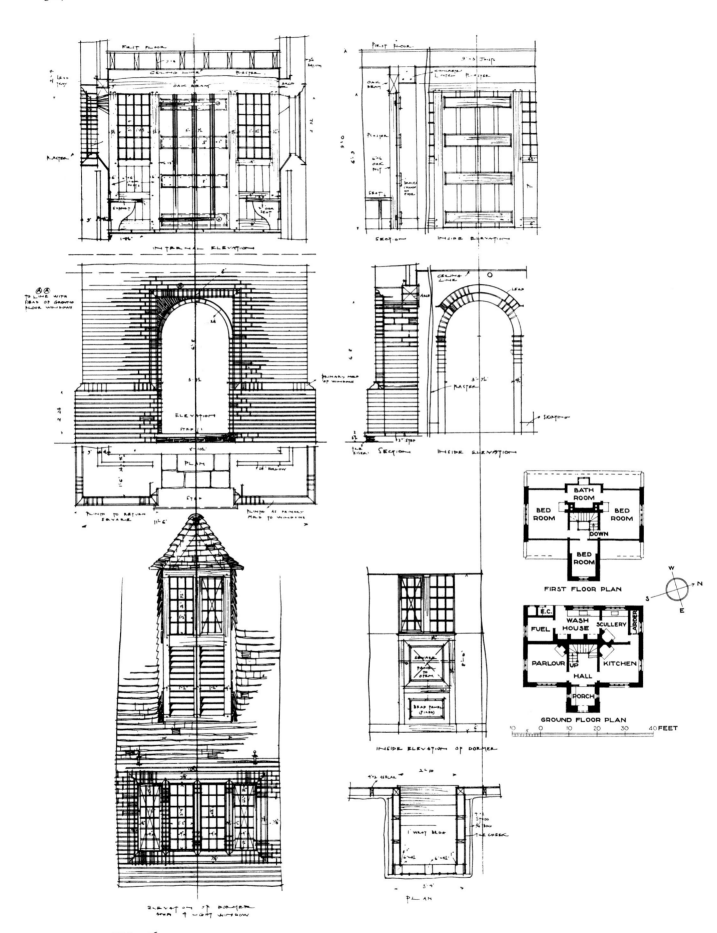

FIG. 563.—THE LODGE, KNOWLTON, CANTERBURY: DETAILS OF DORMER, ETC.

Scale one-quarter of an inch to one foot. The plans of the Lodge itself are furnished with a special scale. Photographs of this Lodge are reproduced on page xxxvii.

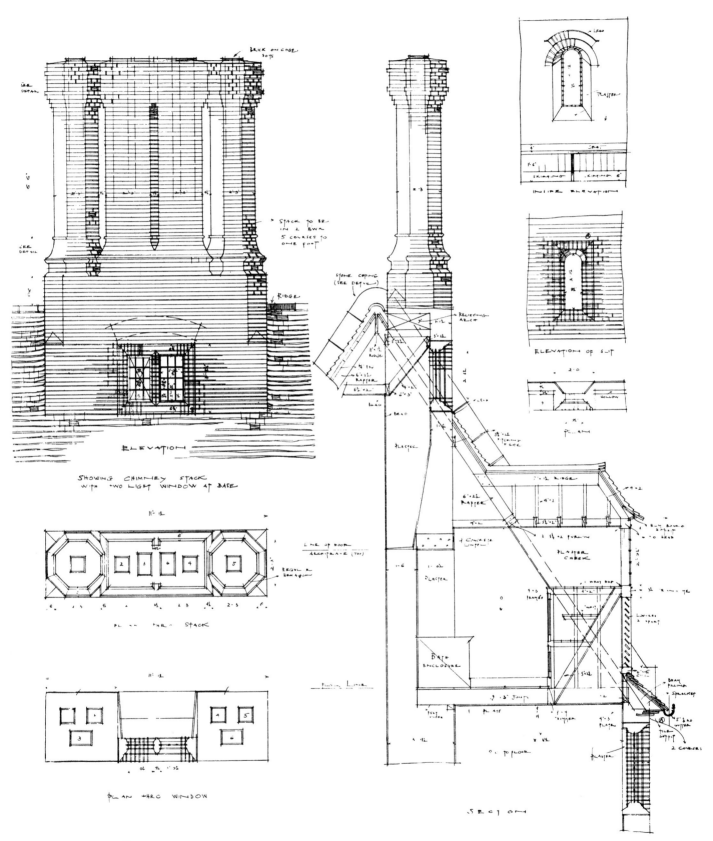

FIG. 564.—THE LODGE, KNOWLTON, CANTERBURY : DETAILS OF CHIMNEY AND ROOF.

Scale one-quarter of an inch to one foot. Photographs of this Lodge are reproduced on page xxxvii.

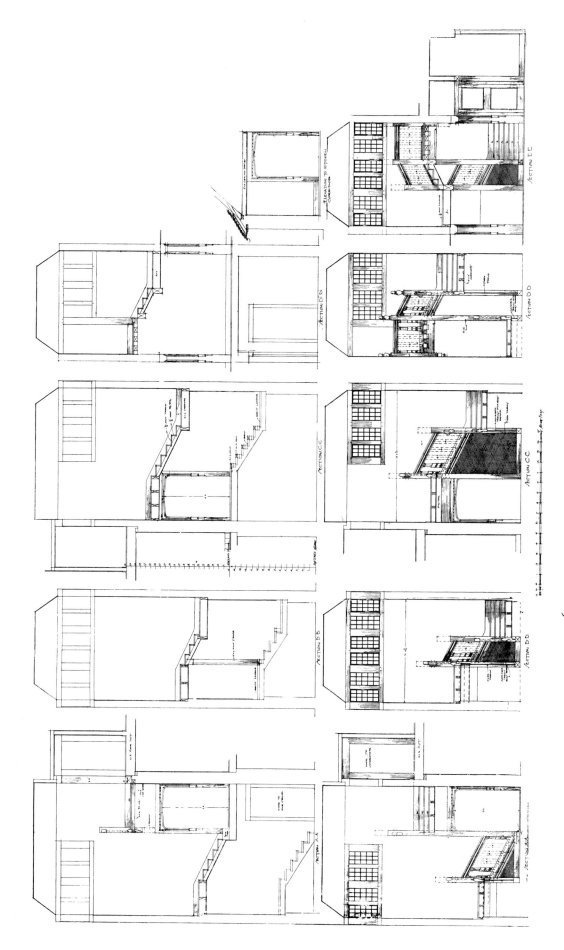

FIG. 565.—FOLLY FARM: DETAILS OF NEW STAIRCASE.

Scale one-eighth of an inch to one foot. Photographs of this staircase are reproduced on page 282.

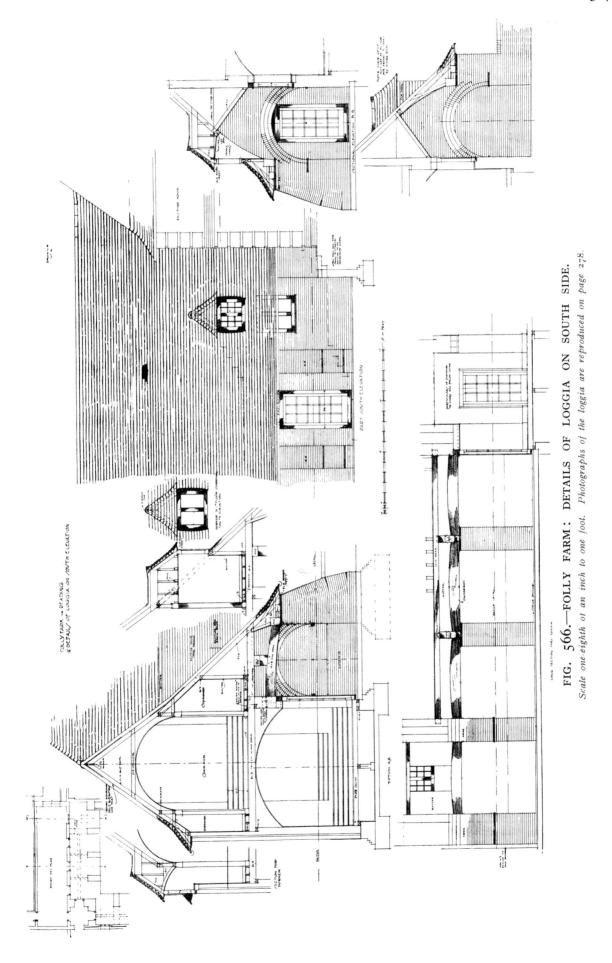

FIG. 566.—FOLLY FARM: DETAILS OF LOGGIA ON SOUTH SIDE.

Scale one-eighth ot an inch to one foot. Photographs of the loggia are reproduced on page 278.

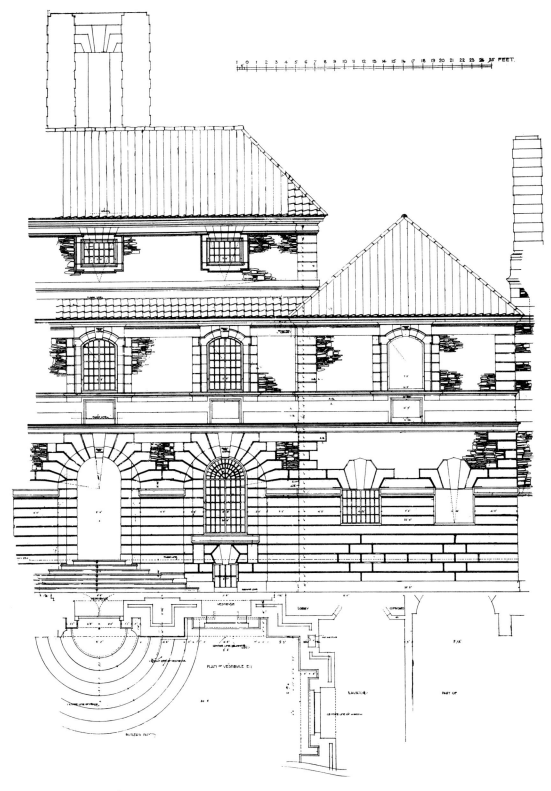

FIG. 567.—HEATHCOTE, ILKLEY : DETAIL OF ENTRANCE FRONT.

Scale one-eighth of an inch to one foot. A photograph of this front is reproduced on page 183.

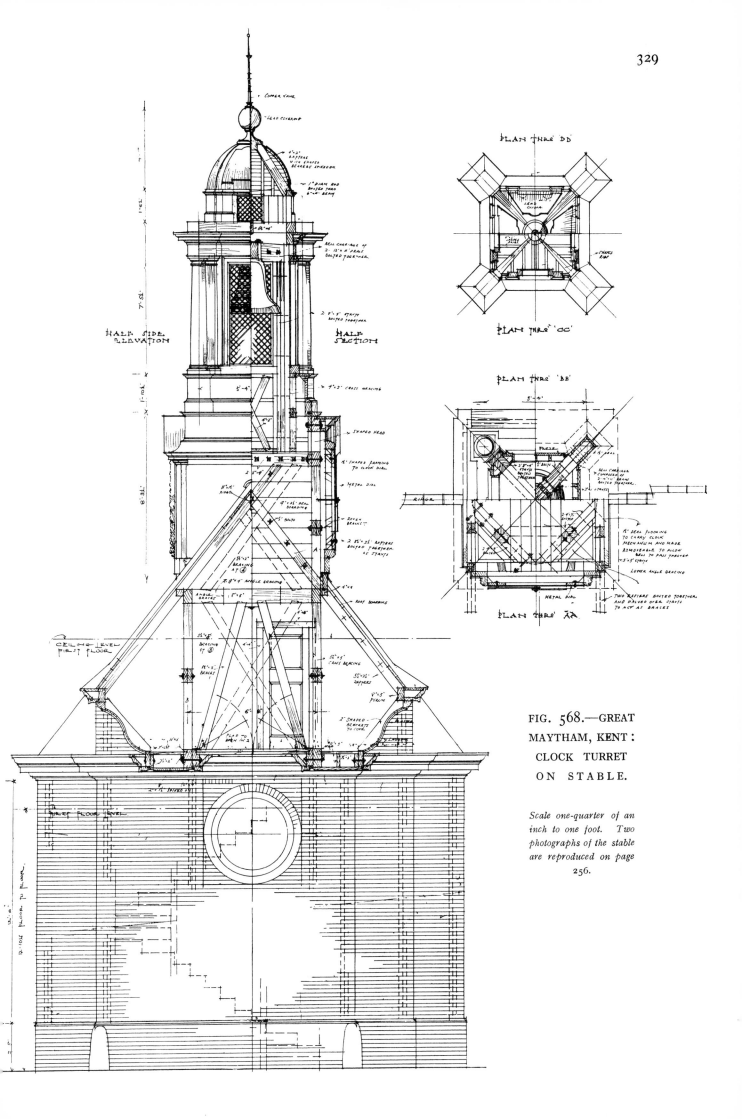

FIG. 568.—GREAT
MAYTHAM, KENT:
CLOCK TURRET
ON STABLE.

*Scale one-quarter of an
inch to one foot. Two
photographs of the stable
are reproduced on page
256.*

330

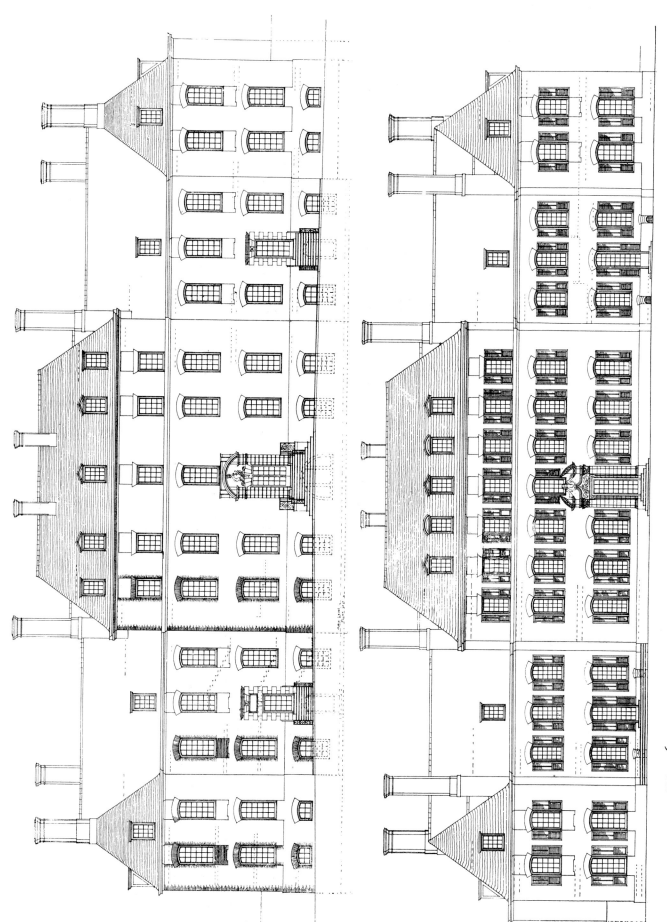

FIG. 569.—GREAT MAYTHAM, KENT: ENTRANCE FRONT (ABOVE) AND GARDEN FRONT (BELOW).
Scale one-sixteenth of an inch to one foot. Photographs of these fronts are reproduced on pages 247 to 252.

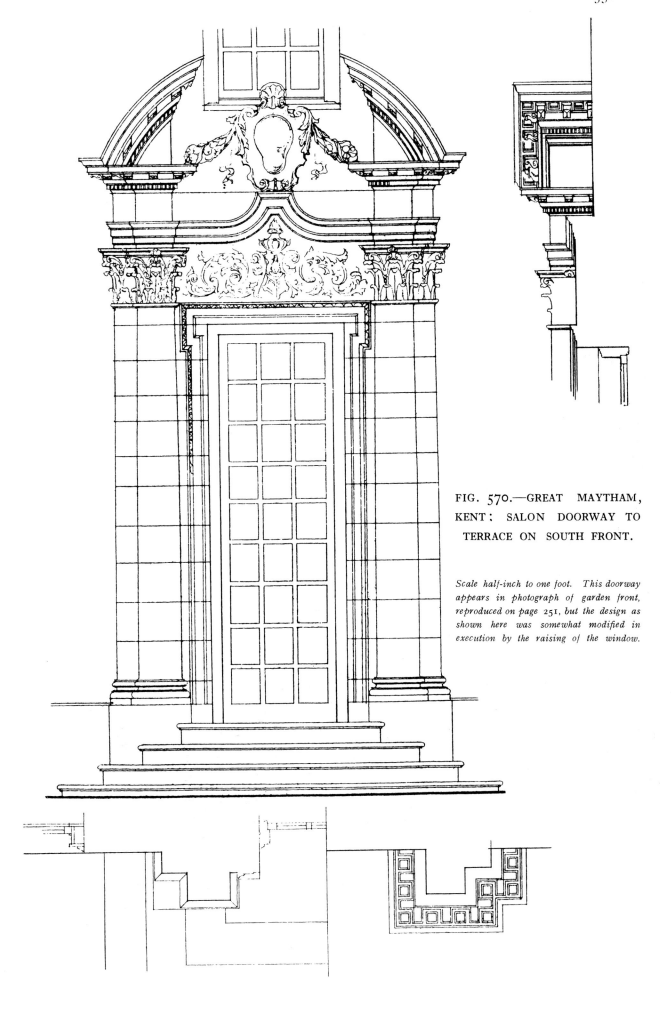

FIG. 570.—GREAT MAYTHAM,
KENT: SALON DOORWAY TO
TERRACE ON SOUTH FRONT.

*Scale half-inch to one foot. This doorway
appears in photograph of garden front,
reproduced on page 251, but the design as
shown here was somewhat modified in
execution by the raising of the window.*

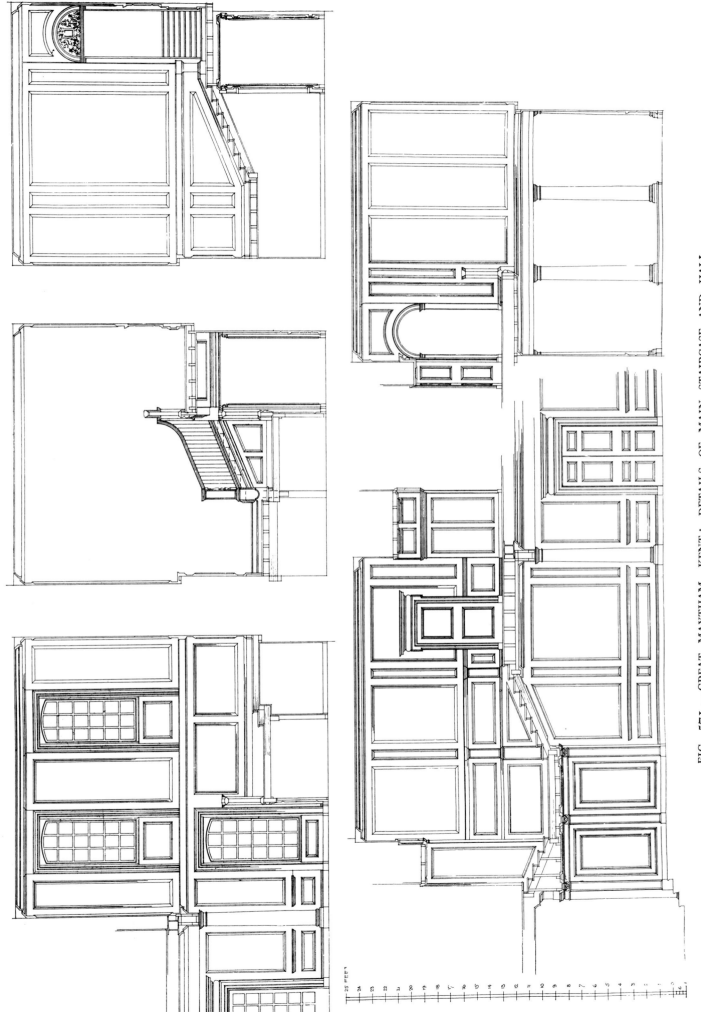

FIG. 571.—GREAT MAYTHAM, KENT : DETAILS OF MAIN STAIRCASE AND HALL.
Scale one-sixth of an inch to one foot.   See scale on drawing.   A photograph of the hall is reproduced on page 254.

25 FEET 24 23 22 21 20 19 18 17 16 15 14 13 12 11 10 9 8 7 6 5 4 3 2 1 0 6

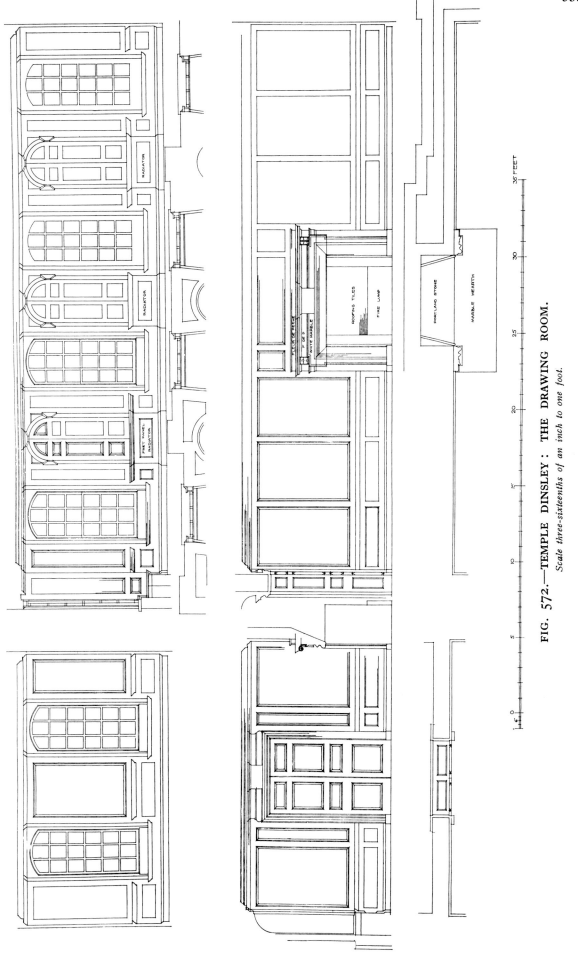

FIG. 572.—TEMPLE DINSLEY : THE DRAWING ROOM.

Scale three-sixteenths of an inch to one foot.

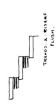

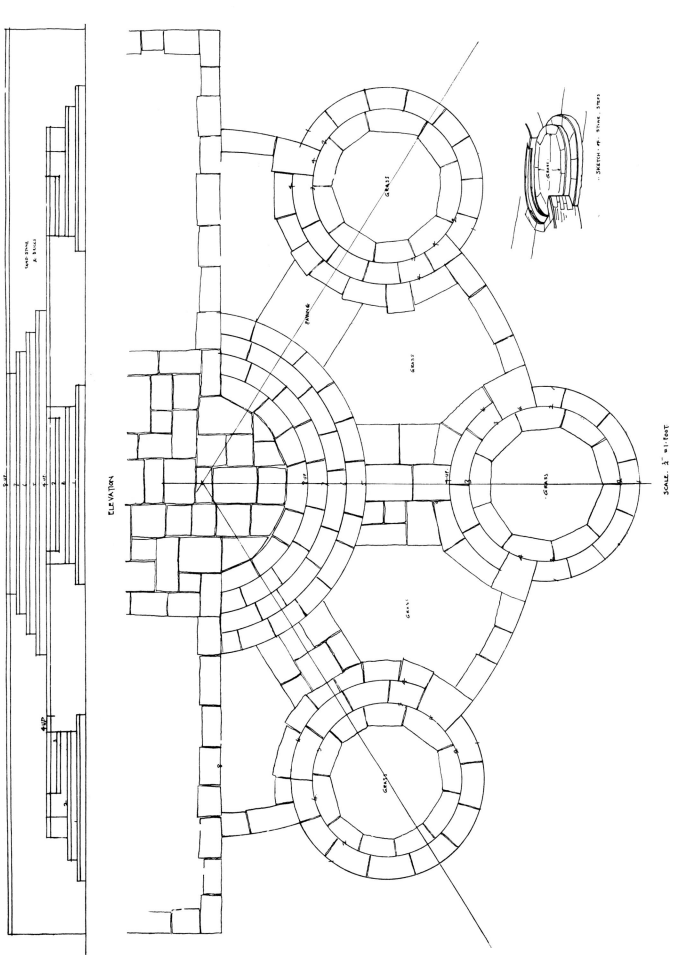

ELEVATION

SCALE. ½" = 1 FOOT.

FIG. 573.—GREAT DIXTER, SUSSEX : DETAILS OF GARDEN STAIRWAY.

Scale one-quarter of an inch to one foot. A photograph of this stairway is reproduced on page 265.

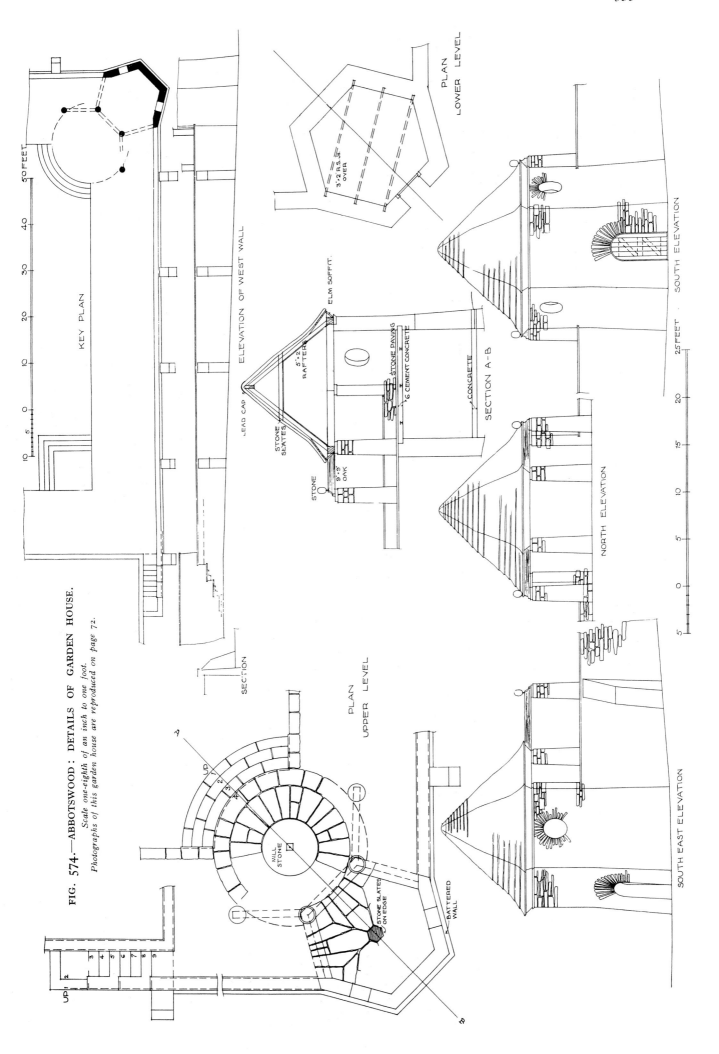

FIG. 574.—ABBOTSWOOD: DETAILS OF GARDEN HOUSE.
Scale one-eighth of an inch to one foot.
Photographs of this garden house are reproduced on page 72.

KEY PLAN

50 FEET

ELEVATION OF WEST WALL

LEAD CAP

STONE SLATES

STONE

5"×2" RAFTERS

9"×5" OAK

ELM SOFFIT.

STONE PAVING

6" CEMENT CONCRETE

CONCRETE

SECTION A-B

PLAN
LOWER LEVEL

3"×2" R.S.J.
OVER

SOUTH ELEVATION

NORTH ELEVATION

25 FEET

SECTION

PLAN
UPPER LEVEL

UP

MILL STONE

STONE SLATES
ON EDGE

BATTERED WALL

SOUTH EAST ELEVATION

A

B

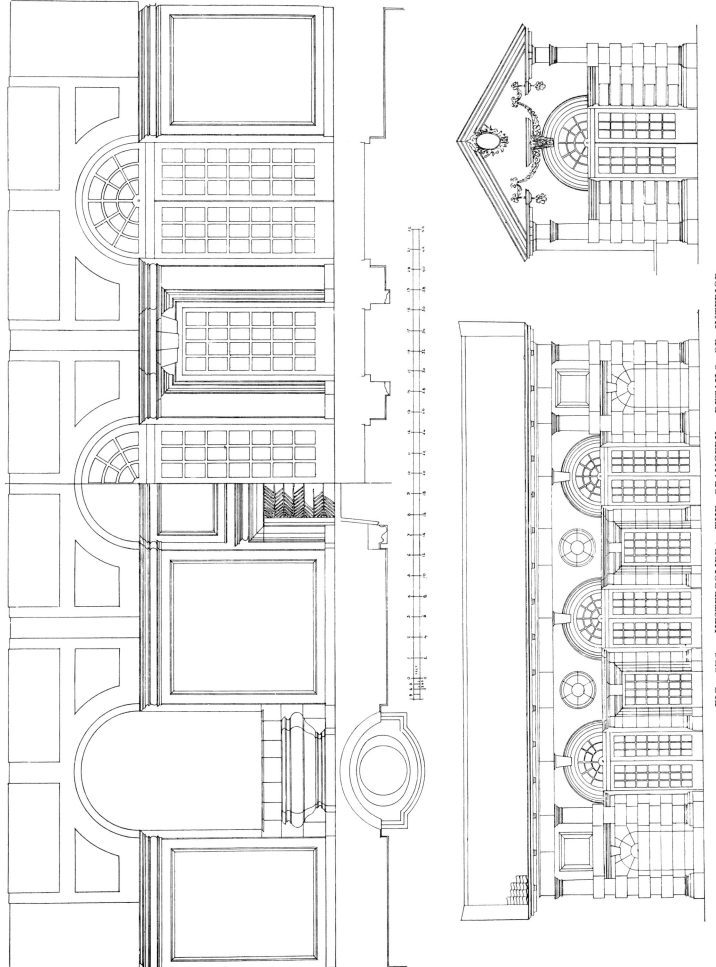

FIG. 575.—HESTERCOMBE: THE ORANGERY. DETAILS OF INTERIOR.

337

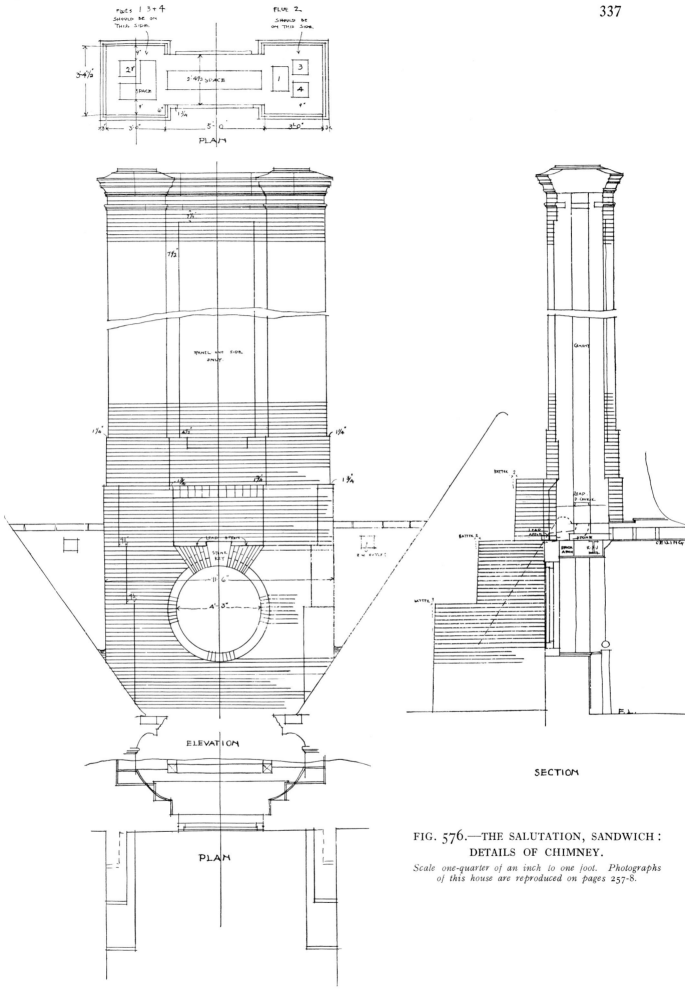

PLAN

ELEVATION

PLAN

SECTION

FIG. 576.—THE SALUTATION, SANDWICH :
DETAILS OF CHIMNEY.

*Scale one-quarter of an inch to one foot. Photographs
of this house are reproduced on pages 257-8.*

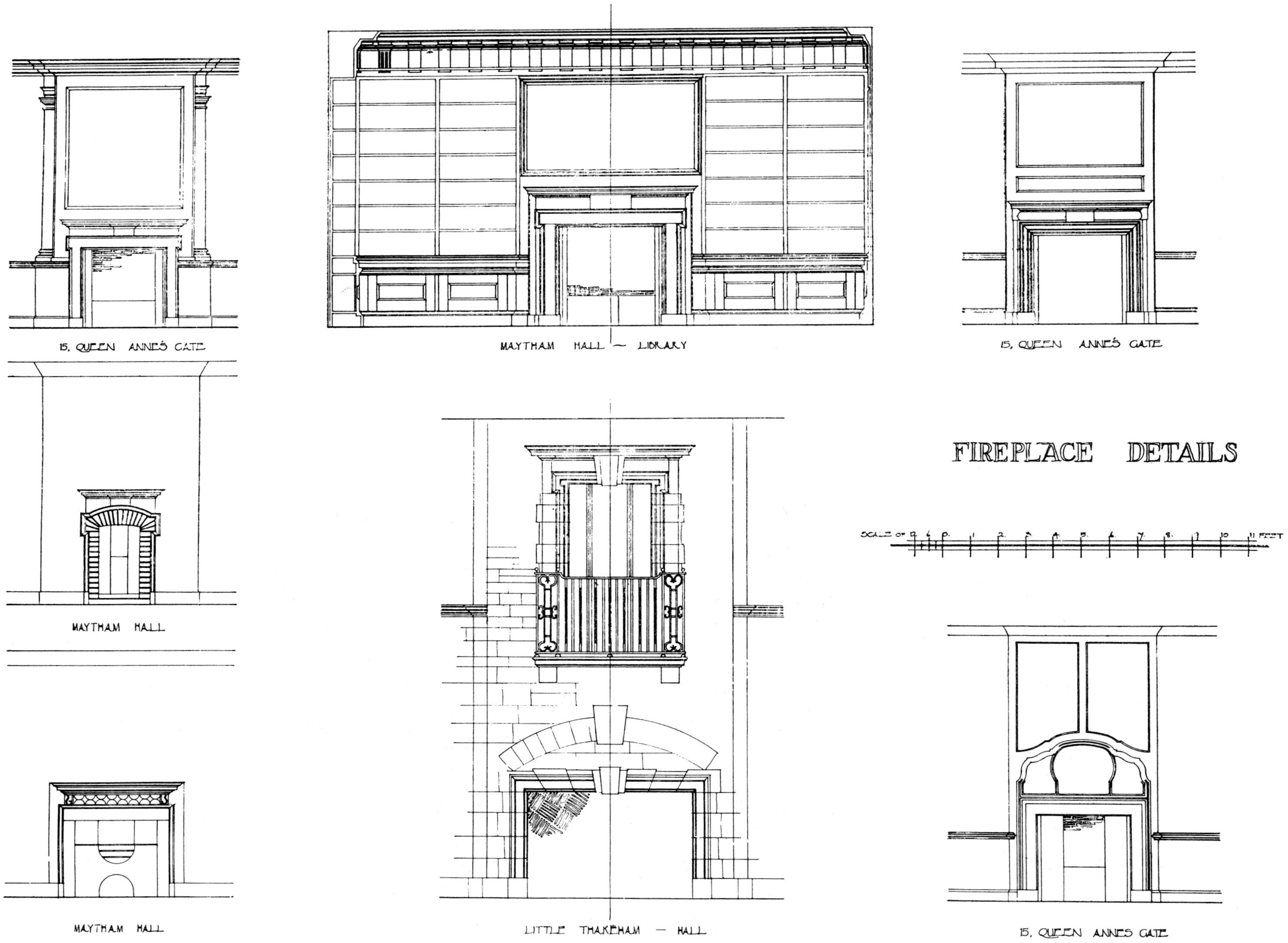
15, QUEEN ANNE'S GATE
MAYTHAM HALL — LIBRARY
15, QUEEN ANNE'S GATE
MAYTHAM HALL
FIREPLACE DETAILS
SCALE OF 12 6 0 1 2 3 4 5 6 7 8 9 10 11 FEET
MAYTHAM HALL
LITTLE THAKEHAM — HALL
15, QUEEN ANNES GATE

FIG. 577.—DETAILS OF VARIOUS FIREPLACES.

Scale one quarter of an inch to one foot.

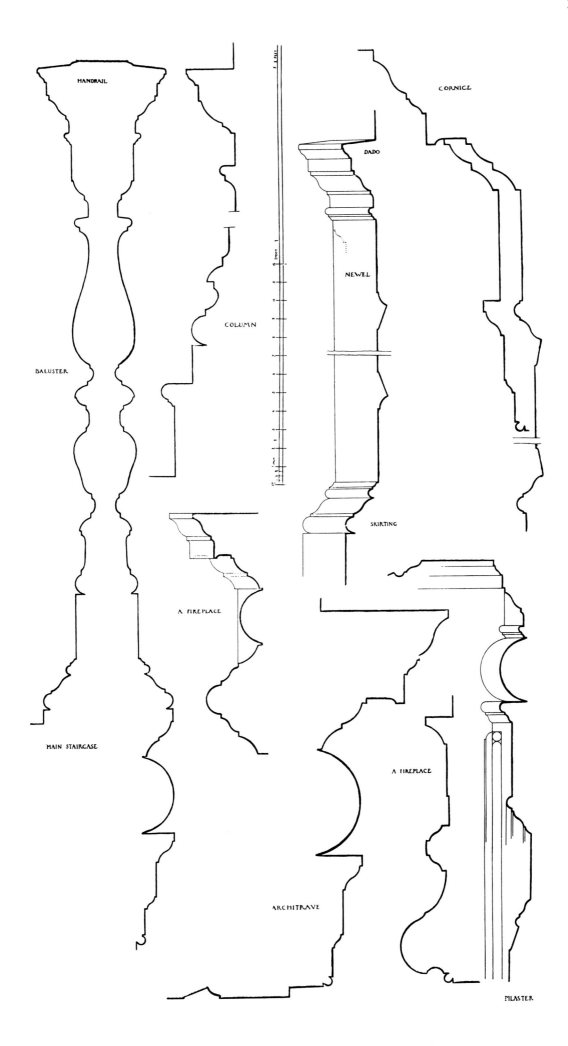

HANDRAIL

BALUSTER

COLUMN

DADO

CORNICE

NEWEL

SKIRTING

A FIREPLACE

MAIN STAIRCASE

A FIREPLACE

ARCHITRAVE

PILASTER

FIG. 578.—GREAT MAYTHAM: QUARTER FULL SIZE DETAILS OF MOULDINGS.

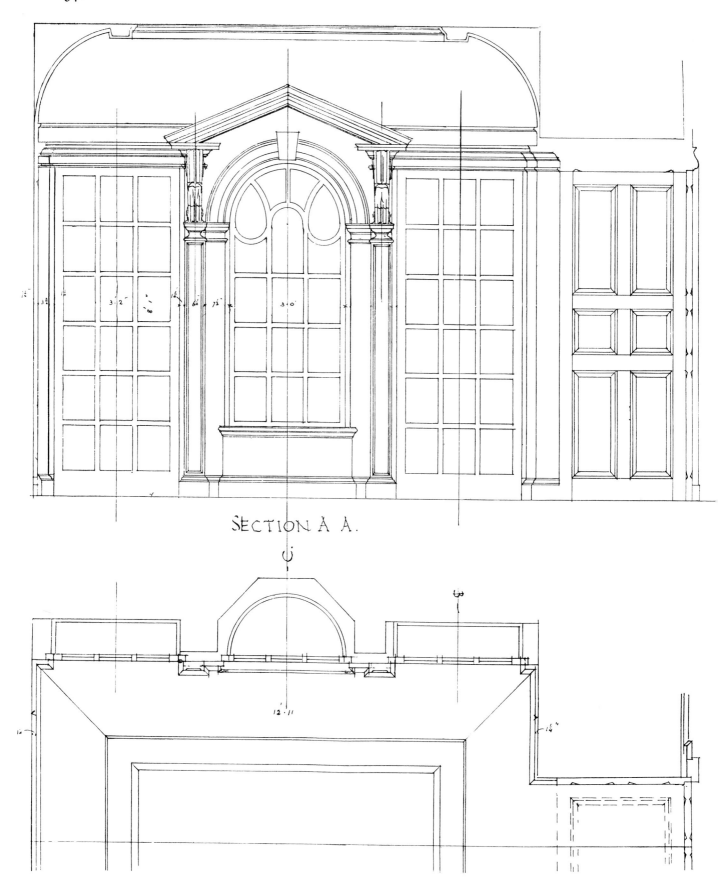

SECTION A A.

FIG. 579.—WINDOWS AT BARHAM COURT.

Scale one-quarter of an inch to one foot.

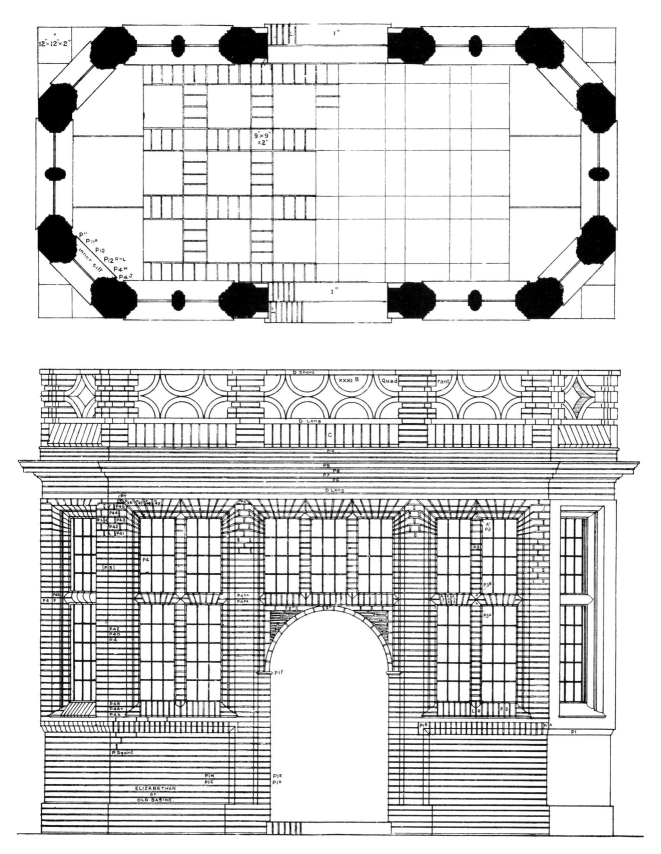

FIG. 580.—PLAN AND ELEVATION OF PAVILION BUILT IN PURPOSE-MADE BRICKS.

The scale is a little less than half an inch to one foot.

INDEX.

NOTE.—*The* SMALL *numerals indicate* REFERENCES IN THE TEXT. *The* LARGE *numerals indicate* ILLUSTRATIONS *of the subject indexed, and refer* NOT *to the Figure Numbers but to the* PAGES *on which such illustrations will be found.*

The author has thought it well not to index the many historical matters and persons to which references are made in the course of elucidating the story of the old buildings repaired and enlarged by Mr. Lutyens. Names of owners of houses are not indexed, as they are given on page 318 in the " List of Works."

NOTE.—*The* Small *numerals indicate* References *in the* Text. *The* Large *numerals indicate* Illustrations *of the subject indexed, and refer* Not *to the Figure Numbers but to the* Pages *on which such illustrations will be found.*

The author has thought it well not to index the many historical matters and persons to which references are made in the course of elucidating the story of the old buildings repaired and enlarged by Mr. Lutyens. Names of owners of houses are not indexed, as they are given on page 318 in the "List of Works."